Rehabilitate, Rewire, Recover!

Anorexia recovery for the determined adult

By Tabitha Farrar

This book is dedicated to the brave people in recovery I have had the pleasure of meeting and working with, and the many of you who read drafts, added your comments, and helped me edit this edition. You know who you are.

Key Terms

Chronic energy deficit: Prolonged energy deficit that has created energy debt.

Compensatory behaviours: Behaviours such as purging, restriction, or exercise that negate food eaten or attempt to create energy deficit.

Energy debt: The accumulation of the effects of long-term energy deficit such as lack of bodily repair and maintenance work.

Energy deficit: When the amount an individual consumes is less than their nutritional needs. A person doesn't have to be in a thin body in order to be in energy deficit.

Mental hunger: Non-physical hunger that manifests as thinking about food.

Nutritional rehabilitation: The process of moving from an underweight or malnourished body to a healthy, unsuppressed body. This is often referred to as "weight restoration" but I prefer the term "nutritional rehabilitation" as it focuses on amending malnutrition rather than weight. Not all people in a state of malnutrition are at a low weight.

Natural weight. Your natural body weight when you have amended chronic energy deficit and are eating without restriction or compensation.

Neural rewiring: The process of changing neural pathways in the brain.

Poststarvation Hyperphagia: The entirely appropriate bottomless-pit hunger that follows a period of starvation.

Restriction: Most commonly pertaining to dietary restriction of food. Can be also used to describe restriction of other energetic exchanges — such as money, and leisure time — that indicate the brain perceives resources to be scarce.

Recovery weight: The higher-than-usual weight that some people need to temporarily be in order for your body to amend energy debt and restore from the effects of malnutrition.

OCD-ED: The OCD generated by anorexia or any other eating disorder. This affects some people with anorexia, not all.

Underweight: A person who is underweight can be underweight at any size if the weight that they are is less than the weight that they would be without restrictive eating. A person doesn't have to be in a thin body in order to be underweight.

Weight suppression: When a person suppresses their body weight via dietary restriction, exercise, or other compensatory behaviour.

A Pragmatic Approach to Anorexia Recovery

Disclaimer: This book is not designed to replace medical treatment. This book is specific to anorexia recovery and doesn't go into comorbid disorders, or other complications. This book is not medical advice. It is not prescriptive, nor is it written by a doctor.

About this book:

If you are reading this book, I am going to assume that you are an adult trying to recover from anorexia nervosa or another type of restrictive eating disorder. For you to have picked up this book is a positive step. It shows you are interested in recovery. However, there is a difference between wanting recovery and being willing to do what it takes to attain it. There is a difference between hope and action. While I do intend for this book to give you hope, I am mostly interested in inspiring action. Recovery is not a magic trick, you have to take action and make changes to get there.

This book contains one major contradiction. I believe in *personalised* recovery, and yet I am writing a *generalised* recovery book. Please keep in mind that this is my best attempt at putting the things that I have learned into one resource. This is not supposed to be a "how-to" guide. Rather, see this book as a self-help tool to open your mind to discovering what you need to do in order to be successful. Above all else, this is not medical advice. This book is general concept, not individual or specific to you. You have lived with your body your whole life. You know your body, and your eating disorder, better than I do.

Therefore it is important that you take the parts of this book that resonate, and leave the parts that don't. We are all different and unique, and your personal recovery path may be different from mine. That's okay. Take what you need, leave what you don't.

Rehabilitate, Rewire, Recover! was built through a combination of my own experience recovering from anorexia, and from the experiences of others in recovery. The text is littered with anecdotes, both mine and theirs, which may help you identify with others who have shared your experiences. While we can share our stories and learn from one another, remember that you are unique and complicated and should not expect yourself to fit into a defined recovery model or pre-set mold. Think of the ideas presented here as a starting point for you to create your own, personalised, recovery.

There is some science referenced in this book, here and there. But to be clear, my personal experience came first. Anything I have researched I have done so because I was trying to make sense of what happened to me — what I felt, thought, and lived through. I'm not someone who trawls through scientific journals for laughs (probably because texts full of long words that I don't understand irritate me) but will do so when I am motivated to understand something better — and I am fascinated to understand what I lived through with anorexia. To have my own experiences of things such as the "recovery tummy," the "bottomless-pit hunger," and my exercise compulsions reflected back at me in the literature when I was struggling through them was incredibly consoling. So while there is science in this book, it is referenced due to my personal experience and the experiences of the people I have had the pleasure of working with over the years.

(This books contains swear words. This is not an apology; I'm just letting you know.)

Section One:

Groundwork

It is not your *fault* that you have anorexia. But as an adult it is your *responsibility* to recover. Yes, it is unfair that something you are not to blame for is your responsibility to fix, but that's the reality.

No blame. Blame serves nobody, least of all you.

Handing The Power Back To You

When I began working as a recovery coach, I didn't expect that the vast majority of the people whom I worked with would have already been through traditional eating disorder treatment a number of times. Most of my clients have been told at some point in the past that they were resistant to treatment or noncompliant. Some have been told that they would never be able to achieve full recovery. To me, this sort of treatment only illustrates the gross ineptitude in the mental health field. Blaming people with anorexia for being fearful in regards to the recovery process illustrates a lack of understanding regarding the mechanisms at work within a person's brain when they have anorexia. Blaming people with anorexia for not slotting nicely into a cookie-cutter treatment mold is plainly disrespectful. We don't blame sufferers of other health issues for their illnesses or less than adequate treatment outcomes. It's time to start treating people with eating disorders like people, rather than delinquents.

Having not been through traditional treatment first-hand, I never had the experience of being made to feel dependent on treatment professionals. Working with clients who have been through rounds and rounds of therapy before contacting me has highlighted something rather alarming: adults with eating disorders are often disempowered by the traditional treatment process.

They have been told that they need a dietician to tell them what to eat, and a therapist to help them cope with eating it. They have been advised that their own opinion doesn't matter because it is always "the eating disorder talking." They have become long-term reliant on treatment providers; terrified of making decisions and taking action in case they do something "wrong." They have had their confidence in themselves eroded to the point they don't feel they can participate in their own recovery process. Such a great shame, because eating disorder professionals should be helping a person in recovery set goals and assisting them in achieving them; it should be a collaboration. (And thankfully, I do know some great eating disorder professionals who do just that.)

Learned helplessness is really tragic, because I am yet to meet a person with anorexia who was unintelligent or incapable. You are not stupid, nor are you unable to know what you need to eat. In fact, you are the only person who knows exactly what you need to eat because it is the food that dances around in *your* head — the food you are scared of most. You are the person with that information. You are the person who needs to be brutally honest and write a list of your fears and then take action to overcome them, again and again and again. Nobody else can do that for you because nobody else is in your brain.

I believe that when professionals support you as an adult in recovery from anorexia, it should be about giving you the tools and the courage to do what you need to do. It should not be about rendering you a quivering wreck because you don't know which filling to put in your sandwich.

Moreover, not everyone needs therapy in order to recover from anorexia. You may want therapy, but that is your *choice*. People have been dying from and recovering from anorexia for hundreds, of years — long before therapists were invented. Sure, you may want to use professional help as a tool to get you where you want to be, but know that there is a difference between essential and helpful. Professional help may be very *helpful* to your recovery. Food and determination are the only components that are *essential* to your recovery. Anorexia (and restriction) affects your whole life — every aspect of you — therefore you will be the person to unravel it.

You are not dependent on anyone for your recovery other than yourself. But greater than that: nobody else can do this for you. You don't have to wait for someone else to come along and "save" you or give you permission to eat.

This is your body, your brain, your life, your illness, and your recovery is your responsibility. The only person with the ability to get you fully recovered is you. Other people should be there to help and support, but ultimately, this is your recovery.

Responsibility

When you are a child with anorexia, you are in a position where other people — adults — can take control and make you eat. That's a different dynamic, and one that tends to work really well for kids. Additionally, when caught early, children have fewer anorexia-generated neural pathways to rewire.

As an adult, you are responsible for your own health. Other people will come and go. This is ultimately down to you. I know that sounds like a lot of pressure, but it's actually a good thing: you will learn how to look after yourself, and that means you'll always be there for yourself too.

That isn't to say that you do this alone. Far from it. Take all the help and support you can get. Support will help you deal with the stress. Community will help you stay motivated when it gets rough. Swallow all the positive energy available to you.

You will learn the skills needed to get yourself to full recovery. You have to. When you can do this, you will not only reach full recovery, but you will have a robust recovery — and your recovery will not be dependent on anyone else.

Accountability

Accountability is a huge part of recovery. Most of us do better if we have external accountability — i.e. other people — to help motivate us to eat when we are really terrified of doing so. However, even while you are using external accountability (which I thoroughly recommend) you remain accountable to yourself for eating.

You are accountable to yourself for doing your very best at every opportunity — whether someone else has told you to or not. You are accountable to yourself for the state of your health. When you understand this fully, you will realise that this is not about pleasing your therapist, dietician, parents, or your partner. This is about you having the ability and the control to follow through with actions that will serve your own health and quality of life.

Anorexia cannot *make* you do anything. It can merely suggest an action. It can deliver very strong thoughts and emotions motivating you to act in a certain way, but anorexia cannot operate your hands and legs. You always have a choice. You are accountable to yourself for eating regardless of what anorexia has to say about it. Anorexia can suggest that you don't eat, or that you restrict, but it cannot make you follow though.

Be the change

Be the change that you want to see in yourself. This means being proactive and taking action.

Recovery should not be a situation of you versus your parents or your partner or whomever else is always telling you to eat more — but for many people it has turned into just that. You're probably sick of people pushing you to eat more food and rest. So take control. *You* should be the person pushing recovery.

I used to spend all day dreading that someone would suggest pizza for dinner. Or that we go out for cake in the afternoon. I used to forever be trying to avoid situations where other people might suggest what I eat. This forever running away from fear is tiresome. You take control by running towards it.

From now on, *you* be the person who instigates pizza for dinner. *You* be the person who suggests going out for tea and cake.

Rather than spending all day wondering if someone is going to try and make you eat something scary or not, decide for yourself that you are going to do it. You'll feel a lot more in control about it all if you are the one pushing for change.

I'm handing the power and responsibility for your recovery back to you. As an adult with anorexia, the reality is that you are the only person who can get you recovered.

★ You are the only person who can make yourself eat.
★ You are the only person who will really know if you restricted or not.
★ You are accountable to yourself to not allow yourself to participate in disordered behaviours.
★ You are the only person who can answer the question *"Did I do my very best today?"*
★ You are the only person who can ask for more help when you know you need it.
★ You are responsible for your own health. You are responsible for getting your body out of malnutrition.
★ If you are suppressing your bodyweight, you are fighting your own biology, and this will never lead to health and happiness.

You are not powerless in recovery. Far from it. You are the person who will make this happen. And that is great news, because you can do anything you set your mind to.

You are an individual. Your recovery is your own

I have my story. You have yours. We can share stories to help one another, but ultimately you will work out your own specific path to recovery.

Anorexia is a complicated illness that affects every part of a person's life. The mind and body become progressively depleted, and fear (chained with energy deficit) becomes stronger and stronger. As the years go on, habitual behaviour becomes more and more entrenched. Recovery has to be geared around you, not the other way around. I have found that when put at the helm of their own recovery and given compassionate, persistent, and abundant support, adults with anorexia do brilliantly — even those previously deemed unable to recover.

I firmly believe that full recovery is possible for everyone. Recovered. Not forever recover*ing*, and not perpetually in recovery. You can get fully, all the way, totally done, over and out, recovered. You can also work your way to being trigger-proof. All the diet talk and food fads in the world wouldn't cause me to reflect on the way I eat now. I'm very confident that there's nothing out there that could influence me to want to lose weight. Getting trigger-proof takes time and effort, but you can and will get there. Don't expect it to happen overnight. The key is to keep trying.

This book will not deliver a one-size-fits-all recovery method because that doesn't exist. I believe in personalised recovery, with a couple of exceptions — food being the primary one. I believe food should be unrestricted and in accordance to mental hunger (that's the constant thinking about food that you do) as well as physical hunger if that is present.

The situation of malnutrition anorexia creates places an enormous toll on the body and mind. We must remember that anorexia has the highest death rate of all mental illnesses and/or "psychiatric disorders." In order for the body to recuperate, amending energy deficit has to be taken very seriously. This requires both food and rest.

The concept of unrestricted eating holds true regardless of body size. Anorexia occurs in people of all body sizes, and a person can be in energy deficit at any weight if they are not eating enough to meet their nutritional needs. These "nutritional needs" may include the additional calories required for your body to repair the extensive damage caused by malnutrition as well as your natural basal metabolic rate. If you were already thinking that unrestricted eating doesn't apply to you as much because you are not emaciated, then think again. The same rules apply regardless of the size of your body. A person can be very sick in a seemingly "normal" sized body.

This book will focus on the following:
→ Nutritional rehabilitation
→ Neural rewiring

Nutritional rehabilitation gets the body out of malnutrition. Neural rewiring allows for entrenched and habitual behaviours to be changed. Both of these things combined lead to mental freedom. It is important to remember that the brain and body function as one.

When a person has had anorexia for a number of years, as most adults with anorexia have, they have not only to get themselves out of energy deficit to flick that genetic anorexia switch off, but they also have to rewire the neural pathways that have been established via years of anorexia-generated behaviours.

I am suggesting a pragmatic, personalised, food increasing, behaviour reducing, project management style approach to anorexia recovery lead by you. This recovery style values:

- Using resources available to you in an agile and responsive manner.
- Reacting to outcomes by redirecting and changing methods as needed.
- Learning and adjusting as the process continues.
- Detached evaluations of your recovery process.

Chapter 1: A Non-Psychoanalytical Approach

Before we go much further I need to make one core concept clear: I do not believe in psychologising anorexia. I think that one of the core problems with the psychoanalytical approach to treating anorexia is that meaning is implied when there is none.

When we are told that there is an underlying meaning behind our anorexia-generated behaviours, it is implied that we will not be able to recover until said underlying cause is remedied. For some people it is more than implied. Some of us are outright told we cannot recover unless we address the "underlying reason" for our illness. I do not believe this to be true. We can refeed the physical body at any time, and we can rewire those anorexia neural pathways even when the other aspects of our lives are not perfect.

Looking for meaning where there is none

Humans love to put meaning over our thoughts and actions. I expect it makes us feel special, and superior to other creatures — quite an egotistical trait if you think about it. Anyway, philosophy and muse are all very well if one has the time, but should not prevail over science, experience, and common sense — especially when it comes to mental health issues. When a person is in a state of malnutrition, he or she does not have time to waste contemplating existential questions. The body has to be brought out of danger by means of nutritional rehabilitation first and foremost.

The quest for meaning, and the projection of meaning upon all human action is likely what brought about the assumption that people who are thin due to anorexia want to or enjoy being thin because it is fashionable to be thin. Just because we place meaning on top of behaviours, and just because it feels like it makes sense to do so, doesn't mean it is true.

Anorexia the chameleon

Anorexia is not about wanting to be a supermodel. Anorexia is a genetically-based illness and has been documented since the middle ages. Back then it was referred to as "Anorexia Mirabilis," meaning "miraculous loss of appetite." Like I said before, people have been dying from and recovering from this illness for a long time.

In the medieval era, religious fasting and starving in the name of God was the cultural mask that seemed to justify anorexia. There were many church leaders and "starving saints" who developed anorexia with the so-called purification via starvation. Anorexia hid behind religion, in the same way that it currently hides in our thin-obsessed society. The "reasons" for anorexia are shaped to fit whatever the culture of the time period; with an appropriate view on both history and science, we see that cultural trends often exist as excuses. I believe that, actually, the illness isn't all that complicated. It has nothing to do with the will of God, nor is it what we seek in fashion magazines. It's really quite simple: anorexia is a genetic response to energy deficit.

In 1380 when Catherine of Siena was starving herself to death, it was said she was doing so with religious intent.[1] In 2002 when I was starving myself to emaciation, it was assumed that I did so in order to be a catwalk model. The illness is a chameleon in as much as both the individual suffering from it and the society in which that individual exists can usually find a reason to excuse the apparently intentional act of self-starvation. The assumption that people with anorexia symptoms want to be thin for the sake of being thin has only been around since about the 1960s — so we can probably blame Twiggy for that. Back in the Victorian era it was popular to assume that people with anorexia were starving themselves to avoid sex. Then along came Hilde Bruch with the idea that it was the fault of their parents. So far, all the most common assumptions about the "why" behind anorexia nervosa share one thing in common: they are all based on psychoanalysis. They're also wrong, in my opinion.

I believe that the reason a person with anorexia develops fear of weight gain is because their genetics react to energy deficit that way — and we will get into that in more depth in the following chapters. That really is as deep as the "why" behind the illness a person with anorexia actions needs to go. And I'd say that one cannot get much deeper than DNA, so that's far enough for me.

That is not to say that wanting to be thin cannot trigger anorexia in a person with the genetics for it. Sure, it can if it leads to dieting behaviour and energy deficit. Likewise, personal trauma can, of course, cause a desire to eat less, and this can lead to that initial energy deficit that will spark anorexia in those prone to it. But anorexia

---

[1] Anorexia And The Holiness Of Saint Catherine Of Siena'. Albany.edu. Retrieved 2014-04-20.

is so much more than a desire to eat less. Only people with the required genetics develop anorexia when they go into significant energy deficit — hence trauma and diet culture can aid the development of anorexia, but they don't cause it.

We do not need to psychologize anorexia to refeed ourselves any more than we need to psychologize cancer in order to administer chemotherapy. This recovery approach is a non-psychoanalytical approach to anorexia recovery. I do not believe that psychoanalysis is required to nutritionally rehabilitate from a physiological state of malnutrition, nor do I believe it is required in order to change behavioural patterns.

Can *You* Recover From Anorexia?

Yes. Absolutely, yes.

Even if you have had multiple recovery attempts. Even if you have had this illness the majority of your adult life. I believe you can recover. Fully.

In my experience, even people refused traditional treatment due to being labelled "difficult" or "noncompliant" can and do recover fully when they are listened to and worked *with*.

There is this weird "motivation" rhetoric that gets thrown around. People getting told that they are not motivated enough to recover. I'm going to assume that if you are reading this book you are motivated to recover — so I don't think that you have a motivation problem.

Unfortunately, even if you are ten-out-of-ten motivated, if your fear is also ten-out-of-ten then it can negate your motivation. The fear will stop you taking action, and this then looks like you are not motivated because you can't change anything. That's a fear problem, rather than a motivation problem. Often I find that we don't need to work on increasing your motivation as much as we need to work on overcoming your fear.

Learning and adjusting

A crucial element to anorexia recovery is learning. In recovery as an adult, you have to learn how to eat well and continue eating well — not just for a stint, but for life. That means that you have to learn what works for you and what doesn't. And I'm not talking large-scale "what works." I'm talking small scale most of the time. The details — these separate us as individuals from other people, and make us unique.

Failure is a gift to learning. I believe that the years of failure I went through in recovery are what have lead me to be as robust in my recovery as I am now. I believe that this is because in getting here I made a lot of mistakes. And I learnt from them.

Failure gives you information that success cannot. Self-disparagement is a distraction you can't afford to indulge in. As soon as something doesn't work, change your tactics and try something new without wasting energy on blame of self or others.

Above anything else, you are smart. If you use your wits against the urges to restrict, and your courage to walk into — rather than away from — your fears, you'll work out how to do this.

You *are* "sick enough"

One thing people often tell me is that they don't believe that they are unwell enough, or thin enough, or in a bad enough state of health to think that the recovery should apply to them.

I'm going to say this now, early on in this book. If any aspect of your life is compromised by an eating disorder, then you are unwell enough to take recovery action. This applies to you. Eating disorders come in all shapes and sizes.

Basically, if you are reading this book, then you are sick enough. This book isn't going to be winning any literary prizes — it's not exactly *Harry Potter.* You're not reading this book about anorexia recovery for kicks and giggles. You picked up this book because something is wrong. So stop telling yourself you are not sick enough and focus on getting better.

Remember:
- You do not have to be thin to be in a dangerous state of energy deficit or malnutrition.
- You can be underweight at any size.
- You can have anorexia at any size.
- Eating disorders affect people of all ages. You can fully recover at any age. Don't tell yourself you are "too old" to recover.
- Eating disorders affect men and women. I personally believe that as many men have eating disorders as women do — they just don't get diagnosed as often.
- Eating disorders affect people from all cultures.

- You do not need to have suffered trauma to have a restrictive eating disorder.
- You do not need to want to be thin to have a restrictive eating disorder.
- Your compulsive behaviours don't have to be extreme to be compromising your freedom. Don't settle for anything less than full recovery.
- You can be eating and still restricting, and any level of restriction can compromise your health and happiness.
- One of the mechanisms of anorexia is that you often don't fully comprehend the extent of your poor physical and mental health.
- You do not need to have an official diagnosis to have anorexia. Many health professionals miss the signs and therefore diagnoses are often only made when a person is an exact stereotypical representation of the illness.
- Orthorexia is just another subset of a restrictive eating disorder and so overly "healthy eating" has to be tackled in the same any any other restrictive eating disorder does.
- Many health — and even eating disorder — professionals don't understand that eating disorders are not just about a low weight. If you suspect you are still unwell, then you have work to do. Even if your doctor tells you what you are fine because your BMI is normal.

You are sick enough. Yes, *you*! Let's get on with recovery.

Before you get started:

This book will tell you things that your anorexia brain doesn't want to know. This book will suggest you do things that will immediately fill you with resistance. Question that resistance, as it is most likely coming from a place of fear. Only you can really know your true intentions, and in order to recover, you have to become incredibly good at calling yourself on your own bullshit.

As a general rule, the more resistance you feel to a suggestion to eat, rest, or break one of your anorexia rules, the more important it is that you do it. Anorexia constructs many rules, and these rules must be broken. The clues to recovery are in the resistance that you feel. Resistance leads you to where your fear lies. Recovery is about running into fear. I know this sounds terribly psychoanalytical, but it really isn't. Fear is a very biologically-based emotion that the body generates in response to perceived threat. Your brain is interpreting eating more food than you are currently eating as a threat. You have to run straight into that fear when you eat more food.

Chapter 2: Understanding Anorexia

You do not have to understand anorexia in order to put your fork to your mouth and eat more food. You may be wondering why I spent so much time writing a chapter on "Understanding Anorexia" if you don't need to understand this illness in order to take the action required to help you recover. I am writing this chapter because it explains the importance of nutritional rehabilitation plus neural rewiring. It explains why you can only fully recover if you reach nutritional rehabilitation. It may also give you a different perspective on your illness, and that may help you overcome your fear reaction to eating more.

Additionally, I think it's easier to conquer something that you understand.

Energy Deficit

It has been shown that anorexia has a genetic base, and that for people who have the genetic predisposition to anorexia nervosa, the anorexia genes are sparked or triggered by energy deficit.[2]

What is negative energy balance/energy deficit?
Energy deficit is like being overdrawn at the bank. In banking, financial deficit is when the funds you have don't cover what you spend. In terms of your body, energy deficit is when the energy you put in doesn't cover the energy you use. The most common — although not exclusive — cause of such an energy deficit in our current environment is going on a diet.

Thousands of years ago, the most common cause of energy deficit would have been scarcity of food: Famine. We'll come back to this later.

When a person loses weight, they do so by maintaining energy deficit to the extent that their body is forced to utilize fat stores. This happens because the energy taken in is not enough to fuel the body on a day-to-day basis. Despite dieting being the most common factor, energy deficit can occur without you actively deciding to lose weight at all. If for example you are unwell, or you have a stressful time during which your appetite is suppressed.

My own initial energy deficit was caused as I wanted to lose a bit of

---

[2] Cynthia M. Bulik et al. Significant Locus and Metabolic Genetic Correlations Revealed in Genome-Wide Association Study of Anorexia Nervosa. *American Journal of Psychiatry*, 2017

weight so that I was light enough to exercise my favorite racehorse. Not all weight loss is about wanting to look a certain way. But for many, the pressure to look skinny provokes intentional weight loss — in that sense, a culture that glorifies thinness can certainly facilitate energy deficit. While this pressure may influence an energy deficit initially, it is a different ball game once an eating disorder kicks in.

What happens when a person with the genetic predisposition for anorexia goes into energy deficit?

If a person with the genetic predisposition for a restrictive eating disorder such as anorexia nervosa goes into a negative energy balance for any reason, anorexia can be activated. The anorexia switch is flicked on. To me, the easiest way to explain this is a shift in operating system in the brain. I felt like I gradually moved from one way of being to another. From a person with a relaxed relationship with food, to a person who saw food as a threat and would go far out of her way to avoid it.

Not only is our relationship with food and other forms of energy compromised when anorexia activates, for most of us many other facets of our personalities are affected also. I will go into much greater detail on this and other aspects of malnutrition in the following chapters.

Why don't all people who diet have anorexia?

That is a good question, seeing as almost everyone you know is probably on some sort of diet these days. It is because a diet, or energy deficit, only triggers anorexia or a restrictive eating disorder in people who have the genetic predisposition for it.

When a person without anorexia genetics goes into energy deficit, they feel uncomfortable — most people dislike being on a diet, and energy deficit makes them cranky and hangry. The majority of people who diet find a pleasant feeling of reward in coming out of energy deficit by eating food. Being on a diet is no fun.

That pleasant feeling that most people get from eating food likely evolved to make humans desire to eat. In times when finding, catching, and exposing oneself to the elements long enough to secure food was a dangerous affair, nature had to bribe us into bothering to eat at all by making eating feel good. Can you imagine how early humans would have had to risk life and limb to hunt or gather food? If you wanted meat you would have to battle a real live animal and kill it — risking being stabbed by an antler or tusk in the process. Gathering food would not have been as immediately dangerous, but would be long, hard, work.

Nowadays, in the western world at least, finding food is not a life-threatening feat, but for most of the last 5 million years it would have been.[3] You could get eaten trying to find something to eat! Our brains had to give us an incentive to want to do that.

For most people, eating food is highly pleasurable. If you have the anorexia genetics, once you get into energy deficit and after the

[3] Int J Obes (Lond). 2009 Jun; 33(Suppl 2): S8–13. Appetite control and energy balance regulation in the modern world. Reward-driven brain overrides repletion signals Huiyuan Zheng, Natalie Lenard, Andrew Shin, and Hans-Rudolf Berthoud

anorexia response to that deficit is triggered, your brain begins to see eating more food than the minimal amount possible as a threat. That doesn't mean that we totally stop getting pleasure out of eating. The pleasure is often still there, but overwhelmed by fear and anxiety.

As I moved into energy deficit, I began to feel a substantial *dis*incentive to eating — crippling fear followed by guilt and anxiety. Anorexia didn't stop food from tasting good, but that was massively outweighed by intense feelings of negativity and discomfort.

"I was just so surprised at how easy dieting was for me. I know some other guys who have dieted and they go on about how hard it is. For me it was so easy, I guess I felt like for that reason it was the right thing to do. I feel so stupid. I could have avoided this whole nasty experience had I not done that diet." - M, adult in recovery from anorexia.

For people with the genetic predisposition for anorexia, what began as a diet can turn into a full-blown, life-threatening, eating disorder. The person will begin to have thoughts inspiring them to move more and eat less, they will start to have a fear-reaction to food, and they will often begin to show signs of weight loss — but remember, a person can have anorexia and be in energy deficit without presenting at the stereotypical low weight.

One of the symptoms of anorexia is not knowing the extent of your problem (anosognosia). The individual will usually be unaware that anything is wrong with them until either the illness has caused them to become physically compromised, or the mental misery of the anorexia thought patterns gets too much to bear. Even then some individuals (like myself) cannot see that they have an eating disorder. This is a real problem with stigma and stereotypes; because those of us who don't fit the mold of the body-dysmorphic, teenage girl rarely get diagnosed. Therefore, we don't get help, and the behaviours of the illness become more and more entrenched over the years. (But don't fear, you can still recover regardless of how long you have been sick.)

Not eating feels good, right, and focused ...

For a person with a restrictive eating disorder such as anorexia, we can feel really calm, relaxed and have a huge sense of wellbeing when we eat less. I used to feel incredibly focused when I resisted eating. It felt good and right to do so. I loved that feeling of safety that I initially got from eating only as little as possible. It was alluring. It felt rather like a game — and one that I was good at! Feeling successful made me want to restrict more and more. I felt powerful.

Eating, however, would make me feel stressed and anxious. Therefore, not eating was also a case of negative state relief.

It was so much easier all round not to eat very much. Whilst the weight loss felt good too, it wasn't as much about that as about the way that restriction felt so right and eating felt so wrong. In a sense, it felt like madness to make myself eat when I didn't want to. Plus then there were the compliments from others. The "Oh, you've lost a little weight ... you look great" sort of comments. Those comments alone would not have been enough to make me continue to eat less, but when I was on that path already, they certainly added incentive. Even my doctor told me I was looking fit and well. Everything and everyone seemed to congratulate my lack of eating. (Apart from my mother, who was on my case from day one. Good for her. Thanks Mum!)

An Alternative View Of Anorexia

I was never able to resonate with any of the psychoanalytical suggestions about my illness. I didn't see how my behaviours could possibly be a response to trauma, as I never experienced trauma. I didn't see how my weight loss could be attributed to bad parenting because my parents were (and still are) wonderful. I didn't see how my restriction was an attempt at controlling my life, because I had never felt particularly out of control in the first place. I didn't see how I was making myself thin in order to avoid sex, because I had no reason to avoid sex. None of these explanations ever made sense. I was extremely lucky growing up, and was a very happy, body-confident kid. I found the idea of blaming my parents, an aversion to sex, a need for control, or some non-existent trauma to be insulting. Insulting to me, insulting to my parents, and insulting to anyone who has actually experienced trauma.

For some people, these suggested psychoanalytical reasons for food restriction and weight loss may resonate because they have been through tougher times than I had before the onset of their illness. I understand and respect that. But even then, even when a person has been through trauma or other complications, does psychoanalysis actually work in helping them reach nutritional rehabilitation?

I am not going to judge the effectiveness of any form of talk therapy for a trauma survivor in this book. This book is not about treating trauma. But, I will say this: treating trauma alone does not amend malnutrition. If a person has suffered trauma, and also has an eating disorder, then the two things need to be treated appropriately. Regardless of the presence or absence of trauma in a person's life, if they have a restrictive eating disorder they have to nutritionally rehabilitate in order to recover. Nutritional rehabilitation will not make the trauma go away either, thus support for that needs to be ongoing. Additionally, there is often a need for high-level professional support when a person who has experienced trauma is going through the recovery stages due to the heightened anxiety in this time. Nutritional rehabilitation has to be the first port of call for a person with anorexia regardless of whatever else is going on, but you have to assess your individual situation and put additional support in place if needed.

"During adolescence, I experienced significant amounts of what the psychological system refers to as trauma—serious sexual and physical abuse, as well as a very bizarre childhood and alcoholic father, etc. I do not deny the experiences, nor the suffering. But the trauma did not cause my anorexia. After one particular event, I shut down and quit speaking, did not sleep, and lost my appetite, completely. I lost weight. A few months later, I had entered fully into Eating Disorder patterns, and slid straight into hell. I was told to blame my parents, and encouraged to talk about the trauma as a way to hit a secret center button of anorexia cure. These things did not make sense to me. I was starving, though I was not hungry, and all I wanted was for someone to tell me to eat! They never did. I could not use any of the dynamics as an excuse or reason. Three therapists dropped me, as I refused to agree with the systematic talking

cure. I lost weight, and that's what triggered the genetic anorexia. My
freedom is in the food." - Stella, adult in recovery from anorexia.

In a sense, focusing on getting a person out of malnutrition will mean
that they are more able to engage in other types of therapy more
effectively. Getting a person into a place of nutritional safety is a win-
win solution regardless of the additional obstacles that person is
facing.

Anorexia is not evil

Anorexia is a genetically coded, energy-deficit provoked reaction that
invokes cascading behavioural, physiological and psychological
reactions, which, if sustained long enough, become habitual.

The personification of the illness that we all (myself included at times)
seem to have normalised may serve a purpose in early recovery. It is
certainly helpful to parents of children with anorexia as it allows them
to separate illness from child, and was helpful to me in my own
recovery in helping me separate my anorexia desires from my healthy
desires. But I don't think it is indefinitely helpful when we start to overly
personify the illness. Anorexia is not a nefarious imp. Anorexia is not a
demonic possession. Anorexia is not your ex-boyfriend. Anorexia is not
evil.

Rather than personifying anorexia and hating it, I found it more
productive to look at my situation a little less emotionally. When I
stepped back to look from a detached viewpoint, I was able to take a
more pragmatic approach to my recovery. In essence, I stopped taking
it personally. There is no point in hating anorexia. Over time I have

developed a sense of compassion for my anorexia — the following chapters may help you understand why. Anorexia evolved for a reason. In some certain circumstances — such as a famine environment — anorexia may have saved my life.

My husband works as a software engineer. When the code is not producing the results that he wants it can be frustrating. However, sitting and arguing with the computer doesn't fix it. That would be a waste of time and energy. To fix it, he has to rewrite the code. When I was able to see anorexia in this way, and when I saw eating more and not complying with disordered behaviours as rewriting the code, I was finally successful in achieving full recovery. I could sit there and argue with anorexia all I wanted, but doing so changed nothing. Taking action put me in a position to rewrite the code.

Let's have a look into why anorexia may have, in certain circumstances, been a lifesaver.

Anorexia As An Evolved Response to Famine

Out of all the theories around the "why" behind anorexia nervosa, Shan Guisinger's *Adapted to Flee Famine Perspective*[4] makes the most sense to me. It is based upon the Darwinian view that biological systems, including psychological functions, have evolved through natural selection because of their contribution to inclusive fitness.[5] There are a ton of examples of situations of migrating mammals in a response to famine and when you consider that for early humans, lack of available food would have been the biggest survival threat, it is no wonder that a migration response would have evolved in some groups of humans. We are mammals, after all, regardless of how superior we like to think we are. And when a vital element to life, such as food, is compromised, our primal instincts take over.

From an evolutionary point of view, it is proposed that as far as the brain is concerned, if you are not eating enough then that must mean that you are existing in a famine or hostile environment.[6] In times of famine, the brain and body are forced into survival mode. For most people, survival mode may look like trying to find something to eat and lying low. For those of us with anorexia genetics, the energy deficit of famine provokes something completely different: migration.

---

[4] Adapted to Flee Famine: Adding an Evolutionary Perspective on anorexia Nervosa, Shan Guisinger

[5] W.D. Hamilton, The genetical evolution of social behaviour I & II, Journal of Theoretical Biology 7 (1964), 1–52.

[6] Caballero, 2007 The global epidemic of obesity: An overview Epidemiologic Reviews, 29 (2007), pp. 1–5

I tend to call this the Anorexia Famine Response, because this is the system that seems to switch on when your body believes it needs to migrate due to scarcity of resources in the current environment.

Certain species of mammals have a migration response when food supplies get low, and I believe that some of us humans do too. In mammals that migrate, a desire to eat can get in the way of the process of migration, so the desire to eat gets shut down while the animal is in migration mode.[7] If a migrating bird stopped every time she saw a worm she would not get very far! She would never make it to the areas of abundant food and therefore, stopping to eat too much along the way may actually be a threat to long-term survival. Hence, for migration, eating is rather a distraction and therefore a migratory adaptation is to not want to feed much for the duration of migration. That's why too much food feels like a threat. In a sense, if you need to migrate, feeding is a threat to your ability to do this successfully.

Guisinger's *Adapted to Flee Famine Perspective* explains why people with anorexia restrict food, are unaware of the effects of starvation, and are often hyperactive. Guisinger presents anorexia as having evolved as an adapted mechanism for fleeing famine — as a migratory response. Not a choice. Not an emotional coping mechanism. Rather, involuntary genetic code that prompts the migratory response of wanting to move; not wanting to eat; and a certain lack of self awareness.

---

[7] Animal anorexias N. Mrosovsky and David F. Sherry (1980) *Science*

I especially love how this theory removes the blame for having the condition from the patient. And the patient's family too.

Genetics

A genetic locus has been found for anorexia.[8] This is fabulous news for those of us who have long been arguing that anorexia is a biologically-based illness rather than a purely psychological one. It makes it a lot easier to advocate for food as the primary treatment for anorexia when people understand that many of the character changes that a person goes through are due to malnutrition. (It bothers me somewhat that the genetic samples are only drawn from people who are stereotypically statistically underweight, because people with anorexia in larger bodies are not usually diagnosed, so don't enter the samples. Hopefully as research progresses we will be able to support body diversity and show that a person can also be in energy deficit at any weight if their weight is lower than that which they should naturally be.)

Of course, genetics alone don't determine if a person develops anorexia or not, as energy deficit needs to be present in order for those genetics to be activated. Anxiety, stress, illness, over-exercising, and dieting behaviour can trip the switch.

One important relevance of genetic evidence in terms of anorexia nervosa is that it shifts the focus away from that elusive "underlying reason" for the illness and therefore gets to the effective treatment —

[8] Cynthia M. Bulik et al. Significant Locus and Metabolic Genetic Correlations Revealed in Genome-Wide Association Study of Anorexia Nervosa. American Journal of Psychiatry, 2017; appi.ajp.2017.1 DOI: 10.1176/appi.ajp.2017.16121402

food — sooner. Less time wasted means the illness is less able to take root, resulting in weaker and less entrenched behavioural neural pathways to rewire. The sooner energy deficit can be amended, the easier it is to unroot the illness.

Now that we have genetic evidence for anorexia and other metabolic illnesses, the *Adapted to Flee Famine Perspective* makes even more sense to me. Evolutionary theories surrounding why we eat in the way that we eat aren't just limited to anorexia projections, there has been shown to be a higher incidence of metabolic disease among populations believed to have experienced famine or other extreme nutritional conditions in the past. *The Thrifty Gene Hypothesis* suggests that for some people, a metabolic response to deprivation that caused them to store body fat would have been a survival advantage.[9] This may also explain why going on a diet makes a person with these genetics gain weight faster. It seems that, increasingly, information is pointing to genes being in control of a person's body shape and the way that they eat.

Genes evolve for a reason, and more and more it looks like anorexia and other metabolic illnesses are down to code that made sense for thousands of years, but became obsolete with the invention of the commercial refrigerator.

Epigenetics

Epigenetics is a mechanism by which the environment directly impacts a person's genes by a process called DNA methylation. In

---

[9] . Beyond Feast–Famine: Brain Evolution, Human Life History, and the Metabolic Syndrome Christopher W. Kuzawa

most basic terms, this is the turning on and off of a gene, or making it weaker or stronger.

Whilst the genes for anorexia may be there, they seem to lie dormant until turned on by energy deficit. The study of epigenetics looks into the turning on and off of such genetic code by the environment. For example, epigenetic obesity theories suggest that for some people, a tendency to put on weight and store fat may be coded into their DNA.[10][11][12]

As an example of this: it has been shown that there is a link between prenatal stress and susceptibility to Binge Eating Disorder in mice.[13] Researchers can simulate prenatal stress by giving female mice a drug that results in a limited supply of nutrients to the fetus in their wombs, thus simulating lack of nutrients in the mother's environment to the baby mouse before it is born. This sets the baby mouse up for being born into an environment of famine. Is it a coincidence that these mice were then born with a tendency to binge eat in response to stress? Maybe, maybe not.

Binge eating is a behaviour that gets a ton of criticism due to stigma and judgement — but the ability to eat a lot of food in one go may be one of the most fundamental survival skills that mammals have. In

---

[10] L. Bouchard et al., Differential epigenomic and transcriptomic responses in subcutaneous adipose tissue between low and high responders to caloric restriction. The American journal of clinical nutrition 91, 309-320 (2010).

[11] L. H. Lumey, A. D. Stein, E. Susser, Prenatal famine and adult health. Annual review of public health 32, 237-262 (2011).

[12] K. Pietiläinen, S. Saarni, J. Kaprio, A. Rissanen, Does dieting make you fat? A twin study. International Journal of Obesity 36, 456-464 (2012).

[13] A Methyl-Balanced Diet Prevents CRF-Induced Prenatal Stress-Triggered Predisposition to Binge Eating-like Phenotype. Mariana Schroeder et al

times before food was so abundant, the ability to binge eat would have likely meant that you survived better in a famine environment.

The environment you are in affects the genes that are active or dormant. And even more interestingly, researchers have found that in mice that displayed binge eating behaviour, an adequate, unrestricted diet seemed to negate it.[14]

So what about anorexia and epigenetics?[15] It has been shown that the longer a person suffers from anorexia, the higher the likelihood in alterations in their DNA methylation — this can cause changes in a person's physiological makeup.[16][17]

It is possible that environments where thinness is promoted lead to an overexpression of genes that suppress appetite and weight gain in people who are genetically vulnerable to weight suppression?[18]

So what does all this mean for you? While the exact recipe for anorexia is as yet unknown, science is beginning to piece together some of the ingredients. The environment plays a role, but only if you have a genetic predisposition. In a sense, your eating disorder is the

[14] A Methyl-Balanced Diet Prevents CRF-Induced Prenatal Stress-Triggered Predisposition to Binge Eating-like Phenotype. Mariana Schroeder et al.

[15] Eating disorders, gene–environment interactions and epigenetics. Campbella et al, Neuroscience & Biobehavioral Reviews, Volume 35. Issue 3. January 2011, Pages 784-793.

[16] The plasticity of development: How knowledge of epigenetics may advance understanding of eating disorders. Michael Strober et al.

[17] Season of birth and anorexia nervosa Giulio Disanto et al. The British Journal of Psychiatry Mar 2011.

[18] Genetics and Epigenetics of Eating Disorders, Yilmaz, Hardaway, Bulik.

result of an unlucky hand of cards. The good news is that you get to reshuffle the deck.

For now, you have to put away the "why" questions, and focus on the process of what you need to do in order to live. This is exactly what we are going to get into.

Summary:
- Anorexia genetics are activated when a person with the genetic predisposition meets the correct environment to turn on those genes.
- When those genes turn on, your brain interprets eating more as a threat to survival, and favors eating less (and often moving more too).
- Food and achieving energy balance seems to be the leading factor in turning the anorexia famine response off again.

Chapter 3: Fear

In this chapter we will explore fear and other such emotions that play a part in anorexia. Research into understanding emotions is a fascinating and evolving field. Researchers are constantly learning and theorising how feelings and emotion affect the way we see the world; our ability to apply reasoning and logical thinking; our problem-solving skills; and our ability to adapt to life changes and events.[19][20][21] It is generally thought that human emotions are made up of many parts — biological, psychological, and sociological.[22][23] Emotions are not silly indulgences or inconveniences that get in the way of with logical thinking. Rather, they are rather brilliant sorting methods where awareness, understanding, and memory are built.[24]

Emotions tell us what is important.[25] If you go and watch a film at the cinema and it doesn't spark an emotional reaction in you, you won't remember it. However, if you see a film that did spark emotion for you, then you are bound to remember it for years after. Therefore, emotions are part of memory and learning. (This somewhat explains why my French, Math, and Geography are so poor.)

---

[19] Clore, G. L., & Huntsinger, J. R. (2007). How emotions inform judgment and regulate thought. *Trends in Cognitive Sciences.*

[20] Vansteelandt K, Van Mechelen I, Nezlek JB. The co-occurrence of emotions in daily life: A multilevel approach. J Res Pers. 2005.

[21] LeDoux, J. E. (2012). EVOLUTION OF HUMAN EMOTION: A View Through Fear. *Progress in Brain Research.*

[22] The Sociology of Emotions: Basic Theoretical Arguments Jonathan H. Turner, SAGE Journals, 2009.

[23] Kováč, L. (2012). The biology of happiness: Chasing pleasure and human destiny. *EMBO Reports.*

[24] Kensinger, E. A. (2009). Remembering the Details: Effects of Emotion. *Emotion Review.*

[25] Clore, G. L., & Huntsinger, J. R. (2007). How emotions inform judgment and regulate thought. *Trends in Cognitive Sciences.*

It helped me a lot when I was in recovery to identify my resistance towards changing my eating and movement behaviours as fear. For some reason, I went years without understanding that it was fear that was controlling me. I thought maybe I was just stubborn, or defiant, but I never used the f-word. When I was able to understand that my inability to gain weight or eat more came down to fear, I immediately understood what I needed to do. You see, due to my ego, I hate nothing more than being afraid. I have always been a person to run towards — rather than away from — things that scare me, so once I had labelled my resistance to change as fear, I knew exactly what I had to do.

Fear of eating

I've lived in war zones, and it still wasn't as hard as this!"- Anon, adult in recovery from anorexia (military).

No fear I've ever felt was as powerful as the fear around eating more than the minimum amount possible when I had anorexia. The fear that you are dealing with as you eat more in anorexia recovery is an instinctual, urgent fear. You can overcome this fear by knowing what it is, why it is there, and learning to ignore it. Needless to say, this is not easy. But you will learn how to do it. You have to.

The fear of eating is a paralyzing fear. A brain-freezing, mind-fogging, non-negotiable, get-me-out-of-here-before-I-hurt-someone kind of fear.

For many of us, the fear we feel when faced with eating more —
despite the presence or absence of a desire to gain weight — is
devastating and confidence shattering. Understanding why the brain
invokes such a crippling fear reaction to eating food, eating more food
than other people, weight gain, and resting can help you categorise
this fear and overcome it.

Why is food a threat?

If someone offered me food, I would feel as if they had pulled a gun
on me. That is how threatening more food felt.

How ludicrous is that?
Was I hungry? Yes, always.
Did I want to gain weight? Logically, yes.
Did I understand that food is not anything to be scared of? Logically,
yes.
Did any of those truths make a blind bit of difference to the level of
threat I would get when faced with more food? No!

If anorexia genes exist as an adaptation that helps us survive in times
of famine and migrate to areas of abundant food, it makes sense that
for that time of migration, stopping and eating "more" than the
minimum needed to stay alive and keep moving that day could be a
threat to your survival. Migrating animals cannot afford to stop too
long. A bird on the wing eats only what it needs to intake in order to
keep going. There is an urgency to migration. Getting to the place of
abundant food is a pressing matter — if you stop and eat longer than

everyone else, the chances are that you will not reach the lands of abundant food at all. If you don't migrate, you die. In that sense, eating more is a threat to your survival — so is resting.

Many of us fear eating "too much" when we are in recovery. Eating more than other people who are also eating gives many of us intense feelings of wrongdoing. From a migration point of view this makes sense — if you stop for too long in a location where there was "some" food but not "abundant" food, you might risk never getting to the areas of abundant food. If you stop and eat longer than the other people in your group you may get left behind. If famine is extreme, you may be in competition with members of your own group in terms of getting to the lands of abundant foods first.

"I wanted to kill my husband this morning because he made himself an egg-white omelette rather than using the yolks. I came very close to purging as it felt so wrong that I had eaten an omelette with yolks in when he didn't." - BJ, adult in recovery from anorexia.

Many of us hate to admit it, but watching other people eat more than we do feels rewarding. As if we are in a secret competition with them over who can eat the least. As far as your migrating body is concerned, you are. You are fighting for your life to get to the lands of abundant food first. This means eating the least, and moving the most. While living in the 21st Century many of us cannot fathom that we might starve to death, for the most of human evolution, famine would have been one of the biggest threats to survival. That's why your brain is so primed to be afraid of it.

This also explains why there is such an urge to move straight after eating something for many of us with anorexia. Don't stop too long. Eat only what you need to survive then move again.

"I eat really slowly ... drag it out ... but as soon as I have finished eating I have to get up and clean the kitchen. I mean even if we have guests or whatever and at Thanksgiving. Everyone else can sit around the table and laugh and talk ... not me. Got to move!" - BJ, adult in recovery from anorexia.

For a migrating mammal, eating more and stopping longer than anyone else could ultimately kill you. Eating more really is a threat. In that sense, it's not so crazy that I would pitch a fit at anyone who tried to get me to stop and eat. Your "irrational" feelings of anger towards people who try to make you stop and eat are totally rational from a migration point of view.

Fear of higher calorie foods

I don't think I need to tell you that people with anorexia generally have a problem eating higher calorie foods. For many of us, lower calorie foods are "safe" and higher calorie foods are "fear" foods.

These days you can buy a burger or a pizza without expending a ton of energy to get it. Historically though, higher calorie and fatty foods would have been much more difficult to attain. In order to eat meat, one would have to kill an animal. This is a large time investment, dangerous, and risky as there is no guarantee that a day spent hunting will result in a kill. Hunting is even less likely to result in a kill in a famine environment. For this reason, I think that when migrating it would make sense that the brain discourages you from the costly and risky activity of hunting for meat. Hence, a disincentive to eating highly caloric foods and incentive for eating or grazing on less caloric, but easier to attain foods such as berries and forage.

Certain species of pig do this too (thin sow syndrome).[26] When they lose weight (energy deficit) they start to move a lot and refuse to eat their higher calorie grain. Instead, they eat their low-calorie straw bedding. That's rather similar to the preference for eating low-calorie foods when you have anorexia, don't you think? Why would a pig, who is losing weight, stop eating grain and start eating straw and pacing? Because she is trying to migrate.

"I used to feel compelled to walk up and down the hospital corridor. I had no idea why I wanted to do this." - RB, adult in recovery from anorexia.

Turns out I have a ton in common with those pigs if I go into energy deficit.

From Shan Guisinger:
"Your fear of eating is not because you are vain. Your weight suddenly feels like life and death because once it was for your ancestors. You have anorexia genes because your ancestors survived by resisting their hunger and moving. Gaining a pound means you have failed to resist

---

[26] Kyriakis S.C. (2001) Anorexia-Like Wasting Syndromes in Pigs. In: Owen J.B., Treasure J.L., Collier D.A. (eds) Animal Models — Disorders of Eating Behaviour and Body Composition. Springer, Dordrecht

your hunger and move enough. Anorexia makes gaining a pound feel like the worst thing. It steals your future to help you migrate today because it was migrate or die in the Pleistocene."

Why does fear override logical thinking?

I know what you are asking yourself at this stage in reading all this: Okay, so my brain thinks it's migrating, but surely logical thinking can tell my brain that I am not really in a famine? Surely part of my brain knows that there is plenty of food around really and hence no need to migrate?

Your survival brain doesn't work like that.

"Deep inside the skull of every one of us there is something like a brain of a crocodile. Surrounding the R-complex is the limbic system or mammalian brain, which evolved tens of millions of years ago in ancestors who were mammal but not yet primates. It is a major source of our moods and emotions, of our concern and care for the young. And finally, on the outside, living in uneasy truce with the more primitive brains beneath, is the cerebral cortex; civilization is a product of the cerebral cortex." — Carl Sagan, Cosmos p.276–277

The brain stem area is your survival brain. It deals with things like food, safety, and sex. If your survival brain feels threatened, it will react without consulting with the cerebral cortex — that's the "rational thinking" part of your brain. Your brain stem area reacts. It doesn't think.

Our brains as we know them now evolved from the brain stem. Some animals, such as reptiles, only have a brain stem area — hence it is often referred to as the "reptilian brain."[27] Your reptilian brain is 'preverbal', but it controls incredibly important functions such as breathing, heart rate, and the fight, flight, or freeze response that we have when we perceive a threat. Brain stem impulses and urges are reflexes — instinctual. This probably sounds very familiar to you if you have anorexia or any other restrictive eating disorder.

Staying alive is primitive brain stuff, not executive functioning stuff. Fear protects us from death. If your brain perceives a threat to your existence, it wants to get you the hell out of danger hence it doesn't mess around asking the prefrontal cortex to sign off on the fight, flight or freeze response. In a sense we become a little daft when we are scared. We can't think logically. Everything boils down to fight (I'll kill you rather than eat that), flight (I'm running away so I don't have to eat more), or freeze (can't move or make a decision either way).

While your logical brain knows that there is a McDonalds on every corner, that is irrelevant because your brain stem isn't consulting your logical brain when it triggers that threat response to food. All it knows is that you went into energy deficit and this signals that you are in a famine environment. Remember, the brain stem doesn't think, it reacts to data. Lack of food coming in is data to support the notion that food is scarce in your environment. It has reacted to your state of energy deficit by triggering anorexia to save you by making your primary focus in life being eating less and moving — migrating. Your brain

27 Curr Biol. 2015 Apr 20; The reptilian brain Robert K. Naumann, Janie M. Ondracek, Samuel Reiter, Mark Shein-Idelson, Maria Antonietta Tosches, Tracy M. Yamawaki, and Gilles Laurent*

stem doesn't give two hoots about what your cerebral cortex thinks as it has perceived a threat and hence is overriding all other brain responses other than "migrate to where there is more food!"

The good news, is that while you cannot control this fear-based response from happening, you can control your reaction to it. The Toolkit section of this book provides exercises that will help you to do just this.

Brain tantrums

Do not expect your brain to be "on board" with recovery at all times. If recovery were easy I would not have written a book about it. When you are in energy deficit and anorexia is active, your brain will interpret eating more as a threat to your survival. It will use negative emotions and panic to try and motivate you *not* to eat more. No amount of talking about why you should eat more, and no amount of science is going to stop your brain from freaking out if you eat more. This is because the fear response is coming from your reptile brain and this will override logical thinking.

- You are going to have to eat more even while your brain is screaming blue murder about it.
- You are going to have to eat more even when it feels like the "wrong" thing to do.

Eating more is going to feel wrong … but it is right. In order to recover, you have to eat a lot of food even while your brain is screaming at you not to. This is the process of rewiring the brain that we are going to be working on in this book — teaching your brain to drop the neural pathways that associate eating with a fear response and stopping the fight or flight reaction.

Tip: When eating is really scary, focus on the mechanics of eating rather than listening to the fear that your brain is throwing out. I used to focus on my hand holding my fork and putting food into my mouth. Chew. Swallow. Repeat. Whilst also using anything and everything (TV, crosswords, books, puzzles) as a mental distraction while I performed the physical actions of eating.

You don't need your brain on board in order to chew and swallow. Your brain can be freaking out and you can still mechanically go through the physical process of eating food. I know this, because I have done this many times.

Neuroplasticity And The Brain: Rewiring Entrenched Behaviours

Learning that the brain is neuroplastic was a game changer for me in terms of recovery.[28] I have been interested in yoga and meditation since my early teens, when I first found a book on it that belonged to my mother. But I didn't really begin to put all the pieces together as to how meditation had been relevant to my own recovery until I moved to Boulder, Colorado.

Boulder is a town where meditation and mindfulness are so commonplace that you can't actually find a place to sit in a park and eat a hot dog without tripping over somebody meditating. In Boulder, every takeaway coffee comes with a side of namaste. Even a cynic like me picked up a load of meditation concepts in the first year I was here, and in doing so I began to understand that many of these mindfulness techniques were things I had intuitively been doing in recovery in order to try and keep myself calm and focused in the face of fear.

Lots of cool mindfulness techniques have been developed in and around Boulder. "Neurosculpting®" is an example of one of them. It's founder, Lisa Wimberger, describes Neurosculpting® as *"the fusion of brain science and mindfulness so even the most insidious mental beliefs can be rewritten."* Her technique is taking the functional aspects of meditation and putting them into exercises that people can use to transform their own default settings. Pretty nifty — and very similar to

---

[28] Buonomano, Dean V.; Merzenich, Michael M. (March 1998). "CORTICAL PLASTICITY: From Synapses to Maps". *Annual Review of Neuroscience.*

the thought process techniques I had been using in my own recovery. It turns out that the little mental exercises I had been doing in recovery were examples of neural rewiring techniques — I just hadn't known it!

For anyone interested, I recommend Lisa's book "*New Beliefs, New Brain*" as while it is not about eating disorders, it tells the story of how pretty much any brain-based reaction can be overcome with neural rewiring.[29]

My interest in rewiring and recovering from trauma led me to take a yoga for trauma course, and from there I went on to found and run a nonprofit organisation that taught yoga to trauma populations for free. For four years, I taught restorative yoga and breathing techniques in women's safehouses, homeless shelters, to "at risk" teens, veterans, and in substance abuse rehabilitation houses. I taught over 1000 yoga for trauma classes in those four years, and it was a wonderful time of inspirational learning for me.

What I learned about myself, and witnessed in others, is that you can change the default way in which your neurons fire by changing your behaviours and not reacting in a way that confirms undesirable thought patterns. Learning how people rewire trauma experiences also helped me to understand why I had been able to recover from anorexia the way that I did, and the importance of what I did. You see, even though I didn't realise it at the time, what I was really doing when I forced myself to eat all the foods I was scared of in recovery, and break all the anorexia-generated rules, was adding neural rewiring to nutritional rehabilitation.

---

[29] https://www.amazon.com/New-Beliefs-Brain-Yourself-Stress-ebook/dp/B00BWDV4WC

I began to understand that my recovery worked because I did both. If I had nutritionally rehabilitated by eating safe foods and keeping all my anorexia food rules in place, they likely would have persisted. Years and years of thinking and acting with anorexia had left me a mental roadmap that meant unless I challenged and rejected all these behaviours I would still wind up doing them.

Why do our anorexia-generated behaviours become so hard wired? Well, I think that if anorexia is a reaction to a perceived famine, the migration response — when it evolved — would have only been required to last long enough to get you to the lands of abundant food. A couple weeks? Many months at the most? Not really long enough for the behaviours that serve migration to become entrenched. A feast would then happen and this would have been the signal to the brain that the famine was over. Job done. You moved. You are out of danger. Get on with life.

In our current environment, diet culture is putting people into energy deficit while food is abundant. This means that there is no natural "end point" to signal the famine is over. Hence some of us are "migrating" for years.

Apparently, habits are formed in the basal ganglia part of the brain.[30] The repeated behaviours of eating very little and moving a lot start to form very strong neural pathways in our brains.[31] These become entrenched behaviours. The neural pathways that lead to these

[30] Yin HH, Knowlton BJ. The role of the basal ganglia in habit formation. Nat Rev 7

[31] Smith, K. S., & Graybiel, A. M. (2016). Habit formation. *Dialogues in Clinical Neuroscience. 18*(1), 33–43.

behaviours can become very solid.[32] Hence, the behaviours are hard to break and often feel like the default setting. Brick walls. They can become so entrenched and strong that they don't feel optional. But they are, and with determination and support you can break them.

This is one of the catch-22's of anorexia recovery. You can put on weight, you can come out of energy deficit, but if all those neural pathways and behaviours are still in place, they are going to pull you back to energy deficit again. We need to rewire and get out of energy deficit.

I rewired anorexia neural pathways and developed new ones by constantly thinking and doing thoughts and actions that strengthened my desired neural "freedom" map. While habits are very hard to break, you do have some executive control over them.[33] Time spent repeating new, recovery-type behaviours, and that old infrastructure has become forgotten, rusty, overgrown, and therefore has less potential to harm me. Many of the exercises in the Toolkit section of this book focus on helping do you just this, and many of them are exercises I instinctively developed in recovery.

Understanding neuroplasticity brought the glorious realisation that I have the power and the ability to switch my default operating system back from the one that energy deficit pushed it into. But I also understood that to do that, I would have to achieve energy balance in order to counter the years of energy deficit, and while I was still on

[32] Endocannabinoid Modulation of Orbitostriatal Circuits Gates Habit Formation (2016) Neuron, Gremel at al.

[33]Smith, K.S., Virkud, A., Deisseroth, K., and Graybiel, A.M. (2012) Reversible on-line control of habitual behavior by optogenetic perturbation of medial prefrontal cortex. Proc. Natl. Acad. Sci. U S A.

anorexia's operating system, eating and gaining weight would feel "wrong" and frightening in the process. Understanding that the things I would have to do would feel alien to me, helped me tolerate doing them while I was in this process.

Summary: Like the code in your computer, the code in your brain can be rewired with a combination of behavioural and mental operations.

Chapter 4: Anorexia And Your Core Beliefs

If you look at this picture, do you see a young woman, or an old woman?

When I first looked at this I could only see the young woman. I knew that there was an alternative perspective, but I absolutely could not see it. I had to google the old woman version, and follow written instructions on how to see the old woman. Even then it took me at least 20 minutes to be able to see the alternative version of this picture.

(Tip: the chin of the young woman makes up the nose of the old woman)

Once the brain has decided on a version of the truth, it can take a lot of work to shift that.

Your perception creates your reality, and your beliefs and mental constructs create your perception. That is why two people can look at the same picture and see different people. That is why eyewitnesses can watch the police camera video of an incident, and see different agents at fault. Even more interestingly, once your brain has settled on a perception about anything, be it a picture or a political belief, it can be exceedingly difficult to see it the other way.

The reality, is that we never really see reality. There is too much information in the world at any one moment for our brains to process all of it, so our brains filter out a lot of what is coming in via our senses.[34] In order to allow us to process information quickly, our brains often make assumptions, and fill in gaps. They draw plausible information from our preconceived notions, our beliefs, and our life experiences. What you have experienced in the past can influence what your brain tells you about what you are experiencing right now, as do any strong belief systems. Take the concept of evolution for example: people with strong religious beliefs draw different conclusions about the markers of evolution than Darwin did. People can be presented with the exact same evidence and draw different conclusions — as influenced by their core beliefs and values.

Politics is a great example of how our concepts shape our perception. Religion is another. Depending on their political beliefs and alignments, two people can read the same political news story and come out with vastly different understandings of what happened. When election results come through, we call people who voted for the other party "crazy." The opposition is wrong. They are the people who are not seeing things correctly. We become adamant that our perception is the correct representation of what is true. Our brains are designed to feel that strong conviction. That is how it keeps us safe and sane.

Until it doesn't.

34 Front Hum Neurosci. 2014;Understanding human perception by human-made illusions Claus-Christian Carbon,

Anorexia changes your perception, and your reality

When I went into energy deficit, my core concepts and beliefs — the way that I perceived the world — shifted radically. The way I perceived food altered dramatically, but it was not just the way I saw food, my perception of everything in my world changed. My internal perception, beliefs, and mental constructs altered in a magnificent way. This shift affected every aspect of my life — so much more than just my weight.

Perception of threat is what sparks our fear response. Our mental constructs and concepts shape what we perceive as a threat. Because your perception creates your reality, it doesn't matter how non-dangerous the thing that you perceive to be a threat is, your body will process it and elicit a fear response.

Take for example, a person who is afraid of snakes. My little sister had a pet snake as a teenager. He was called Archie, and he was harmless. It didn't matter how harmless Archie was, if a person was afraid of snakes, no amount of reassurance was going to get them to pet Archie. And regardless of how unafraid I was of Archie, my own perception relays nothing about the very real fear of him that someone else might have. We don't get to judge other people's levels of fear as insignificant based off our own. Fear is fear. With anorexia, my brain processed food as a threat. Food is not a threat. But my brain processed it as one, and that was therefore my new reality.

If energy deficit is the trigger, is the answer as easy as energy balance?

Yes, and no. Not quite. It depends how long the anorexia neural pathways have had to form and become entrenched.

The longer that a person "uses" the anorexia neural pathways of restrictive thinking, OCD-ED, and energy deficit seeking behaviours, the stronger those pathways become. As a person moves out of energy deficit and towards nutritional rehabilitation, the underlying drive to restrict food may begin to wane, but the neural pathways are still there — in a sense, this is the habit aspect of the illness. The good news is that without the drive to restrict it is much easier to rewire the brain and teach it new neural pathways. Behaviours and reactions that seemed like solid brick walls before feel softer and more negotiable.

It is hard to change your behaviours if your beliefs are not in line with them — but this is exactly what you have to do in recovery. And the good news is that the more you eat and the more you move out of malnutrition, the easier it becomes as you begin to shift away from seeing food as a threat.

Energy Debt

Nutritional rehabilitation isn't simply a matter of eating more food for a couple of days, because you are not only in a state of daily energy deficit, but a state of chronic energy deficiency — an accumulation of years and years of wear and tear that your body has not had enough energy to address.

Imagine we are talking about money. Your house costs $100 a day to run. For ten years you have only been earning $50 a day. That doesn't just put you $182,000 in debt, because over those ten years you haven't been able to do any upkeep on the house, and you need a new septic tank, plumbing, and a roof. You owe $182,000 + the general upkeep and repair work that you haven't been able to do. Earning $200 a day will put you in a daily surplus, but it will still take a lot of time before you have paid off your debt and also forked out for all the repairs that need doing. It's like the difference between gross profit and net profit.

Achieving daily surplus is one thing (gross energy surplus), but it has to be sustained long enough to not only allow your body to recover from being underweight, but also to make all the healing repair work (net energy surplus).

I believe that the hardest part of this entire process is sustaining a state of daily energy surplus long enough for the process to be completed, and therefore reaching a state of true energy balance. Don't be surprised if your desire to eat a lot of food continues for a while into the process. Trust that if your body is asking for food that is knows what it is doing, and provide it with the nutritional resources it is asking for without judgement.

Running Into Fear

I remember once, I think it was around year three into my illness, I went to a village hall function with my parents: Harvest Supper. It's a casual village meal cooked and served by the ladies on the Parish Council. I remember the main course coming out and being placed in front of me. It was lasagna. I still remember now the fear that rushed through my body as I saw in front of me something that I couldn't fathom eating. The panic rose from my chest up my neck until my ears felt hot. I felt claustrophobic. I felt like I was going to puke. I was surrounded by people. My parents were there. Everyone was laughing and chatting as if this were the most normal situation in the world — which I guess it was. But not for me. I was alone in my fear.

The negotiations were running thick and fast through my panicked brain. How could I get out of eating this? Could I pretend I was sick? A million thoughts all at once negotiating, plotting, trying to figure out a way to make the panic subside. The fear felt like a blowtorch on my face and I had to get away from it.

"What's wrong?" someone might ask me as they happily noshed away. And how does one answer that question without sounding like a lunatic. How would I tell the truth in that situation? *"I'm scared of the lasagna,"* feels like a ridiculous thing to say. But that was the truth. My brain would throw out a hundred reasons to try and tell me that my resistance to eating lasagna was totally justifiable. But it still all boiled down to fear. I was afraid of the food.

Fear and data

If a person's brain holds the belief that snakes are a threat, that person will likely scream and run at the sight of a snake. Doing this reinforces the fear of snakes, as it gives the brain additional data to support the notion that snakes are a threat (you screamed and ran, and you only do that if something is scary, so therefore snakes must be scary).

A person scared of snakes can know logically that a pet snake, like Archie, is not poisonous or dangerous. They are still likely to want to scream and run when they see Archie. Thus, illustrating that the fear response bypasses logical thinking.

To get that person past the fear of snakes, they need to spend time looking at, being with, and even handling snakes. When they do this, they reduce the fear response because they are accumulating data points. Every time they touch a snake and nothing bad happens, the brain has another data reference to counter the data references it has telling it that snakes are to be feared. They are rewiring that fear response. Over time, and with enough positive data points, that person will stop having a fear reaction to snakes because their brain no longer sees snakes as a threat.

Google Search for your brain

Google Search (other search engines are available) pulls the answer to any given search term by referring to an algorithm that takes into account your previously used search terms, and the most common words and answers (both locally and globally) used for that search term.

Try this. Open a browser and type in "Pizza is…" The algorithm will start to suggest things that are commonly written after people write the words "Pizza is." You can do this for any word, and Google will show you what is commonly associated with those words, as it calculates the likelihood that you will also want to search for these commonly searched word combinations is high.

Your brain does a similar process as Google Search does with stimuli that you encounter in the world. If you think of pizza, your brain will draw on your previous reactions or outcomes that are associated with pizza. When you have had anorexia for a while, the reactions that your brain assumes are appropriate for pizza are usually not so nice — but that's because those negative associations are what anorexia has thrown out as data points. The task in recovery, is to heavily counter these negative data points with different ones until the brain starts making positive associations with food.

A brain in anorexia-mode perceives food, or certain types of food, as a threat. It creates a fear reaction to these things. If you respond to that fear by not eating, or by only eating a restrictive amount, you reinforce it. The Harvest Supper night that I didn't eat the lasagna, and got into a subsequent argument with my mother about it, I gave my brain data to support the notion that lasagna was a food to be avoided. I have had to eat a lot of lasagna over the years to counter that notion.

Anorexia recovery involves consistently giving your brain data to weaken the perception of threat. You do this by running into the fear that you feel, rather than away from it. Every time you run into fear and survive, you give your brain information that whatever it was that sparked the fear reaction is actually safe.

If you have had anorexia for a while, chances are that you have a bit of a data problem when it comes to food.

Your Brain In Anorexia Mode

Experts such as Dr Laura Hill have helped me to understand a little more about the functioning of the brain.[35] There are studies to show that when a person has anorexia, things can function slightly differently.

The amygdala is the part of the limbic system responsible for the response and regulation of emotions — especially fear. The amygdala has been shown to activate in patients with anorexia and elicit a fear response to seeing their weight-restored bodies.[36] Interesting that energy deficit would cause this reaction ... an aversion to wellness. I can only assume that this is because when we are supposed to be migrating we are not supposed to be feeding, and weight gain represents feeding. Many of us who reach full recovery look back at our anorexia-influenced bodies with horror, so this aversion to well-looking versions of ourselves is often reversed with recovery. Now, when I look at pictures of myself when I had anorexia, I want to march that version of me straight to the hospital. I looked terrifying, and while I knew I was underweight at the time, I could not see the full truth of my situation then.

The amygdala has been reported to be involved in the way that people with anorexia process food and body image representations, as have other brain areas such as the insula and the medial prefrontal

[35]http://tabithafarrar.com/podcast/tabitha-talks-dr-laura-hill-neurobiology-behind-eating-disorders/

[36] Body image distortion reveals amygdala activation in patients with anorexia nervosa – a functional magnetic resonance imaging study. Gert Seegera. Neuroscience Letters Volume 326, Issue 1, 21 June 2002, Pages 25-28

cortex.[37] It has been shown that people with anorexia have stronger activation of the insula when asked to rate how satisfied they are with pictures of thin bodies.[38] This indicates a far greater emotional investment in such a task than people without anorexia show. It has also been shown that people with anorexia overestimate their own body sizes, and that this may be due to a problem in the way we process information about our own bodies.[39][40]

Interestingly I have found that while people with anorexia can look in the mirror and not view themselves as underweight, when shown photographs of themselves they are more able to see it (some people, not all). For some reason a photograph sometimes provides a level of distance that allows us to see the illness more clearly. All in all, we see ourselves as fatter than we are.

"Personally, during my sickest periods in the past I never thought of myself as fat per se. I've never associated myself with the idea of body dysmorphia at all. That stock image photo of a thin woman looking in the mirror and seeing a fat reflection is very reductive and not the vast majority of people's experience, surely?.. however, what I see when I look in the mirror and what I see in photographs is starkly different and quite disturbing, to be honest. I can look at a photograph and then look in the

[37] Eur Eat Disord Rev. 2012 Processing of food, body and emotional stimuli in anorexia nervosa: a systematic review and meta-analysis of functional magnetic resonance imaging studies. Zhu Y1, Hu X, Wang J, Chen J, Guo Q, Li C, Enck P.

[38] Psychol Med. 2010 Separating two components of body image in anorexia nervosa using fMRI. Mohr HM1, Zimmermann J, Röder C, Lenz C, Overbeck G, Grabhorn R.

[39] Eat Weight Disord. 2015mBody size overestimation and its association with body mass index, body dissatisfaction, and drive for thinness in anorexia nervosa.Hagman et al.

[40] Psychiatry Res. 2014 Body size estimation in anorexia nervosa: a brief review of findings from 2003 through 2013. Gardner, Brown

mirror and see 2 totally different people; it's very disconcerting... on a bad day it can be quite the challenge to recovery, because I can look in the mirror and think 'mate you look fine today!' And then (today for example) see a candid shot of me someone's taken and think 'that's bloody grim!!"
- Anon, adult in recovery from anorexia

The insula

The insula has to balance out the parts of the brain that deal with the external environment with those responsible for maintaining homeostasis.[41] Its connections in the brain are vast. It's easier to list the parts of the brain that the insula is not connected with than those it is. It's like Waterloo Station in London — connected to everywhere. It's a communication hub! Anyway, the insula is relevant in your body representation, and your perception of self — that is, the way that you think of your body. It works with other brain areas such as the somatosensory cortex involved in perception of self. In doing this, the insula stores an integrative model of your own body. It is a bit like Google Maps in that sense.

It is usually thought that for people with anorexia, a faulty representation is given that makes a person perceive their body as different — bigger — than it really is, and this theory is behind body dysmorphia.[42][43] Not every person with anorexia has the same level of body dysmorphia, but most of us have some form or major or minor

---

[41] Menon, V. & Uddin, L.Q. Brain Struct Funct (2010) 214: 655.

[42] J Int Neuropsychol Soc. 2000 Sep;6(6):673-81.Characteristics of memory dysfunction in body dysmorphic disorder.Deckersbach et al.

[43] Saxena S, Feusner J. Toward a neurobiology of body dysmorphic disorder. Primary Psychiatry. 2006;13:41–48.

incongruence between the way we are and the way that we think we are.

For some reason, as I was nutritionally rehabilitating, I actually found it comforting to know that my perception of self was out of whack. It calmed me to think that my perception was skewed, and that the things I was feeling were inaccurate.

Chapter 5: Effects Of Malnutrition/Starvation

This chapter will explore the effects of long-term malnutrition.

You may have seen, or experienced, many of the issues outlined in the following pages. But you may not have considered them to be natural responses to energy deficit and malnutrition. There are significant things that happen when a person goes without enough food. Frankly the more I learn about how brilliant the human body is, the more in awe I am of it. And thankful that it did its job and kept me alive despite the constant strain it was under due to lack of food.

How energy deficit affects your metabolism

Let's get one thing clear. You cannot "break" your metabolism. Your metabolism is not a china vase. When your metabolism reacts to energy deficit by slowing down, it is not broken. It is actually doing its job of conserving energy in times of energy scarcity perfectly.

Your metabolism is reactive. It responds to a combination of the external and internal environmental data it is given. If that is an environment that creates energy deficit, it will slow in response. If it is an environment of energy surplus, it will speed up in response. Your body is really flipping smart!

During initial calorie restriction, you go into energy deficit, which means that you are expending more energy than you are taking in. In this initial phase, you may lose weight pretty fast. The second phase is when your rate of weight loss decreases, but will continue until fat mass is depleted. After this, if energy deficit continues, your body starts to metabolise your protein stores.[44]

Metabolic rate decreases

As you eat less and your body weight falls, your body reduces your metabolic rate in order to run more efficiently — rather like the way that you would make an effort to spend less money if you got a pay cut. You fire the maid and the butler, sell the horses, and opt to live in a 1-bed apartment rather than your mansion in the countryside. Right?

The human brain is expensive to run and is said to require around 25 percent of the energy we consume. As malnutrition continues, the prefrontal cortex and "higher brain" or "executive functioning" areas get less fuel.[45][46]

There are a number of ways in which your body economises, one of which is slowing down the movement of food through your intestines, or delaying gastric emptying. This makes sense really. If the production line of food going through your body is low, you don't need

[44] Curr Obes Rep. 2016;Changes in Energy Expenditure with Weight Gain and Weight Loss in Humans Manfred J. Müller, et al

[45] To Favor Survival Under Food Shortage, the Brain Disables Costly Memory, Pierre-Yves Plaçais, Thomas Preat

[46] Int J Eat Disord. 2015 Neuropsychological function in patients with anorexia nervosa or bulimia nervosa., Weider et al.

a conveyor belt that is running at the rate of knots. Better to save energy while there is not much food coming in by slowing that whole digestion operation down.

Your endocrine system has various ways that it economises — such as decreasing thyroid hormones, insulin, testosterone and leptin; and increasing levels of cortisol and ghrelin.[47][48] All-in-all, this results in decreased heat production (hence you feeling cold a lot) and reduction of your overall metabolic rate. The implications here for the thyroid hormones are intense, and can lead to hypothyroidism such as slow heart rate (bradycardia), hypothermia, and ultimately the thyroid gland can shrink in size.[49] Many of the hormones that control appetite are affected, and this contributes to the illness by making us feel less hungry.

It was noted by Ancel Keys, that food restriction results in a very considerable set of adaptations by the human body. However, miraculously the life of the organism is maintained closer to "normal" than would be thought possible:[50]

Man, therefore, can achieve a not inconsiderable adaptation to the caloric restriction. The manner in which the adaptation is achieved, however, is, in part, quite different from the way in which the body adapts

[47] J Int Soc Sports Nutr. 2014;Metabolic adaptation to weight loss: implications for the athlete, Eric T Trexler et al

[48] J Int Soc Sports Nutr. 2014;Metabolic adaptation to weight loss: implications for the athlete, Eric T Trexler et al

[49] Evidence of diffuse atrophy of the thyroid gland in patients with anorexia nervosa.. Støving et al. Int J Eat Disord. 2001

[50] Adaptation to caloric restriction. Henry Longstreet Taylor and Ancel Keys The Laboratory of Physiological Hygiene. University of Minnesota, Minneapolis

to such stresses as high-altitude exposure, heart disease, or an increase in the environmental temperature.

It is clear that much of the adaptation is an automatic consequence of the use of the body itself as fuel for the metabolism. The life of the organism is prolonged or maintained closer to normal than would otherwise be the case by the rather desperate expedient of reducing the mass activity of the organism. - Adaptation to Caloric Restriction Henry Longstreet Taylor and Ancel Keys The Laboratory of Physiological Hygiene, University of Minnesota, Minneapolis

Most of the time you have no idea how much distress your body is actually in. Whilst all these things were going on inside my body, I had little knowledge of them. I was so fixated on restriction and exercise that I thought of little else. I was simultaneously self-absorbed and alarmingly unaware of myself. This makes it even more scary in a way, as it enabled me to keep going despite being in a state of malnutrition. We can kid ourselves that it's okay because we feel okay. It isn't.

If anorexia is a survival adaptation to a famine environment, why is the malnutrition it creates so very bad for us? Surely this is maladaptive?

Well, I imagine that if it were for migration purposes, then anorexia's urges to move a lot and eat very little would serve to get you to where the abundant food was. Then when abundant food was met and feasting began, that would signal to the body that the migration response could be switched off. An end point. In the modern world where energy deficit is instigated not for reasons of food scarcity, there is no natural shutoff point. The state of malnutrition can go on for years and cause serious damage and even death.

Malnutrition is stressful

A starving animal is paranoid, irritable, hyper-alert, mean, defensive, possessive. What does a starving animal do with food it can't eat? It hoards it. It steals it. Many of us with anorexia start hoarding food and other resources and are unable to spend money or even allow ourselves to wear our "good" clothes for fear of ruining them.

"I have this leather jacket in my wardrobe. I've never worn it. Instead, I continue to wear the scrappy old jacket I bought it to replace. I never used to be weird about wearing new clothes before anorexia."- BJ, adult in recovery from anorexia.

My "hungry brain," was preoccupied with food and directed all my sensory energy towards finding potential food sources, smelling, and tasting food.[51] Hence, in combination with anorexia, which inhibits actual eating, I developed all manner of odd behaviours; such as, cookbook obsessions, grocery store frequenting without buying, and tasting food before spitting it out. I didn't know it at the time, but cookbook porn, an obsession with cooking programs, and a tendency to nibble at or smell foods when nobody was looking are all very common in anorexia.

The malnourished brain is also pretty wary of change, and anxious about the future — be it five minutes or five years along the line. For

---

[51] Int J Obes (Lond). 2009 Appetite control and energy balance regulation in the modern world: Reward-driven brain overrides repletion signals. Zheng et al

people with long-term anorexia, this can actually work to make us fearful of the change that recovery may bring. For all of us, it looks like inflexibility. For some of us, we don't like going on vacation, we don't like things like holidays, or anything that is a change from the normal day. We future-trip and allow the "*what ifs?*" to put us off taking action. Hesitation to change means that we get deeper and deeper into energy deficit. As we cannot think clearly, the cycle continues.

In short, for many of us, the combined effects of starvation and the anorexia response elicit a shift in character. Over the years, I assumed that this anxious and stressed out personality was "me." But thankfully it wasn't. I returned to being a carefree, happy, relaxed person when my brain and body come out of malnutrition. This happens when we come into energy balance and stay there for a prolonged period of time.

Minnesota Starvation Experiment

The effects of malnutrition were documented quite nicely a long while ago in the Minnesota Starvation Experiment.[52] To summarise for those of you who have not read the study: it was a clinical analysis performed in Minnesota between November 19, 1944 and December 20, 1945, by a bloke called Ancel Keys. Keys wanted to see what happens when people are not given enough food, and how quickly or not humans can recover from malnutrition.

---

[52] 32. Keys A, Brozek J, Henschel A, Mickelsen O, Taylor HL. The Biology of Human Starvation. University of Minnesota Press: Minnesota, 1950.

After a control period on a "normal" diet of 3,200 calories, the 36 male participants in that study were put on a short-term starvation diet (~1570 calories for 6 months) and with the weight loss they began to display all sorts of out-of-character behaviours.

(Note that this "normal" amount of 3,200 calories that the men were fed in the control period is now, in our diet obsessed culture, considered over the recommended caloric requirements for the average person. I would argue that recommending caloric restriction across the board as many "health" bodies have done has only contributed to many health problems (physical and mental) today. But that's a whole other book!)

In the semi-starvation part of the experiment, the men reported feeling irritable with one another and family. They were paranoid. They hoarded food. They obsessed about food. They displayed many of the traits that are typical of anorexia, yet they did not have anorexia. From this we can see that many of these traits associated with anorexia are in fact due to the effects of starvation. And the good news is that they are reversible with nutritional rehabilitation (aka lots of food).

Food. Water. Oxygen.

"If any one of these basic needs were not met, life would be put in jeopardy." - NASA fact sheet

There are three substances that every human needs in order to live: food, water, and oxygen. This is another reason why it is so preposterous to me that talk therapy for anorexia often focuses on a person's relationships with others and ability to love oneself. A person who is missing enough of a vital human survival element such as food doesn't need to talk about love. They need to eat!

"You've got oxygen, and water, and food would be your third most pressing need. It is pretty remarkable to think that people would be psychologically just overcoming that innate drive to eat ... that's pretty shocking really." - Michael Lutter, psychiatrist and researcher on eating disorder genetics.

The above statement is from a conversation that I had with researcher Michael Lutter the week after he published the research study "*Novel and ultra-rare damaging variants in neuropeptide signaling are associated with disordered eating behaviors.*"[53] It's not just shocking, it's ludicrous that for decades it has been thought that people with restrictive eating disorders will override all feelings of hunger and starve themselves to death on a whim.

Incidentally, the above study is among only a few that have looked into linking neurotransmitters involved in feeding and appetite to eating disorders. Lutter told me that what seems rather an obvious finding — that the neurotransmitters that govern feeding behaviour are disrupted in people with eating disorders — hadn't been found before ... because nobody looked for it. The field of research has been so focused on looking for psychological reasons behind anorexia and

---

[53] http://tabithafarrar.com/2017/09/eating-disorder-science-variants-neuropeptide-signaling-associated-disordered-eating-behaviors/

other eating disorders that the most blatant biological connections are only just being explored.

Effects Of Malnutrition — ones you may notice in yourself

Malnutrition has to be treated as a serious, life-threatening, medical emergency. Here are some of the most commonly observed effects. Of course, there are more, and there are things specific to you that I may not have noted. Additionally, don't expect to have all of these effects, and not having them doesn't mean you are not in malnutrition. We are all different.

Sensitivity to noise, crowds etc.

Many of us find we develop a hyper-awareness of our environment when we are in malnutrition. Disliking the sound of other people eating or breathing is common. I hated being in crowded public spaces but it was more the noise that got to me than anything else. I also developed a strong intolerance to the sound of road traffic, or other forms of white noise. This effect reduced with recovery. I still don't love noise, but my aversion to it is not nearly as strong as when I was in energy deficit. It doesn't get under my skin and make me fractious like it used to.

I've also heard some people become very sensitive to the smell of cooking when they have anorexia.

"I had an extra extraction fan fitted in the kitchen because I hate cooking smells." - RB, adult in recovery from anorexia.

Many people with anorexia have told me that they cannot abide to hear other people eating. I don't remember this being a thing for me, but frankly that is probably because I was so isolated all the time I rarely had anyone else to eat with anyway. But in case you have noticed this about yourself, yes, it is a fairly normal anorexia trait, and your sensitivity to noise should reduce as you recover.

"Even listening to my kids eating annoys me. Makes me feel like a bad mother." - EJ, adult in recovery from anorexia.

Edema

Swelling is most common in the ankles, feet, under the chin, cheeks, and around the eyes. I've known plenty of clients who experience swelling in their legs and arms. This can happen during restriction or during phases of recovery. With refeeding, edema (and general swelling) is common. This can be painful and is awkward at the best of times.

Here is something I learned about edema from Dr Jennifer Gaudiani: Edema can actually be due to an overcompensation towards dehydration by the body. The way I understand it (in non-doctor speak) is if you have been purging via vomiting or laxative use etc then sometimes the edema can be extensive, because when you purge, your body gets massively dehydrated and low in salt. To guard against losing more water and salt, a hormone called aldosterone gets produced — this hormone stops you losing as much salt and water in your pee. When you stop purging and start to rehydrate overproduction of aldosterone by your body can lead to the huge water retention that some people see. This is usually short lived but if it goes on too long it is not optimal and there are medications that you can take to reduce it. If your MD is not savvy to these effects of purging, then ask them to look into high production of aldosterone (something that is called Pseudo-Bartter Syndrome).

"My legs are swollen and painful. I'm tired. I feel like ten years of exercise just caught up with me" - EJ, adult in recovery from anorexia.

Any significant throbbing, discoloration, or dizziness should be presented to a medical professional for observation.

Dysphagia (difficulty swallowing)

This is not something I have experienced myself, but I have heard about it from others. Apparently, it feels like foods are getting stuck in your throat.

Funnily enough, it was explained to me by my dog's veterinarian, that when animals are very sick and don't eat enough sometimes the muscles that they use to swallow food become weak. We were talking about an elderly dog at the time, but it clicked for me then that this is what this difficulty swallowing business that some people had told me about was. If you go to your doctor about difficulty swallowing and they are not eating disorder informed they may look for causes of this but it is likely that it is due to your state of malnutrition.

Impatience and irritability

Malnutrition, a state of stress for the body, often causes significant personality shifts, markedly with general impatience and irritability. I used to be particularly antsy and cranky. I think that hunger makes one this way, but I can also speculate that impatience would be a healthy trait in a famine environment. I hated any circumstance that meant I had to wait, as this would be time wasted standing still or sitting when I felt that I should have been moving or exercising. The general irritability I felt played into the same time pressures. Even when talking to friends I would be hoping that the conversation would end so that I could walk again or get back to doing whatever OCD-ED ritual was next on my mental list.

Many people in recovery have spoken to me about finding their levels of irritability distressing. Needless to say, this is often heightened around mealtimes. But for some of us it is far more than that. I found I was rather like a bratty teenager and particularly unable to be nice to people whom I was close to. Mainly my parents, and my mother certainly bore the brunt of my snarkiness. I think a lot of this was because she was the greatest threat in that she was always pushing me to eat more. I always loved her deeply, but as soon as she walked into the room I would be catty with her.

"I hate how mean I am to my husband. I miss him while he is at work, but as soon as he is home I am nasty to him. Almost like I can't control it. All he has to ask is "how was your day?" and I snap at him! Like I feel my skin crawling with annoyance and all he did was walk in the door! I don't

want to be this bitch I am turning in to." - J, adult in recovery from anorexia.

What "J" describes above is similar to how I felt towards many people I was close to when I was in severe energy deficit. I didn't know when I went into recovery that my irritable personality would alter, but it did. Turns out I have the capacity to be loving and patient with people when I am not in a state of prolonged starvation. Who would have thought!

"But I don't WANT 3 eggs in my omelette, I only want 2"; "it's not FAIR that I have to have another snack, YOU don't have to have one; "why won't you let me run? I hate you, you're ruining my life!". Are these the ramblings of an adolescent, outraged teenage girl? Nope, these are the comments that I, a 40 year old woman says to her husband on a daily basis. Because I have an eating disorder and am therefore also a teenage brat." - SF, adult in recovery from anorexia

Depression

When your body is under-resourced for a prolonged period of time, it is bound to get to a point where it feels depressed. There have been studies showing that low serum lipid levels are associated with increased suicidality, and death via suicide is higher in populations of people with anorexia than it is the general population. [54][55] In short, lower than average levels of blood cholesterol — common for people

[54] Wu, S., Ding, Y., Wu, F., Xie, G., Hou, J., & Mao, P. (2016). Serum lipid levels and suicidality: a meta-analysis of 65 epidemiological studies. *Journal of Psychiatry & Neuroscience: JPN*,

[55] Pompili, M., Mancinelli, I., Girardi, P., Ruberto, A. and Tatarelli, R. (2004), Suicide in anorexia nervosa: A meta-analysis. Int. J. Eat. Disord.

on low-fat diets — have been linked with a greater risk of being depressed and/or suicidal.

Unfortunately, I never allowed my depression to stop me from exercising. I think I heard once that the best thing for depression is to get up and get going, so I took this advice to the extreme. Turns out that this wasn't the "best thing" for me at all! The more tired and depressed I felt the more I pushed myself and the less that I ate. I have since learned that this is not the way to deal with malnutrition-induced depression. Eating and resting is the way to deal with a tired, undernourished body and mind. And yes, this can be another aspect of recovery that gets worse before it gets better.

Depression is common in recovery, and there is a bigger section addressing this later.

Lanugo and feeling cold

As your metabolism lowers, your body has less fuel to use for central heating. You'll notice that you can't get warm, and your hands, nose, and feet get a purple or white tint a lot of the time. I was cold all the time when I was underweight. Even in the summer! Painfully cold. One of the best parts of recovery is not feeling the cold any more. There is a fancy name for the cold, white, hands and feet that many of us get: acrocyanosis.

"I can't wait for the day when I don't have to practically sit on the radiator" - LG, adult in recovery from anorexia.

In order to try and keep warm, many of us develop this fine hair over our bodies called lanugo. It's not the most attractive of things. Lanugo tends to come around the cheeks and arms first and the back. Thankfully this gradually goes away with recovery. I hated the lanugo; it drew attention to the poor state I was in. People noticed it, and this would make me squirm if questioned about it.

Dulling of senses and emotional responses

I swear that as I progressed through recovery I began to see the world as a brighter place — literally. Colours stood out more. Music had more appeal. I hadn't noticed my own lack of depth of sensory processing until it improved again. Energy may be redirected away from sight, sound, touch, and taste sensitivities when we are in a state of malnutrition. I didn't notice this as I slid into energy deficit, but I did notice my senses getting brighter on the way out. Colours seemed more colourful the more I ate!

I also noticed that other than the emotions of paranoia, irritability, anger etc, I was rather emotionally inept while I was in energy deficit. I don't think I cried for years other than when I was screaming at someone who tried to make me eat. It was a tremendous shock to me that one day in recovery I started to blub watching the film *Love, Actually*. I didn't know whether to be embarrassed by my own sappiness, or relieved that I could finally display convincing human emotion.

Paranoia and defensiveness

A starving brain that thinks it is in a threatening environment has to be on the offensive in order to protect itself from danger. I was unreasonably paranoid that the entire world was in collusion with the sole mission of making me stop and eat more, or exercise less. Anyone who showed up with food as a gift was a suspect. Anyone who caused me to be late to exercise was on my hit list. When asked why I was not eating I would readily launch off the handle in an aggressive defense of my choice not to eat.

"When I was picking the kids up from school yesterday another parent stopped and was chatting to me. The whole time I was talking to her I was mad at her as I was aware it was getting dark and I would not have time for my run after we got home. A part of me felt like she was stalling me on purpose to stop me running. I know that's so illogical but I auto-hate anyone who may accidentally cause me to do less exercise." - EJ, adult in recovery from anorexia.

Being made to eat more or move less was not all I was paranoid and defensive about. I was generally a very uptight person. It didn't take much to make me feel attacked and hence I often picked fights where they should not have existed. I was also one to escalate things quickly. If someone said something I didn't like I would often push the situation into a full-blown argument. That is not who I am. I am naturally a laid back and relatively easy-going person. I am happy to report that reaching full recovery has seen a return of the true me.

From an adult in recovery:

"OMG I blew up, I mean exploded , yesterday because my friend asked me why I had chosen our local school for the kids rather than the one her kids go to. I can't seem to control my reactions to questions that bug me. I never used to be like this. Is this normal? Is this the AN?"

Possessiveness/hoarding

Hoarding food is common for people in malnutrition. Reports on the Minnesota Starvation Experiment show that cookbooks and food related items were hoarded, but some participants also began hoarding non-food items.

I stockpiled all sorts of things, including food. I squirreled my "safe" food and God-forbid anyone else in the house accidentally touch my supply of low-calorie granola bars! One of my clients maintained a month's supply of yoghurts in the fridge — something that greatly annoyed her partner. Someone else I know collected plastic bags so that she didn't have to pay 10 pence at the grocery store. Another stacked every inch of space in the cupboards with dried fruit. Some people hoard foods that they won't eat too — for one client, he needed to have loads of crisps and cookies in his kitchen, knowing full well he would never touch them. This goes with many items — clothes, cleaning items, books, magazines, etc.. For whatever reason, it is a sort of comfort to the massive anxiety, to "have enough."

"In hospital, I kept hoarding food in my draws. Anything I could get! They shouted at me so many times and would randomly inspect my draws and empty them." - RB, adult in recovery from anorexia.

Many of my clients (and I did this also) felt an OCD-like urge to replenish their "stash" on a daily basis. One thing eaten means replacing the missing bar/egg/banana asap or before another item of the same can be eaten — like a one out, one in deal. I certainly did this with things like low-fat yoghurts and other safe foods. I could only eat one that day if I had bought one (in the marked down for quick sale section of the store) regardless of how many I had!

"I have enough raisins to last one year. I go through a XXg bag in a month so I always have to buy a new bag every month to make sure I have over 12 bags in the cupboard at any time. It's not just raisins - dried apple and apricots and the "safe" gingersnap biscuits that I am allowed." - Anon, adult in recovery from anorexia.

Part of my hoarding was due to my reluctance to spend money. I would salvage plastic plates and cutlery, paper napkins and all sorts of odd things. I once remember having a huge argument with my mother as to why I washed and saved used pieces of cling film and tin foil. She thought it was weird (and it was) but I went off on a waste-reduction lecture about how I was saving the planet whilst she was contributing to global warming. That's one of the problems with anorexia, many of the behaviors are frugal and praiseworthy ... but still weird. Of course it is right to recycle. But my motivation at that time was not for the collective conscience. We tend to see this at play with veganism, exercise, and many other traits that are arguably okay for people without eating disorders, but dangerous for those with.

Preoccupation with food aka "Mental Hunger"

You may notice that you are thinking about food all the time. This is due to a greater allocation of mental energy towards food.[56] This is what I mean when I talk about "mental hunger." Mental hunger is a sign that your body is in energy deficit. The hormones that regulate your appetite are higher than normal when you are underweight, as the body tries to signal to the brain that more energy is required.[57] Of course with prolonged malnutrition physical hunger signals may be absent, but the mental hunger remains. Many of us become distressed about the mental attention that we pay to food all day and often in the sleepless nights.

It is important to understand that mental hunger is not just thinking about eating food. It is any thinking that involves food — so could be thinking about not eating. Or looking at cookbooks, or wanting to cook for others, or thinking about exercise (as exercise is a means to eating more).

Mental hunger can be observed by anyone who is in energy deficit regardless of whether they have anorexia or not. Sadly, people often interpret it as a food obsession that proves they have to be very restrained around what they eat. In reality you only have mental hunger if you are not eating enough or are restricting what you are allowed to eat. It is unfortunate that the diet industry thrives by putting

---

[56] All I saw was the cake. Hunger effects on attentional capture by visual food cues Richard M. Piech, Appetite 54 (2010) 579–582

[57] Ghrelin and Eating Disorders- Atalayer et al Prog Neuropsychopharmacol Biol Psychiatry. 2013

people in a state of energy deficit to the point that they become utterly preoccupied with food.

"As starvation increased ... cookbooks menus, and information bulletins on food production became intensely interesting ... " - D.M Garner. The Effects of Starvation on Behavior Implication for Dieting and Eating Disorders.

Mental hunger can also include a tendency to be overly interested in what other people are eating. I certainly used to get a weird pleasure out of watching others eat, but that was only true if they were eating more than me or eating something that I judged as "bad" or "unhealthy" food — foods I would not allow myself. It would make me cross to see other people eating a salad or low-calorie food. That felt like a direct threat or insult to me.

"I live with my family. We spend most meals together. I always watch carefully what they eat and always make sure that I eat juuuust a little less or, if I eat more, that it's not evident or it's only "healthy" food. E.g. if we have pasta at lunch and the others eat a second portion I won't eat that second portion, I'll eat a bowl of cherries instead. That way I feel "better" and "superior" - only to feel a miserable idiot slightly afterwards, because it's clearly so disturbed and sad and it's the complete opposite of what I would have done when I was healthy and didn't give the slightest fuck about what other people ate." - Anon, adult in recovery from anorexia

Having to eat less than others is not the same as watching other people eat, but the feeling I would get, especially from seeing another person eat, was a very similar feeling of betterness. As in, I was stronger because I didn't eat the fatty delicious food that the other person had succumbed to. Another extract from Minnesota Starvation Study about watching other people eat:[58]

"[The volunteers] often reported that they got a vivid vicarious pleasure from watching other persons eat or smelling food."

Trouble sleeping

Insomnia is often present in people who are malnourished. I had chronic insomnia for the duration of my illness. Arguably, if a body is supposed to be migrating, then sleep takes a back seat for the duration of the process. Food, as one of those substances vital to life, takes priority over zzz.

Conversely, some people find that they sleep really well when they are very malnourished, only to have trouble sleeping once they start restoration. I think this may be a little like the elusive hunger signals that for many of us only come when we are eating more. When you are not eating barely anything your brain concludes that the famine is so bad it may as well let you sleep as there is no point keeping you awake to eat as there is no food to eat. When you begin to eat more, your brain assumes that you are now in an environment where food is present and therefore it wants you to stay awake and eat all night.

---

[58] 4. D.M Garner. The Effects of Starvation on Behavior Implication for Dieting and Eating Disorders.

Not sleeping is painful. I had awful, *awful* insomnia when I was in malnutrition. The worst part is that sleepless nights were coupled with relentless fantasies of food. I would lie there tormented by all the foods I wanted to eat but wouldn't. I am thankful to be able to report, that nutritional rehabilitation brought with it restful sleep.

Delayed gastric emptying (feeling full)

Delayed gastric emptying (gastroparesis for those who like long words) is when the stomach empties slower than normal.[59] This means that you can feel full for ages after eating. This is another genius engineering feat that your smart body does in order to slow metabolism. If there's not enough food coming in, it doesn't want to waste energy by clearing the stomach so often.

Feeling full is an annoyance when you are trying to eat a lot of food in recovery. But it won't stay like that forever. You have to train the system back up by continually putting pressure on it to function faster by increasing your demand for its services — yes, by eating more!

Amenorrhea (in women)

Amenorrhea — a fancy long word that I always struggle to pronounce — means "loss of menstrual cycle," as resources are directed away from processes that are nonessential. It indicates hormonal disruption. The loss of your period is likely the tip of the iceberg in terms of the endocrine system response to insufficient intake, but it is the most noticeable.

---

[59] Determinants of delayed gastric emptying in anorexia nervosa and bulimia nervosa. ROBINSON et al

Loss of menstrual cycle is never a good thing. Egregiously, not all medical professionals know that amenorrhea can be a symptom of malnutrition. When I went to the doctor age 19 with no periods, he put me on the pill rather than suggest I gain weight. This is the same story for many women. I have even heard of doctors telling patients that they are lucky not to have a period.

"My doctor told me I was the luckiest girl in the world because I don't have my period." -FB, adult in recovery from anorexia.

Amenorrhea can affect your bones, your general cognition, and many other systems in your body. In the long term potentially resulting in infertility. It has to be taken seriously.

Side note: if you have not lost your period, that doesn't necessarily mean that you are not in malnutrition. I also have had clients whose periods return at very low weights — while this is a sign that things are moving in the right direction, it doesn't mean you are all recovered yet!

Low sex drive

Whether you are male or female, if your body is in a state of malnutrition and your endocrine system is lacking in fuel, the last thing on your mind will be sex. While not having a sex drive is not life threatening by any means, it can signal that your body is out of sorts.

Food. Oxygen. Water. If any of these are in deficit then the brain will not focus attention on much else. Reproductive needs come further down the hierarchy of needs. Your brain will likely want to focus your thoughts on food, hence you have a lot of mental hunger, and a lack of sex drive.

Especially people in relationships (a problem I never had when I was very sick) tend to really resent the lack of sex drive, for pretty obvious reasons. While I certainly did not miss my sex drive when I had anorexia (I was too busy thinking about food to miss anything much) I very much enjoy having it back!

Thinning hair, cracked nails, bad skin, and poor teeth

These are some of the most egregious bodily symptoms of malnutrition—and they are the ones most of us complain about most frequently. Many of us don't connect these physical reactions with malnutrition, and will likely seek any possible solution—other than food. For example, I would plaster my nails in "nail hardener" and use "thickening" shampoo on my hair rather than do the eating that I know now was really the required course of action.

Reallocation of resources away from nonessential-to-life processes impacts the appearance as well as the health of skin, hair and bones.[60] You may also notice discolouration of your fingers, nose and ears. This is caused by the body directing blood flow to organs in order to conserve heat energy more centrally. My hair got horribly thin until I almost had a bald patch. Very happy to say that my hair is now back to

[60] Strumia R. Dermatologic signs in patients with eating disorders. Am J Clin Dermatol. 2005;6:1–10.

its pre-anorexia thickness — but this took years of energy surplus and eating very well for my hair to look healthy again.

For some people, hair loss only occurs during the recovery phase. This can be alarming, as only when you start to eat more food does your hair shed faster. It seems this is the body getting rid of weak, old hair to make room for new stronger hair. Obviously, you should always be consulting your doctor if anything in recovery alarms you.

I got this horrid yellowing skin (carotenemia) which became very noticeable. One person asked me if I had been painting with orange paint as the insides of my hands were so orange looking. Much of that comes with over ingestion of fruits and vegetables containing beta carotene. I am no longer orange because I eat more than just carrots.

"I've had itchy skin a lot. Mostly in my lower legs. It's been worse at night but seems to happen randomly, other than it has definitely been something that has arrived along with increasing my intake." - anon, adult in recovery from anorexia.

I didn't have any increased itchiness when I was in recovery, but I have known plenty who did. I did have very dry skin both when I was in malnutrition, and throughout recovery, and I guess that the itchy skin that some people feel in recovery is something to do with rehydration. I've also been told that lack of fat in the diet can lead to dry itchy skin. I've had a number of clients who have experienced tingly, itchy, sensitive skin in the recovery process, but not when they were restricting. This can add to the paranoia that one is doing something wrong by eating more. If you do get itchy skin in recovery, don't allow it to give you cold feet too!

"I want to scratch so much I am worried people will think I am a junkie"- LL, adult in recovery from anorexia.

Eczema, scabies, acne, dandruff, slow healing wounds, under eye bags — these things happen when the body does not get enough food. The remedy will not come in an expensive bottle of hair conditioner or nail varnish — it comes in the form of food.

Weak bladder

Need to pee a lot? Malnutrition can weaken pelvic floor muscles, as can excessive exercise and low estrogen levels. This can be embarrassing and inconvenient. I am happy to say that nutritional rehabilitation has led to me being able to go longer without a trip to the loo!

Kleptomania

Let's make this very clear. Not everyone with anorexia has the urge to steal. I am just pointing out that I think there is a higher prevalence of people with kleptomania among people with anorexia than the general population.

Stealing is likely a more generalised symptom of starvation.[61][62] I was arrested and detained twice when I was at university for stealing. It is hard for me to talk about because this is the biggest insult to my authentic self imaginable. I am honest to a fault — except, apparently, when I am in a solid state of malnutrition.

I only ever stole things that I could afford, which makes the whole business even stranger. I stole things like toilet roll, apples, small grocery items. I got arrested in John Lewis in Edinburgh for shoplifting a single-serve packet of instant mushroom risotto. I was pitied and let off by the judge. They should have put me in hospital.

I have had periods during the ED where I have stolen money. From my parents, my ex-boyfriend and work colleagues. It was 2007, but I feel the guilt nearly every day. One work colleague caught me and I had to speak to my supervisor. I explained the situation to them. They didn't tell the police, but they said to that I had to go to a therapist. I visited a therapist, but I left the job, too, because I felt to guilty and ashamed. Always I stole the money for to buy food... It is so pitiful. - Anon, adult in recovery from Anorexia

The urge to steal as a symptom

The urge to steal food was still very great for a long while after that arrest. However, it was trumped by fear of getting caught. It didn't go away until I was in long-term energy balance. That aspect of me, like so many others reversed with adequate nutrition. The urge to steal

---

[61] Comorbodity of kleptomania and eating disorders Bryukhin et al

[62] Harv Rev Psychiatry. 1995 The relationship between stealing and eating disorders: a review.Baum

and hoard feels so distant now but I know it was strong when I was ill.

As with any illness, there are various symptoms and a person can have some and not others. Not all people with anorexia have the urge to steal. It is likely only a minority of us. Never accuse a person of stealing just because they have anorexia. But be there and listen and support them should they disclose that they have this symptom. It doesn't mean that they are a thief. It's also usually highly disturbing to those of us who do steal.

Dumpster diving

What I call "dumpster diving" is relevant here too. There were many occasions where I ate food that someone else had thrown in the bin. I worked in a restaurant when I was sick with anorexia, and I would salvage uneaten food from the plates as they came in if nobody was watching. I was deeply ashamed that I did this. Turns out I am not the only one.

"I took a donut out of the bin at work today. I brought it home with me and ate it. I don't know whether to feel proud for eating a donut — something I have not eaten in years — or utterly disgusted with myself." - Anon, adult in recovery from anorexia.

This sort of thing seems to be more common in those of us with money spending problems. It was easier for me to eat food someone else had thrown away because I didn't have to buy it. So yeah, it's a scarcity mindset thing. My starving brain trying to get the food that it so badly wanted and having to use unorthodox methods because I wouldn't just go out and buy it.

Thank goodness, with nutritional rehabilitation, my urge to rescue food from the bin is no longer present.

Kleptomania or compulsive spending

Anorexia doesn't only affect the most obvious flow of energy (food). It also often affects the relationship with money for many of us, and other things. Spending money was painful. But ... I also wanted to gather and hoard food. Not being able to spend money and a strong drive to gather food is what leads to stealing food.

People who steal when they are in chronic energy deficiency are not people who steal. If you asked me to steal a roll of loo roll right now I wouldn't do it. Mostly because that's just so dumb. Loo roll costs nothing, I'd just buy you a roll. But when I was sick, stealing felt instinctual. That is not to say I didn't feel incredible shame about it. I did.

The energy imbalance can also cause the pendulum to swing the other way. I experienced an inability to spend money, urges to steal, and urges to hoard. Other people experience compulsive spending. I think that whatever the reaction, full nutritional rehabilitation can sort it out.

Effects of Malnutrition — the ones you likely won't notice

Catabolism

Catabolism is when the body breaks down muscle and tissue for energy. It happens in order to keep your vital organs going when there is not enough food coming in. It's a bit like if you lost your job and had to start selling your furniture in order to pay the mortgage. If that goes on too long you'll have an empty house.

The metabolic cycle should be a balance of catabolism (breaking down) and anabolism (building up). In energy deficit we don't do the building up part. Many of us enter states of chronic catabolism or long-term energy deficit. While you cannot feel this happening, you feel the resulting fatigue, irritability and anxiety associated with a body in a state of catabolism. It hurts my heart that some diet "gurus" market catabolism as a weight loss tool.

Anemia

Anemia is due to lower than adequate numbers of red blood cells. This is a symptom of malnutrition. Your starved bone marrow no longer has the resources it needs to produce cells. I spent 10 years in and out of the doctor's office due to anemia. My doctor kept on upping and changing the iron supplements she was giving me. She would also tell me to eat more red meat, but that was about as far as she went with associating my chronic anemia with malnutrition. Once the body is past a certain state of energy deficit all the iron supplements in the world aren't going to help. I needed to give my body more fuel overall so that it could produce resources for me.

A couple of years post nutritional rehabilitation and my iron levels are just fine.

Reduction in heart size

It's not just the fat and muscle on your body that gets eaten up by energy deficit. Your organs suffer too. The heart loses muscle mass in starvation. In the Minnesota Starvation Experiment, it was estimated that heart volume of subjects decreased by an average of 17 percent. And those guys were only in semi-starvation for 6 months![63]

Additionally, the heart reduces its workload when the body is in a state of malnutrition by reducing resting heart rate: Bradycardia. There are some incredibly scary cardiovascular consequences to malnutrition; bradycardia is common, and I have that. I also have developed some arrhythmia. The most severe consequence here is sudden death by cardiac arrest — a terrifying thought but it happens!

Obviously one would notice something like a cardiac arrest, but you may not notice the stress and strain that malnutrition places on your heart otherwise. Malnutrition is a huge insult on the physical body, and every part of you will be affected by it in some way.

---

[63] Adaptation to caloric restriction. Henry Longstreet Taylor and Ancel Keys The Laboratory of Physiological Hygiene. University of Minnesota, Minneapolis

Hypoglycemia

Low blood sugar is a common medical complication with anorexia.[64] This can leave you feeling dizzy or have blurred vision and inability to concentrate. Not everyone gets symptoms when they have hypoglycemia, but if you do it tends to be things like shaking and trembling, sweats, and brain fog. Symptoms or no symptoms, hypoglycemia is a big deal so don't hesitate to talk to your doctor. Severe hypoglycemia has been associated with sudden death because it indicates liver failure and a depletion of substrate to maintain safe blood glucose levels. As with most of these malnutrition results, There can be very serious implications: In one study of nine AN patients with severe hypoglycemia, six died. [65][66]

Please take this seriously. This is one of the reasons I think that it is highly inappropriate that people with anorexia are referred only to therapists and not medical doctors who specialise in malnutrition. Get a check up.

[64] Anorexia nervosa – medical complications. Philip S Mehler and Carrie Brown Journal of Eating 2015

[65] Rich LM, Caine MR, Findling JW, Shaker JL. Hypoglycemic coma in anorexia nervosa. Case report and review of the literature. Arch Intern Med. 1990;150:894–5.

[66] Hypoglycemic Coma in Anorexia Nervosa Case Report and Review of the Literature Lisa M. Rich, MD; Marc R. Caine, MD; James W. Findling, MD; et al

Brain Atrophy

Cerebral atrophy (also known as "starved brain") can occur with malnutrition. It indicates a reduction in grey matter.[67] Symptoms are things such as general brain fog, bad memory, inability to concentrate. While this has been studied mostly in people with eating disorders, I think the role of malnutrition in these alterations is worthy of investigation. There is evidence that cerebral atrophy returns to normal with recovery.[68] It has been suggested that this reduction in grey matter can contribute to some aspects of anorexia such as body dysmorphia.[69]

"It feels like the radio is on, the TV is blaring loud, and someone is talking to you all at the same time but all you can think about is food. It is so hard to concentrate on anything!" - RB, adult in recovery from anorexia.

One study used MRI scans to show that the average gray-matter volume of people with anorexia was about 648 milliliters, compared with about 680ml for healthy individuals. This increased to an average of 663 with nutritional rehabilitation.[70]

---

[67] Cerebral atrophy in anorexia nervosa, The Journal of Pediatrics, 1980, Nussbaum

[68] J Comput Assist Tomogr. 1977 Reversibility of cerebral atrophy in anorexia nervosa and Cushing's syndrome.Heinz

[69] Gray matter decrease distribution in the early stages of Anorexia Nervosa restrictive type in adolescents. Gaudio et al

[70]Brain tissue volume changes following weight gain in adults with anorexia nervosa.Roberto et al. Int J Eat Disord. 2011

Bone density reduction

The endocrine system is severely affected by malnutrition, especially the thyroid and pituitary glands, gonads and bones.[71] Bone health can be severely compromised and up to 90 percent of women with anorexia are said to have reduced bone density.[72] I would assume this is the same for men with anorexia, but the studies I've looked at tend to only collect data on women. Excessive exercise perpetuates hypothalamic amenorrhea leading to associated bone loss, which is somewhat ironic considering most of us have been told at some point that exercise aids bone density — which it does when you healthy.[73]

Loss of bone density is considered an irreversible complication of anorexia once a person is a little older (post early 20s) so all the more reason to get into recovery eating as soon as possible. It is never too late to stop further damage.

Hypercortisolemia

Cortisol is a hormone the body creates in order to deal with stress. Individuals with anorexia can have hypercortisolemia or heightened levels of cortisol in the blood. Elevated cortisol for long periods of time can have many detrimental effects on the body, and you will likely notice the byproducts of this in your stress and anxiety levels.[74]

---

[71] Endocr Pract. THE ENDOCRINOPATHIES OF ANOREXIA NERVOSA, Usdan et al.

[72] Grinspoon S, Thomas E, Pitts S, et al. Prevalence and predictive factors for regional osteopenia in women with anorexia nervosa. Ann Intern Med.

[73] Medical complications in adolescents with anorexia nervosa: A review of the literature. Katzman MD.

[74] Hypercortisolemia Is Associated with Severity of Bone Loss and Depression in Hypothalamic Amenorrhea and Anorexia Nervosa. Lawson et al. J Clin Endocrinol Metab (2009)

Effects of Anorexia

All the effects I have listed above are those that could be seen in malnourished people —whether they have an eating disorder or not. What I will list in the following section are some of the effects of *anorexia*. That is, these are effects that I consider to be specific to people with anorexia, rather than straight up malnutrition.

Fear of eating "too much"

This is the foundational fear that most other fears associated with anorexia stem from. Your brain interprets the action of eating as a threat. Considering migration response theory, this would be because your brain interprets eating anything more than the smallest amount needed to survive and keep going that day as a threat to your ability to migrate, and therefore, your survival. The less you can stop and eat, the farther you will travel and the sooner you will get to the place of abundant food. Your brain strongly feels that in order to survive, you have to move as much as possible and stop to feed as little as possible; it uses the fear emotion to motivate you not to eat more than the most minimal amount possible.

Even if you don't like migration theory to explain anorexia, you will probably agree that fear of eating more food than judged as necessary is one of the principal fears of anorexia. Do not underestimate the strength of this core fear of eating. It is a deep survival-based fear. Survival fears are emotions that trump all other emotions and desires because the brain values surviving over anything else. This fear of eating will shape every aspect of your life over time.

Fear of weight gain

Migration theory explains that your fear of weight gain amplifies when you have anorexia because your brain interprets weight gain as an indication that you are eating "too much" and therefore failing at migrating. Despite the fact that your logical brain may know that you need to gain weight, the brain-stem based fear response will override logical thinking and tell you that weight gain is a threat to survival. Hence, many of us dread the incredibly strong feelings of remorse and guilt that we get if the number on the scale increases. The fear of weight gain is not just limited to the number on the scale; clothing size, comments from others — basically anything that indicates weight gain. Anxiety around weight gain often leads to body checking and constantly looking for signs that you might have gained weight.

"I'm so bored of my brain. Someone can look at me the wrong way and I think that they are thinking I have gained weight." - BJ, adult in recovery from anorexia

This fear of weight gain is often interpreted as a vanity issue. It is assumed that we are scared of gaining weight due to wanting to look a certain way. This always perplexed me. I had never been particularly aware of my weight before I was in a state of malnutrition. The notion that I was so into looking thin that I would willfully starve myself felt incorrect — yet it was hard to defend myself against that accusation given my actions. I think it is even more difficult to convince people that your anorexia is not a vanity issue if you initially instigated energy deficit in order to look slimmer — which most people do due to the pressures from society to look a certain way. Even if your energy deficit started with a diet, anorexia is so much more than this. The idea you could willfully override your need for one of life's vital substances just to look a certain way is ridiculous.

Anorexia is not about wanting to be slim — even if it feels like that. Anorexia, and the fear of weight gain associated with the illness, was around long before it was fashionable to be thin.

Fear of stillness

The migratory effect. Migrating animals don't sit still; they move!

A migrating animal will migrate no matter what. The only animals that get left behind are those that are too sick to move and therefore they die. This is a very non-negotiable compulsion to move. I remember watching the geese flocking in the winter and getting ready to migrate as a child and thinking *"how awful to have to fly all that way, surely they don't want to do that."* Well, of course they don't want to do it. Geese probably don't feel like there is a choice to their migration. Whilst I was compulsively running when I had anorexia, I didn't feel like I had much choice either.

When anorexia is activated (by energy deficit) in those of us with a migratory-like response, the brain allocates energy resources to your limbs in order to enable migration to a place where there is food. This is your body assuming that you need to move your legs to walk yourself to somewhere that there is food. (Movement will be covered in much greater detail in the following chapters.)

"I can't not move. I feel trapped if I have to sit in the car. Or sit at all. I stand at the back of the room in lectures. I hate it but I have to do it." - J, adult in recovery from anorexia.

I used to be more scared of stillness than I was of eating. I would fidget and jitter if I had to sit down at all during the day. That's not to mention all the exercise. For many of us, overcoming the urge to move is the biggest struggle of recovery.

Please note, not all people with anorexia get the urge to move. Some people seem to get the fears of eating more and fears of weight gain without the urge to move, but, in my experience, this is the minority.

Fear of nutritionally dense or "unhealthy" foods

This is an interesting one, as it differs slightly depending on the individual. Some people are able to eat nutritionally dense foods, but only in small quantities. Some people have more of a fear of "unhealthy" foods. Regardless of your individual specifics, it still results in a restriction of food eaten.

I think that the fear of nutritionally dense foods is fascinating. I used to think I was simply into "healthy eating," and that by coincidence nutritionally dense foods happened to be considered "less healthy."

But then I realised I would happily eat a low-fat yoghurt which was crammed with artificial sweeteners, and so that doesn't really fit with the "healthy eating" muse. Pretty hypocritical really that I would spend ten minutes lecturing my dad for piling butter onto his toast, then sit down and eat a "lite" yoghurt. Typical anorexia. It was less about being "healthy" and more about an intense fear of calorically dense foods. That didn't stop me climbing aboard my high horse and telling other people what they should and should not be eating — which is ironic when you consider I was the one scared of a piece of buttered toast.

I have a bit of a theory on this. I've no proof for it other than the best explanation of my own experience merged with what I know about migration theory, but hear me out: Before we had the ability to farm and produce meat as efficiently as we do now, in order to get nutritionally dense foods such as meat, humans would have to stop and hunt. A migrating human doesn't have time to stop and spend the day hunting. Hence, nutritionally dense foods are a threat to migration.

In our modern world where food is readily available, nutritionally dense foods are still feared by people with anorexia. We go to the most plausible and logical explanation that we fear these foods because they are more likely to promote weight gain, but I believe that there is a deeper, more migration-specific reason that people, and animals that migrate tend toward the low-calorie foods that can be grazed on and shy away from nutrient dense foods.

Pigs are not "scared" of weight gain. Pigs don't read Vogue and want to be supermodels. But when in energy deficit, certain breeds of pig are prone to "wasting pig syndrome" where they ignore their feed to eat straw and pace incessantly — sounds like migration to me![75]

Migrating animals favor the sorts of lower-nutrient foods that they would be able to graze on while on the move.

Even if you don't buy migration as an explanation for anorexia, I think that you will agree that on the whole, people with anorexia tend to fear nutritionally dense foods, especially in large quantities.

Eating becomes highly emotional

I am not talking about "emotional eating." At least not in the sense that term is usually used. Let me explain why being in a physical state of malnutrition makes eating emotional, and how anorexia contributes to this.

Emotions are what our brains use to motivate us into action. When you have anorexia, eating becomes highly emotional because your brain needs to motivate you into action regarding your state of malnutrition. There are two majorly conflicting sources of emotion:

1. **The anorexia response,** which works to use emotion to disincentivize eating. It generally uses incredibly strong negative feelings of threat, shame, disgust, regret, fear, guilt, and anxiety around food to motivate you to eat less and move more. Additionally, the anorexia response uses positive

---

[75] J. L. Treasure, J. B. Owen, Intriguing links between animal behavior and anorexia nervosa. *Int J Eat Disord* **21**. 307-311 (1997).

feelings of success and reward when you restrict food and move to incentivise these actions.

2. **Malnutrition**, which uses the emotions of lust, desire, wanting, etc to make you seek out food in order to counter your malnourished state. This a normal reaction to malnutrition, and people without anorexia become highly focused and desiring of food when in energy deficit. For those of us with anorexia, our seemingly uncontrollable lusting after food scares us, whereas for a person in malnutrition who doesn't have anorexia, it motivates them to find food and eat it.

For a person *without* anorexia, the more prominent emotion pertaining to food after a period of restriction or scarcity is the desire to eat a lot. For a person with anorexia, there are very strong, conflicting emotions. Years of negotiating between our strong desire to eat, and our equally strong fear of eating, is utterly exhausting — and most of us develop OCD-ED habits, rituals and rules that are in a sense, in place to negotiate; so, we eat enough to not die, but not enough to really live either.

Our fear emotion trumps all other emotions because fear is supposed to save our lives in times of danger. Hence, fear is the emotion that is followed for the most part. In recovery, you have to walk straight into that cripplingly strong fear as you respond to the desire to eat.

One of the blessings of achieving energy balance is that your brain no longer needs to use emotion so strongly around food. As a result, eating stops being such a big deal. I no longer lust after food and spend my day obsessing about it, and I no longer feel incredible guilt after eating. Eating food is about as emotionally charged for me now as getting dressed in the morning is.

One of the answers to the question "*when will I know when I am weight restored/ out of energy deficit?*" is that you will no longer feel so strongly emotional about food. It won't be a big deal or something that causes you much pause in life. Eating becomes unremarkable. Just another enjoyable part of your day.

Eating anxiety

Due to the fear that you have around eating "too much," eating becomes a highly anxiety-provoking event. On the one hand, you have a desire to eat a lot, and on the other, you have a crippling fear of eating "too much," so you consistently opt for eating smaller amounts. Many of us feel enormous pressure to "Goldilocks" the amount that we are eating — we want to get it "just right." Our anxiety around doing this causes us to constantly plan what we are going to eat, plan the amount of movement we need to do in order to counter our intake, and of course, count calories.

Over time, the conflicting messages that we receive a) from our own brains, and b) from society, about how much and what to eat result in a very limited amount of "safe" foods in controlled quantities. We also regiment what we are eating and when in order to reduce some of the anxiety. This often gets misinterpreted as a need for control. Rather, it is a way to reduce the anxiety — or at least keep it to a bearable level. Being overly controlling is more about negative state relief, than it is about actually being controlling.

The "Goldilocks effect" often plagues people as they are trying to allow themselves to eat more food in recovery. We try and eat more ... but not "too much" more. Which turns into a rather impossible and very stressful game. It is important to know that much of your anxiety is around your fear of eating "too much," and that there is no such thing as "too much" food when you are in recovery and past the risk of refeeding syndrome.

Eating regret and guilt

Many of us feel intense guilt after eating anything that we perceive to be more than the minimal amount possible when we have anorexia. Guilt is a negative emotion that anorexia is generating to try and disincentive eating. The intensity of eating guilt usually increases with the higher nutritional value of the food.

Eating regret is most commonly present when you eat a food and it doesn't taste as good as you thought it would, was different from the usual, or was higher calorie than what you usually have, or for whatever reason isn't as perfect as you hoped it would be. Then you get a huge overwhelming feeling of panic and regret. This is often accompanied by an intense urge to negate it with a compensatory behaviour — typically purging or exercise or restriction but sometimes other forms of self harm are used.

The feeling of eating regret is one of intense frustration and borderline panic — I used to shake and would feel like a livid screaming energy pulsing through me. Like I was so furious with myself I wanted to break out of my own skin. Unfortunately, eating regret happens often as we challenge ourselves more and eat more in recovery simply because we are doing just that: trying new things.

The good news is that the intense eating regret goes with full recovery. I can eat something that doesn't taste fabulous and shrug it off now. In the meantime, be aware that if you eat something that wasn't all you had hoped it would be, it is a normal anorexia response to feel devastated about it — but you have to ignore that and not allow it to affect you. Certainly don't allow it to make you compensate with things like exercise or restriction or purging. Don't even allow it to ruin a second of your day. Instead, see it as a double victory, because not only did you try something, but you ate something that you didn't like that much and then went on to not allow it to pull you down.

Like most anorexia-generated reactions, eating regret will only be able to persist if you allow it to affect you. Incidentally, I found I had a similar reaction to spending money or buying something that wasn't as perfect as I had hoped. I was the queen of taking purchases back to the store.

Body dysmorphia

Not all of us have the stereotypical extreme body dysmorphia where we look into the mirror and see ourselves as huge. I for one was always painfully aware that I was unattractively underweight. However, even for those of us like myself who don't see ourselves as overweight, there can be a degree of separation from reality. I was not as privy to the reality of my situation as I thought I was. I didn't look at myself in the mirror and panic about how underweight I was. I thought that other people were overreacting. I could not see what they saw.

I do now. If I look back at pictures of myself when I was underweight I am shocked. I want to scream at myself to eat more. I look awful. I look like I should be in a hospital. I can see that now in a way I could not see then. So, yes, even me — someone who knew that she was too thin — had some degree of body dysmorphia.

Some people with anorexia have very severe body dysmorphia and see themselves as much larger than they actually are. Many are on the level that I was on, and know that they are thin, but just seem protected from the reality of it. Either way, you have to understand that you cannot trust your brain to deliver a reliable perception of how you look. There is freedom in knowing that because when your brain is freaking out telling you that you have gained too much weight, you can find peace in knowing your judgement is out of whack.

Hyper-awareness of food and movement

Before I had anorexia, I couldn't give a toss what anyone else ate. That's normal.

With anorexia I became increasingly observant, and judgmental of what others consumed. That's not normal.

If those whom I was dining with ate more than me, I was thrilled. My brain rewarded me for this with strong feelings of achievement. If, however, I ate more than other people, I was punished with feelings of guilt and shame and a strong desire to purge via exercise or restriction.

Incidentally, this desire to eat less than everyone else conflicts with the desire to be eating all the time. As a result, we tend to eat very slowly. As it is painful to be not eating when others are still eating. When you eat deliberately slowly, you avoid the conflict of wanting to eat more while you wait for others to finish. Even if you are eating alone, the time and space after your rationed-out food is eaten is often painful, so you tend to eat slowly and savor every bite.

I found when I was eating with others, my anorexia brain was constantly clocking what they were eating. It feels very stressful to be eating more than anyone else. Many of us find that this conflicts strongly with our desire to eat a lot, and as a result we "push" more food onto other people. If whomever you are with eats more, you are allowed to eat more. This can also be true for rest. I used to find I could sit and rest for longer so long as everyone else around me was sitting and resting. Should anyone else get up and move, and I would have to move also. Another unfortunate effect of this is getting irritable and angry with people who don't eat more than you do. In a sense, when someone else eats only a little, it feels as if they are causing you to have to eat even less. Most of us desperately want permission to eat more, and when someone else doesn't eat very much it feels like that permission has been retracted.

It is not "normal" to be hyper-aware about what other people eat. It is a sign that you are in malnutrition and your brain is focusing on food. The comparison part, and the insecurity around eating more than other people comes from the anorexia response.

Increased general anxiety

It is often suggested that anorexia is an anxiety disorder. I can see why, as people with anorexia display incredibly high levels of anxiety. I mean, if your brain believes you are in a famine environment it has every right to be anxious about things. Additionally, we are often in a state of confusion in terms of having on the one hand a desire to eat a lot, and on the other hand a fear of eating. Caught in the middle for years will turn you into a nervous wreck! However, once in full recovery, these signs and effects of anxiety usually decrease incredibly.

I certainly had very high anxiety when I was in a state of malnutrition, and for good reason. I was exhausted, but driven to continue with relentlessly high levels of exercise. Nowadays, in long-term energy balance, I would say that I am no more anxious than the person next door. I'm probably actually more laid back than most. I don't catastrophize things like I used to when I was malnourished. Compared to living with anorexia, I feel that I can handle anything life throws at me.

Unfortunately, anxiety is one of those things that sometimes gets worse before it gets better in recovery. If you think about recovery as running into fear and resistance, I am sure you can understand why. Your brain fears increased eating and weight gain and that is exactly what you have to do. I do think it is important to be prepared for the increase in anxiety that often comes when one starts eating, resting, and combating behavioural urges. Anxiety holds you hostage. And, if you think about it, if you are not eating enough to feel anxious about it as you nutritionally rehabilitate, then you are not eating enough.

Isolation tendencies

You may notice you are more reclusive when you have anorexia; a starving brain has more important things to think about than being social. But, more than that, interaction can feel like a threat. Social life often means sitting down for extended periods of time and eating. Neither of these things serve migration. Hence, they feel "wrong," and awkward. I used to find if I went to social gatherings I would want to leave after a couple minutes of sitting and talking. I would make excuses to stand rather than sit as this reduced my anxiety, but I was also very aware standing when everyone is sitting is rather odd. In the end I just gave up and stopped going out.

I'd make excuses for not meeting friends. This reduced the stress of it, and also allowed me to be alone and indulge my little rituals and odd food and exercise habits. For a time, I really did feel quite happy to be left alone to do my anorexia-driven rituals. By the time the loneliness of the illness really hit me, it felt too late to change.

The following was written by an adult in recovery:

"Anorexia needs isolation to grow — a bumper of space distance that keeps people and responsibilities away so that it can plant seeds and cover my brain. In the early stages, it kind of hibernates in my brain, as it works at changing the physical body. Once weight is being lost and its process is underway, the isolation becomes more automatic. People stay away because we don't think we need them. Also, they have been pushed, or are possibly intimidated. Disgusted. Saddened. Perhaps we don't even seem to exist anymore, or matter. Anorexia is the veil.

For a while, we desperately need isolation. We do everything we can, through secrets, manipulation, and resignation, to have the private time we need in order to serve the mental illness. Meanwhile, it constructs its bizarre kingdom and builds fence after fence--not so much as to keep others OUT, but to make sure that we stay IN. Some people run to make space, others hide food and perform massive ritualization. Others, like me, just seem to die. Everything stops. It's all a coma.

Years go by, and those fences harden. They grow moss and rust, and things like bulimia and OCD add barbed wire. We even let anorexia place guards with guns at different check points. No one gets in.

Then one day, when the sun is out, the sufferer gets a sideways glimpse of life beyond the fences. What's that? Family? Friends? People having vacations, children, holidays? Meals? And we aren't invited, we aren't there. They stopped asking us a very long time ago. We only wanted to be home with Anorexia, cleaning the floors and reorganizing the spice drawer. But that one vision of freedom, the something beyond the mental fuzz--it makes a tug on the heart, on the soul. Anorexia does not work with the soul, so this is a very big problem for the illness. The soul is out of it's control. And the soul is what gives us the gift of loneliness. When we finally see that we are sick, and know there is a better way, we embrace loneliness. Little by little, the loneliness encourages other emotions, such as desire and boredom. These are other signals that want for us to reconnect with the outside world.

And then there comes the point when wanting to participate hits in direct conflict with Anorexia's dear isolation. They cannot live in the same body. So the sufferer has to choose--listen to the world, or put back Anorexia's headphones? Perhaps this is when we decide to seek help. We move a few steps beyond Anorexia, even for just an afternoon, and share our problems. Help is the first break from isolation, but it makes us leave the eating disorder cocoon. We go from black and white to Technicolor, and it can be terribly frightening. But the energy is something new, and we keep going, despite the tremulous fear. We know what to expect in isolation. But loneliness, this beautiful thing provides possibility." - Mindy, adult in recovery from anorexia

Prone to form habitual behaviours

I was extremely habit-driven, and, for years had a strict schedule of tasks and timings — doing the exact same things, every day. My life was like a black hole of ritual. I was never like this before I had anorexia, and am not ritual-driven now. I think that in a state of malnutrition, part of my brain's survival-mode response was to from habits and rituals that appeared to keep me "safe" and reduce anxiety.

Some people who work during the week and have weekends off find that they follow routine in what they do on a workday compared to what they do on a day off. I found that I was very environmentally triggered into habitual behaviours. At work, I was only able to eat at certain times and certain things; at home the rules were different.

Many of us also have habitual behaviours that depend on the day of the week. For example, every Tuesday is the same lunch as the Tuesday before. I used to do this too. It's incredibly tiresome!

"Sometimes my brain flicks back to thinking "you would have been swimming by now this time last week" or "you didn't eat a morning snack yesterday, you don't need one today". I keep telling myself - I don't need to do that any more, this is how I live now. This is the new normal. I keep thinking of all the energy debt I have built up over the months and years, all the times when I skipped meals or snacks or stopped eating before I wanted to." - L, adult in recovery from anorexia

Increased ability to lie

Mum: "*Did you eat breakfast?*"
Me: "*Yes, I had two pieces of toast with marmite and a boiled egg,*" *I would lie.*

When I was in malnutrition, I felt not an ounce of guilt for lying about what I had eaten. I honestly didn't feel it was even lying. Why not? Because things that allow for eating less and moving more feel right when you have anorexia. Anorexia sits above other moral code and can have the effect of trumping other moral rights and wrongs. That's why someone who is not a liar can tell lies if those lies benefit anorexia. If those lies enable eating less and moving more they didn't feel wrong in my head like lying to my sister about wearing her new top would have.

My brain believed that I needed to feed as little as possible and move as much as possible in order to survive. Survival instincts that are most relevant in any given situation override less pressing morals and values. That is why people who are not killers will kill in self defense. That is why people who are starving will steal. You get the picture. When we are desperate, threatened, our morals get fuzzy.

Once your body is out of energy deficit, once the urge to feed less and move more is turned off, you no longer have to protect it. There is no reason to lie about food and exercise any more. If you are hungry you will eat. If you are tired, you will rest. It becomes nobody else's business because you can manage your own nutrition and rest.

Martyrdom

"No, no. You sit down. I'll do the dishes, I don't mind. Really ... Sit, Down!" -
Me, all the time when I was in a state of malnutrition.

Anorexia places a lot of value in doing the most. Egregiously, this often
expresses itself by being the person who is doing the most exercise,
but it can also develop into lower-level movement aspects such as
cleaning, and non-movement chores. I used to certainly get a feeling
of reward for being the person to run the farthest, but also always
being the person to rest the least, and do the most housework. Not all
people with anorexia have the martyr affect, but I see it more often in
those of us who have had the illness for years and years and been
"functional" with it. Especially those of us who are with partners or
living with family/children.

For me, it wasn't just about wanting to help out. In the same way I
received a reward in my brain for eating less than everyone else in the
house, I felt the same reward when I did more. To the extent that it
would make me seethingly angry to come home to find that someone
else had dared to empty the dishwasher and robbed me of the
chance to do it first.

*"Whenever we have a family dinner like at Christmas I'm the one
washing up and tidying the kitchen whilst the rest are playing scrabble
and having fun."* - S, adult in recovery from anorexia

Increased pain threshold

Interoceptive awareness (sensitivity to stimuli originating within the body) is known to be impaired in eating disorders such as anorexia.[76] Basically that is saying we become rather numb to our physical bodily signals. I certainly felt like a lot of my senses were dulled when I was underweight. My ability to detect hunger was one thing, but not just that. I got frostbite a number of times due to being out running in the cold and dark. It sounds odd, but whilst things like that were painful, my reaction to the pain was not the same as it is now. It was as if I didn't tend to move away from pain signals in the same way I do now. I was so used to being uncomfortable, that pain and hunger didn't seem like things I had to try and resolve. That is not me saying I was seeking pain, I wasn't. I was simply less able to use it as a signal for me to alter anything.

It has been shown that people with anorexia have higher than average pain thresholds — which makes sense from an evolutionary perspective as a high tolerance to pain would mean we could continue with migration. [77]A bird can't exactly just stop flying because her wings started to ache.

"My senses were definately dulled by anorexia, there were times when I was able to go out running despite suffering from a migraine, it was as if I couldn't feel the pain and certainly the urge to move was greater" - LC, adult in recovery from anorexia.

---

[76] Interoceptive awareness in eating disorders: Distinguishing lack of clarity from non-acceptance of internal experience Rhonda M. Merwin et al. (2010) Cognition and Emotion

[77] Biol Psychiatry. 1999. Elevated pain threshold in anorexia nervosa subjects. Raymond

Toolkit

I am putting the Toolkit in here, as the tools described in this section will be referred to throughout this book. The concepts in here are mostly to aid you in the process of neural rewiring. Or at least, these are some of the things that helped me. Use them as inspiration as you develop your own, personal, rewiring techniques.

While I am still absolutely awful at meditation — let's be frank, I hate it — I am so glad I learned the skills that I will share here.

Core Concepts

You have the ability to control your reactions and actions. Regardless of what your insula or any other part of your brain is doing or not doing, and regardless of the thoughts and fears that are being thrown at you, one thing remains true: you have the ability to control your reaction to your thoughts. Please note that I didn't say that you have the ability to control your thoughts — but you have the ability to control your reactions to your thoughts. It is also important to note that the more nutritionally rehabilitated you become, the easier controlling your actions and reactions becomes.

Where your attention goes, energy flows. There is a balance to be had between working through something in a positive manner and then dropping it, and continually indulging in negative thought loops. Obsessing about the things that you don't like about your body is not going to help. All that will do is strengthen these negative thought patterns. I made that mistake many times. For example, that *"oh, that's new"* thought at feeling the flesh on my arm, would quickly spark all sorts of other, less innocent and more judgmental thoughts.

A thought is just a thought. Having a thought doesn't mean that thought is true. Having a thought doesn't mean that you have to believe that thought. Having a thought doesn't mean that you cannot choose, in that instance, to dismiss that thought without further ado. When you invest your attention and energy into negative thoughts, you strengthen the neural pathways that spark them. The more energy you give those thoughts, the stronger and more prevalent they become. A large part of recovery for me was learning to shut negative thoughts down. Stop.

This takes some mental discipline. It gets easier with practice. You never, ever, have to allow a thought or emotion to dominate you. You are the wizard in control of your own brain.

Rewiring The Brain: Neural Pathways

Neural pathways are the linking of thought patterns and processes. They are learned outcomes. For example, if I write the word "burger" this fires off a load of neural pathways to other words that your brain associated with the word "burger." These are not random, they are all words and thoughts that your brain has learned are often occurring alongside the word "burger."

When you learn something, neural circuits are altered in your brain. These circuits are composed of neurons that communicate with one another through "roads" called synapses. When we talk about neural pathways, we are talking about the strength of these synapses. And like your muscles, synapses get stronger the more that you use them.

This is why in order to learn or get really good at something, we have to repeatedly do it over and over. When we repeat an action or a thought, we strengthen the neural pathways that fire off. We get faster and better with our responses.

Anorexia changes the way that you perceive the world, and when we start to favour eating less and moving more, we start to repeat a whole load of thoughts and behaviours that also favour eating less and moving more. Eating enough food to "weight restore" is obviously primarily focused on nutritional rehabilitation, but the act of eating more and new foods starts the process of rewiring the brain's reaction to food and eating too. There is one hell of a lot of behavioural rewiring going on there.

Mental and behavioural rewiring occurs when we reject all restrictive thoughts, behaviours, and OCD-ED urges. In doing this we weaken the neural pathways that anorexia built, and strengthen the healthy brain processes that we are attempting to replace them with.

This section will be full of tools to help you further this neural rewiring.

Implicit bias, and why it doesn't matter anyway?

First I want to address implicit bias, as we all have it, and this is one thing that anorexia is not really to blame for. It is important as a common "what if" question that comes up, is *"what if it wasn't totally anorexia-generated thoughts that are making me scared of gaining weight? What if the true me is biased towards thin? Will I always hate myself?"*

The answer here, in short, is that once and neural pathway is formed, it doesn't matter how it was formed or why it was formed. It is there. Once it is there, we weaken and rewire it the same way. It may well be that you were fat-phobic before you developed anorexia. It would make sense if you were, as we live in a fat-phobic society. That doesn't mean that we can't change that now. Or it may be that you were not fat-phobic before you developed anorexia, but you are now as a result of the illness. Same process, we will be rewiring that response either way.

Implicit bias is usually used to describe underlying stereotyping — such as racism and sexism — but it exists in almost all our thoughts and actions.

Egregiously, western culture associates positives with a low weight, and negatives with a higher weight. Likewise, culture labels foods as good and bad. Implicit bias to food and weight is, unfortunately, normal and not unique to people with anorexia.. Anorexia, however, strengthens these biases as their values align strongly with those of energy deficit.

Anorexia switches you into an operating system that rewards eating less and moving more. This proclivity towards dietary restriction and movement strengthens the already existing implicit bias that you have towards "healthy" foods, exercise, desire for thinness, and other concepts that were already placed there by society. Hence anorexia is not caused by society, but the implicit biases in society strengthen the learning connection in your brain that eating less and moving more is good.

The original source of your fears and reactions doesn't matter. We'll still be able to "re-route" you. The tools that follow are all ones that I used to help me do this. You will likely find that you develop your own tools as you get into rewiring your brain. But start with these to get you going:

Tools

"Your beliefs become your thoughts,

Your thoughts become your words,

Your words become your actions,

Your actions become your habits,

Your habits become your values,

Your values become your destiny."

— Mahatma Gandhi

Spam Folder

Rather than analysing and paying attention to anorexia-generated thought patterns, I am going to suggest you shut down anorexia thoughts without giving them further attention. Giving attention to these thoughts spends valuable mental energy, which only reinforce those neural pathways. You absolutely cannot afford to waste energy in this way. Remember, where your attention goes, energy flows. Do not give anorexia thoughts your mental energy.

Anorexia thoughts are like spam

I compare this to someone sending you spam emails. You cannot waste time and energy opening every spam email that you get in your inbox. Instead, you delete them as soon as they come in. If you regularly get spam from the same sender, you can set up a filter to auto-trash them, or block the sender completely. When you train your brain to ignore anorexia-generated thoughts, you are auto-trashing them.

Sometimes I feel like many forms of therapy work the wrong way. Rather than labeling spam thoughts as junk, the therapist tells you to deliberately open your spam folder and read and analyse all the rubbish mail you have in there. That is asking for trouble, and wasting precious time. What good can it be, to spend hours (and money) asking questions such as *"I wonder why the spammer sent me this mail and what does it mean about me?"*

Opening spam mail only means that you get more of it as the sender can tell if you clicked on it. They then count that as a successful send and will throw more and more spam at you. Where your attention goes, energy flows.

Don't open spam mail unless you want more spam.
Don't open anorexia thoughts unless you want more anorexia thoughts.

Spam mail is designed to be tempting. *"Win a free holiday ..."* in order to get you to click through. Eating disorder thoughts can be tempting too. Don't open them! Don't get sucked in.

Shutting down thoughts takes incredible mental discipline. There is a technique in this toolkit called "Back to Black Meditation," and I suggest that you practice this at least four times a day to help you build up this skill.

Staying Present

Meditation taught me the useful concept of staying present. Thankfully, you don't have to spend years sitting on a round sequined zafu in order to grasp this concept. In a nutshell the idea is that you quit fretting about the future, and worrying about the past, and instead concentrate on the moment that you are in right now. Revolutionary, I know.

Part of shutting down the "monkey brain" overthinking is pulling yourself back to the present. What is true in this moment right now? You'll notice that all of the anorexia fears and "what if" worry thoughts circle around the past or the future. *"I'm scared I'll be a binge eater,"* or *"I'm scared nobody will accept me in a larger body,"* or, *"I'm scared to eat something different for lunch because rice cakes is what I've always eaten in the past,"* and *futuretrip, futuretrip, yadda, yadda, yadda.* When you notice yourself doing this, pull yourself back to the present. What is true right now in this very moment?

Eat for the moment you are in right now rather than eating for what you fear might maybe happen in the future. Make decisions based on the truth of the moment that you are in, not on what you have always done on the past. It may be that you have always eaten rice cakes for lunch in the past. But if your present truth is that you want a burger and fries today, then that is your truth and that is what you should have. (But be smart, because when it come to the crunch your anorexia-brain will try to convince you that you don't really want the burger at all, so be ready to follow through with the pro-recovery burger even if you seem to suddenly change your mind.)

"Eat and Forget"

This is less of a tool and more of a rule really, but I want to add it in here because it is an example of using the "Stay Present" concept when you are eating. "Eat and Forget" means that you don't post-mortem what you have eaten that day, and you don't base future food decisions or eating on what you have already eaten that day either. What happens at a meal or snack time, stays in that meal or snack time. It's like fight club in that sense. This takes a lot of mental discipline.

No counting. No comparing. No compensating. Eat. Forget. Eat again.

Back-to-Black Meditation

This is a tool that you have to practice using multiple times a day. Start now, as it will generally help you with the overthinking problem that most of us have when we have anorexia. The investment is worth it, as being able to detect and reject thoughts is a key part of the neural rewiring required for anorexia recovery. Don't be put off if you find this tool difficult to practice. It *is* difficult. If not getting caught up in thoughts were easy, then overthinking wouldn't be a thing. Overthinking is a thing. Not thinking is incredibly difficult. Hence we have to practice.

I am very bad at meditation. I don't enjoy it. However, there are functional aspects of mediation that were critical to my recovery. This is one of those tools. This, what I call the "Back to Black" meditation (nothing to do with Amy Winehouse I promise), was how I trained myself to drop thoughts I didn't want to be thinking.

The meditation is about sitting still, concentrating on the word "black" and the colour black, (any word or colour will do) and trying to do that without allowing other thoughts to distract you for 3-5 minutes. If you can do longer, great!

The real brain training here comes in when you notice a thought coming in and have the discipline to drop it and refocus on black. It is hard to do! The thought will seem so interesting and tempting and alluring … but that is the whole point. To have the power and mental discipline to reject a thought no matter how seductive it is. Get good at and practice doing this in a meditation setting so you can bring it into the real word and shut down the overthinking about food and worrying about the future when you notice yourself doing it. You will be able to pull yourself out of those eating disorder neural rabbit holes.

(Note: any word or colour can be used as your focus word. The actual word doesn't matter.)

Practice:
1. Close your eyes, take 2-3 long slow deep breaths. (Long slow deep breathing activates parasympathetic nervous system.)
2. Think "black" over and over again.
3. When you notice your thoughts hijacking you, snap it straight back to black immediately. Don't continue or finish the thought. Just drop it.

Detect. Reject. Redirect. (DRR)

When you give a thought mental attention, you reinforce it. Therefore, the biggest and most effective action that you can take to weaken a neural pathway that you don't want any more is to not give it any of your attention, and therefore not give it any energy.

Detect. Reject. Redirect. Means that you notice a thought or behaviour, you stop it, and then you put your attention somewhere else. Think of it as directing traffic.

Detect

The first step to changing a thought or behaviour is to be able to detect it. Self awareness is key here. If you are a nail biter, you will know that you can place hand in mouth without even realising it. When we have anorexia, we think and act on anorexia urges without knowing it too.

As you go through this process you will be drawing up a list of behaviours and thought patterns you wish to change. This will help you with the detection part. As will using other people as canary birds to tell you when you are acting in a way to favour anorexia.

Detection is a lot about self awareness, but it is also about listening to others and asking them to be aware of what you are doing when you can't. If you are unaware of something you cannot change it. Don't be afraid of asking a loved one to inform you if you are doing something that you know you should not be doing. (And try not to bite their head off when they do!)

Reject

As soon as you have detected a thought or behaviour, you can reject it. This doesn't have to be a big deal, and you certainly should not attach any judgement. Don't get cross with yourself. Just stop.

Note: When you reject a thought, you do not argue with it. You do not spend 10 minutes justifying why you should not do what it says. Arguing with thoughts is still giving them mental energy and you will still strengthen them unwittingly. Rejecting thoughts is like putting up a big red stop sign to that thought. It is like a wall blocking that thought. It is like a barrier that means you cannot give that thought another moment of your energy.

Redirect

Redirect that energy to a positive neural pathway. Every time you redirect a thought or behaviour you weaken the existing, undesirable neural pathway, and you start to create and strengthen another, desirable one.

Redirecting often looks like doing the opposite of what the thought wanted you to do. For example, if your thought was to leave some food on your plate and not eat all that you wanted to, then you would simply have to ignore the thought completely and continue to eat. Or, if the thought was a desire to exercise, you would redirect it by ignoring it get comfy on the couch.

Always respond to thoughts of restriction by doing the opposite of what they wanted you to do. This comes back to the concept or running into fear, as often the restrictive thoughts are sparked off by fear of weight gain.

Important note: Redirection is not the same as "fighting the anorexia thoughts." You are not fighting anorexia thoughts as much as ignoring them and taking positive action.

Nervous System Switching

Before we go much further, I should distinguish the two nervous system responses that we are dealing with here:

- **Sympathetic nervous system:** this is the "fight/flight/freeze" hypothalamic–pituitary–adrenal axis response that is very helpful when we are in a truly dangerous situation, but totally inappropriate when it happens in response to food and eating.
- **Parasympathetic nervous system:** this is the "rest and digest" nervous system that indicates all is well in the environment and that no immediate danger is present. This is where we want to be when we eat.

Imagine if you got bitten by a dog. The experience of being bitten would put you in your sympathetic nervous system. You would likely feel a prang of fear next time you see that dog, as your brain now associates the dog with something to be scared of. If you never pet a dog again, this fear will remain with you, as you have not updated your brain with more positive data to prove to it that dogs are not to be feared. This is the reason we get right back on the horse if we fall off. The longer you leave it, the harder the fear is to overcome.

The fear response that anorexia provides us with relating to food and eating places us in our sympathetic nervous system (the fight or flight one) rather than the parasympathetic nervous system (the rest and digest one that we are supposed to be in when we eat). The fact we are even having a sympathetic nervous system response to eating, tells our brain that eating is to be feared. It is a bit of a catch-22 situation, as we are scared of eating, and this tells our brain that eating is something to be scared of.

Likewise, the regret, guilt and anxiety that anorexia throws at us after eating further trains the brain that eating is not a pleasant experience. This further primes it to try and make us avoid eating, in order to avoid the nasty feelings afterwards.

We need to start giving our brain lots of signals to tell it that we are not scared of eating so that it stops associating food with fear. We need to weaken the bridge between food and the sympathetic nervous system response, and strengthen the bridge between food and the parasympathetic nervous system response. The main techniques I used to do this were breathing, and something I call "Parasympathetic Nervous System Practice," or PNSP.

Breathing

Breathing slowly *really* works in reducing panic and stress. It has to work actually, because it is how you body is designed. It is impossible to freak out when you are breathing long and slow deep breaths. This is because long slow breathing places you in your parasympathetic nervous system. Conversely, short, sharp breaths place you in your sympathetic nervous system.[78][79]

---

[78] Ma, X. et al. (2017). The Effect of Diaphragmatic Breathing on Attention, Negative Affect and Stress in Healthy Adults. *Frontiers in Psychology.*

[79] Kox, M., van Eijk, L. T., Zwaag, J., van den Wildenberg, J., Sweep, F. C. G. J., van der Hoeven, J. G., & Pickkers, P. (2014). Voluntary activation of the sympathetic nervous system and attenuation of the innate immune response in humans. *Proceedings of the National Academy of Sciences of the United States of America,*

You will notice that when you start to panic or feel stressed that your rate of breathing increases. This is your body going into fight or flight mode and getting you ready to run from danger! In order to slow down again, you have to slow your breathing.

How to slow your breathing:
1. Take an inhale and count the seconds it takes to breathe in.
2. Exhale and see if you can make the exhale last longer than the inhale.
3. Inhale again and see if you can make the inhale take longer.
4. Exhale and repeat until feeling calm.

Parasympathetic Nervous System Practice (PNSP)

You can practice strengthening your parasympathetic nervous system response and consequently weakening your sympathetic nervous system response to any given stimuli. In doing so you are creating positive associations with whatever the situation or thing that you are having problematic reactions to is — e.g. fear foods or situations — by mentally rehearsing. In a sense, every time you imagine eating a fear food and feeling calm and relaxed about doing so, you are giving your brain data to support the notion that eating that food is nothing to be afraid of.

Method
1. Close your eyes and take 2-5 long slow deep breaths. This places you in your parasympathetic nervous system.

2. Take your time picturing and mentally going through the process of eating the food/situation that you are wanting to challenge.

3. The whole time, keep your breathing long and slow. This keeps you in your parasympathetic nervous system.

4. If you feel your breathing, heart rate, or anything else that indicates you are feeling stressed increase, then you are going into your sympathetic nervous system. Stop the mental rehearsal and concentrate on long slow deep breaths to bring you back to your parasympathetic nervous system. Once you are calm again you can resume the mental rehearsal of eating the food/situation that you are wanting to challenge.

5. Play out the whole experience of eating and make sure you get right to the end of the meal and then also imagine being calm and not having feelings of guilt or regret after eating.

6. Repeat this mental practice many times a day for any food item or situation that you are trying to alter your reaction to.

Every time you run through this process of imagining eating while your body is physically calm, it gives your brain a data point to reinforce that this is not actually a situation or food that warrants a sympathetic nervous system response. It weakens that neural pathway's association, and starts building another one — one that is much more appropriate.

I used this a great deal in my recovery. From mentally rehearsing eating a piece of cheese, to mentally rehearsing going into a shop and buying whole milk rather than skimmed. This PNSP was a game changer for me. It taught me that changing my fear response was a matter of training, and therefore something I had control over.

The "Fuck It!" Attitude

I considered trying to keep this entire book swear word free so that it would garner more respect in professional circles. Then I thought "*fuck it!*"

Hear me out. This is science.

The "Fuck It!" attitude is too important a tool to leave out. It takes care of so many of the niggles, and that "*what if*" questions, and confronts the worrying. The simple attitude of not giving a flying fuck will enable you to ignore whatever thoughts of doubt that anorexia throws out at you.

When I started eating more, the doubts, second-guessing, what if's, and the worrying thoughts got so loud I thought I was going to go insane. I remember one day standing there in my kitchen contemplating spreading butter on my sandwich bread for the first time in over 8 years. I had already made so much relative change in that I was 1) actually eating bread, 2) actually eating a sandwich, 3) actually eating a sandwich with filling in. That final part of buttering the bread seemed so, superfluous. Surely I was doing enough already? Surely I didn't need to push any further? Turns out, there was a long way left to go.

My healthy brain — small as that part of me felt at that time — knew I had to do it right. A part of me knew I was scared of that butter and therefore I had to make myself challenge that fear and eat it. A part of me knew that this was important.

But the questions ... the "what if's" ... the fear. I stood there for what seemed like an eternity looking at a pack of butter and this rather sad, not-yet-assembled sandwich.

Fuck it! What is the worst that can possibly happen if I butter my bread? Fuck it! I'm not listening any more.

That was when I found my "Fuck it!" attitude.

Swearing is important because ...

I could have said *"Darn it"* or *"Sod it"* or *"Jolly hockey sticks I don't care."* But those don't have the same effect on the brain as profanity does.[80][81] Profanity shifts something in the brain especially when used in this sort of context. It served to shock me out of the mindset I was stuck in.

When used flippantly, profanity makes us smirk or smile or giggle a bit. This is the important part. When I thought *"Fuck it!"* I would snap out of that tunnel of indecision and fear in a way that would not happen if I thought *"Sod it"* or something less swear-worthy.

---

[80] The Science of Swearing: A look into the human MIND and other less socially acceptable four-letter words. Harvard Review

[81] Jay, T., and Janschewitz, K. (2008). The pragmatics of swearing. *Journal of Politeness Research.* 4. 267-288.

The shock-giggle effect of swearing is nothing to do with being prudish or naive. It is said to be due to early verbal conditioning.[82] It has nothing to do with the literal meaning of the word and more to do with the way that our brains are conditioned to react to that word. In my brain, my reaction to the word fuck — when used in a non-aggressive context — is to lighten up and smile.

Swearing has an undeniable emotional component to it. I can prove this because you reacted differently to the title of this section than you did to any other title in this book so far. You likely were either surprised, mildly apprehensive, appalled, tickled, or delighted to see the word "fuck" in a section title. Whatever your reaction was it was an emotional reaction on a different level to that of any other single word you have read in this book so far.

Studies show that the brain processes swearing in a different area from where it processes regular language.[83] Specifically, swearing involves the limbic system, which also houses emotional reactions. Some scientists argue that swearing is more about expressing an emotional state than articulating an actual linguistic idea.[84][85] And this is exactly what I am trying to get at here. When you develop a "Fuck it!" attitude to all the what ifs that anorexia throws up every time you try and change something, you shift from an inner emotional

[82]Bowers. J. S., & Pleydell-Pearce, C. W. (2011). Swearing, Euphemisms, and Linguistic Relativity. *PLoS ONE*,

[83] WHY WE CURSE A NEURO-PSYCHO-SOCIAL THEORY OF SPEECH TIMOTHY JAY

[84] Jay, T., and Janschewitz, K. (2008). The pragmatics of swearing. *Journal of Politeness Research*. 4: 267-288.

[85] Swearing and the Expression of the Emotions Richard Hirsch

standpoint of fear to one of cocky disrespect for those thoughts. You remove the power they had over you.

The possible pain-relieving benefits of swearing have also been studied.[86] It is speculated that we let off steam when we swear, and therefore are able to think more clearly. If you think that swearing helps you make more pro-recovery choices, then don't be afraid to use it as a tool in recovery. But remember, you don't have to swear out loud for the benefits to work. (Although sometimes, I have to admit, swearing out loud is much more satisfying.)

Humour

I want to mention humour here as it certainly can be a fabulous recovery tool. I don't need to tell you how to "do" funny. You already know how to make yourself laugh. Laughter was incredibly helpful for me in my recovery. I have a cynical, dry, non-politically correct, sense of humour and I was able to use it to pull myself out of anxiety pretty regularly in recovery. My husband was also fantastic at saying something witty that he knew would pull me out of my stress-state. Laughter shifts something in the brain, that's for sure.[87] I suggest that you use it any way that you can.

---

[86] Swearing as a response to pain; Richard Stephens, John Atkins and Andrew Kingston

[87] Strean. W. B. (2009). Laughter prescription. *Canadian Family Physician*.

Urge Surf

Urge Surfing is a technique that is attributed to a psychologist called Alan Marlatt.[88] A client who worked in addictions counselling told me about it. This is like DRR, but with less of the redirect action or thoughts. Urge surfing is when you don't react to a sharp urge to do something. This may be the urge to throw away a piece of food, or the urge to get up and start moving due to feeling like you ate a lot. Ride it out. Breathe. Do nothing and before you know it the urge has passed.

Urge surfing is in essence doing nothing and riding the wave. Riding over the top of it and letting it go rather than jumping in head fast and going with it.

You feel the urge to exercise? Feel the urge to obsessively clean the house? Call a friend. Eat a cupcake. Sit down and write. Get in the car and go for a drive. Do something else (but make sure it is not something that creates energy deficit).

My recommendation is to eat something anytime an improper or harmful urge occurs. Replace the crazy with sane, and feed your already starving brain. It will be a proper distraction, while helping the cause that you are committed to fighting.

---

[88] Bowen, S., & Marlatt, A. (2009). Surfing the urge: Brief mindfulness-based intervention for college student smokers. *Psychology of Addictive Behaviors, 23*(4), 666-671.

Distraction

Distraction tools are those which help you to ignore a thought, or to redirect and then move away from a thought. It is all very well to tell someone to reject a thought, but without some distraction tools in place they may find that they are constantly bouncing back to it.

Mental distraction

I kept a mental supply of fond memories to use at the ready, when I needed mental distraction.

For example, if I began to get anxious when thinking about something trivial and stupid, such as all the non-organic food I was eating in recovery. I would use DRR, then distract myself by thinking/ daydreaming stories and memories that I knew were very easy for me to get lost in.

Mealtime distraction

One of the reasons that I started an online meal support service is because I know how anxiety-inducing mealtimes can be.

In my own recovery, I got through mealtimes with crosswords and sudoku puzzles. I didn't really understand it at the time, but I knew I could only eat when doing a puzzle. Now it is obvious to me that I was attempting and succeeding to lower my anxiety around eating by distracting my mind away from the food. Personally I think that mindful eating techniques are the last thing a person with anorexia needs to focus on. You're already hyper-focused on food for Pete's sake! You need to practice mindless eating, not mindful eating!

We have found with the online meal support coaching service that the most common reasons people say meal support is helpful to them are accountability — having to show up as they have an appointment to eat — and distraction. That is, having someone to talk to about non-food and non-eating disorder topics while they are eating. Human interaction distracts on a higher level than television, reading, or crosswords.

Distraction counter-activities

You feel the urge to exercise? Feel the urge to obsessively clean the house? Call a friend. Eat a cupcake. Sit down and write. Get in the car and go for a drive. Do something else — but make sure it is not something that creates energy deficit.

Urge distraction has to be specific to you. And so long as it doesn't create energy deficit or provoke another OCD-ED behaviour then it can be anything that works. My cat was very well groomed when I was in recovery because for a while I responded to movement urges by brushing her. I also used writing a lot.

Action: Make a list here of distraction ideas:
(I've done the first two for you)
1. Eat a cupcake.
2. Text someone.

Force Feeding Yourself

I understand that alongside all these other tools, this one feels out of place. The concept of force feeding seems brutal, and unintuitive, but when you have anorexia, this skill is a game changer. Deep down you know your healthy brain wants to eat, you just get scared when it comes to it.

Many of us find that when we are not around food, that we can think of all the glorious food we want to eat. That is because when food is not present, you are in your parasympathetic nervous system, and you are relaxed and your healthy brain can talk to you. But, when you walk into the kitchen, it evaporates. The threat of imminent eating puts you into your sympathetic nervous system, and you opt for your safe food choices despite your best intentions.

Force feeding yourself seems merciless, but it is an act of self love. It is committing to your healthy brain thoughts, and following through with eating even when you suddenly don't feel like you want to any more. This was me, committing to eating pizza, and then following through even if I didn't want to when the time came.

Often in recovery, I had to force myself to eat the foods that I really desired. I have cried, shaken, and sobbed whilst eating fear foods many times, but with repetition, my brain learned that these foods were nothing to be afraid of. In time, I was thoroughly enjoying them. This really is a skill. I credit much of my sustained recovery to my ability to to make myself eat when I don't feel like it.

Functional Detachment

Functional detachment = looking at the recovery process from a detached viewpoint

You cannot subtract emotion. Becoming cold and unresponsive is not the point. This is about *functional* detachment — being able to step back from the emotional reactions that you have and feel and looking at your own recovery from the seat of the observer. So basically, being detached enough that you don't make fear-driven decisions, and look at your own recovery process objectively.

It occurred to me one day, just before I really let go and jumped in to unrestricted eating, that I am a person who gets shit done. If given a task, I usually get it done and out the way immediately. Yet, I'd been "trying" to gain weight for 10 years and not really made much progress. This struck me as completely ridiculous. I realised then, that I had not been treating my recovery in the same way I would usually treat a project, and that I had been too caught up in it all emotionally to be able to take action. That's how I learned to detach myself emotionally from my own recovery project — not completely, just enough so I could actually get on with it.

I found that when I was all caught up in the emotions around my recovery that I couldn't be pragmatic about it. When I reframed my recovery effort in my mind as "project management," I was able to look at it more in the same way that I would look at a project my boss gave me to do at work. Functional detachment is different from not caring. I still cared, but I was able to see the big picture and more importantly able to take my ego out of it.

When we subtract ego from the equation, it can be easier to make better decisions. Ego can be a factor that prevents you from asking for help. Pride can be a serious barrier. Getting on with recovery with less emotion means that if you need help to get it done you ask for it, just in the same way I would ask a colleague for help if I needed it at work.

In an ideal project management situation, every person involved in that project wants what is best for the success of the project, even if that means admitting that they were wrong about something, or asking someone else to help. We do this at work all the time. I found that when I approached my own recovery from this detached standpoint, I was able to make better decisions and work with others as a team better too.

Teamwork requires removal of any unproductive emotional reactions, such as self-disparagement. If something doesn't go to plan, you should not waste energy on blame of self or others, instead, go straight to the problem solving and learning phase.

The most relevant example I can think of here, is monitoring your reaction when a loved one asks you to eat more. There was nothing I hated more than being asked to eat more. My emotional reaction to that was always one of anger and irritation. When I was able to functionally detach from my rage, and step back, my rational brain would have a chance to step in. I would be able to see the request not as an attack, but rather as a pro-recovery project suggestion. I was then able to sit down and eat more rather than getting into an argument about it.

I also had to face this rather uncomfortable truth: I am very emotionally volatile when in a malnourished state — that goes with the territory — and there was no point in blaming myself for that either. That state was temporary, and long-term nutritional rehabilitation brought a refreshing stability to my disposition.

Section Two: Nutritionally Rehabilitate *And* Neurally Rewire

Nutritional Rehabilitation + Neural Rewiring = Full Recovery

Recovery from anorexia could be as straightforward as shutting up the thoughts in your head and eating unrestricted amounts of food while resting. As one of my younger clients says, *"not exactly rocket science, is it?"* While the concept is simple, that doesn't mean it is easy.

If you can close this book right now and sit down and eat unrestricted amounts of food whilst also going against all your restriction rules and OCD-ED compulsions, then you do that. You don't need to read any further. Go for it!

I've said that there isn't a one-size fits all recovery approach and I mean it. However, nutritional rehabilitation and neural rewiring are the core areas of focus that I think are most helpful overall. Within these, there are spin offs and tangents specific to the individual. For all, the first element of reaching nutritional rehabilitation has to be weighted (pun intended) with importance, as full recovery is not possible without achieving energy balance. After all, it is the energy deficit that triggers the anorexia genetics to fire, so you can't very well recover while that is still going on.

As outlined in Section One, many of the things you are feeling are side-effects from malnutrition/starvation. Therefore, nutritional rehabilitation is key.

Recovery focus:
The core areas of focus are:
- ★ Full nutritional rehabilitation
- ★ Neural rewiring by eliminating restriction and OCD-ED behaviours.

Remember, underweight does not always present itself at a low weight. If you are restricting food then it is likely you are underweight, and this is true regardless of what you weigh. I am assuming that you are underweight for the remainder of this chapter, but first I will address those of you who may believe yourselves weight restored but still have a high volume of disordered thoughts and behaviours.

But I'm already "weight restored" so does this apply to me?

Firstly, weight restored according to whom?

And what does "weight restored" actually mean anyway? That some chart says you are within the healthy BMI range and therefore blanket statement assumes that your body is suddenly now healthy regardless of the physical and mental symptoms of malnutrition that you are showing?

Your body doesn't care two hoots for the charts and graphs on the wall in the doctor's office. Your body doesn't care if it is fashionable to be a BMI of 19 or 20. Your body doesn't give a tinkers if the calculations or statistics say you should be recovered already. Your body gets to decide when you are nutritionally rehabilitated. So with that in mind, are you really "weight restored," or are you still weight suppressed but just at a higher weight than before?

Secondly, it is possible to gain weight while still restricting. For example, I can be eating 8,000 calories a day, but if I am an adhering to an anorexia-generated rule that tells me I can only eat two pieces of toast a day, I am still restricting. If I'm eating orthorexically, I am still restricting. If I don't allow myself to eat a second slice of chocolate cake when I wanted, I am still restricting. If I am choosing granola bars when I really want chocolate bars, I am still restricting.

If you are at a good weight for your body, I'm not saying that you have to force feed yourself ridiculous amounts of food that you don't want. I am just saying that you have to let go of restriction. We restrict in many more ways that just quantity of food.

Anorexia provokes the generation of many rules, as well as compensatory behaviours such as movement, purging etc. Over time these develop into forming neural pathways in the brain when we act on them, and develop thought and behaviour patterns. If you are still using the anorexia-generated neural pathways while you are in the nutritional rehabilitation phase of recovery, they will likely still be there when you are at a higher weight. In order to get out of the rut of restriction, you have to form and reinforce alternative neural pathways. So there may still be work to be done in this area of recovery for you.

Thirdly, if you are reading this book, I will hazard a guess you are not yet fully recovered — hark back to the "you are sick enough" lecture at the intro.

So yes, even if you think you are "weight restored," if you are still governed by restriction, OCD-ED, and other anorexia pathway remnants, you have work to do in order to reach full recovery.

Chapter 6: Hunger

This section will address the following aspects of hunger:

- Physical hunger cues
- Mental hunger cues
- Eating-induced hunger cues
- Poststarvation hyperphagia
- Hunger FAQs

Malnutrition affects hunger cues

Normally when your average Joe eats less, neurochemical signals of hunger ago up and signals for satiety and activity go down.[89] However, researchers have found that for people with anorexia, most neuromodulators and hormones influencing hunger, satiety, and activity are present in unusual concentrations that are opposite to those found in normal starvation. In other words, people with anorexia have funky happenings afoot when it comes to the starvation response to hunger.

These findings are consistent with the theory that these responses are adaptations to turn off eating and turn on traveling, or the migratory response. They are also stand alone endocrine system changes that explain appetite suppression. Additionally, they are consistent with my own experienced lack of *physical* appetite when underweight.

---

[89] Ahima, R. S., & Antwi, D. A. (2008). Brain regulation of appetite and satiety. *Endocrinology and Metabolism Clinics of North America, 37*(4).

Physical Hunger Cues

Anorexia messes with physical hunger cues. Studies have shown, that in a person without anorexia, the reward centres of the brain show activity when they are hungry. In a person with anorexia, this is not so much the case. Brain studies have illustrated that hunger doesn't involve the reward and motivation circuits in the brain in a person with anorexia, and also that when a person with anorexia is hungry, there is more activity in the executive "self control" circuits of the brain.[90][91] This would make sense as to why we are able to respond to hunger with restriction, rather than being motivated to eat. I absolutely know that when I was restricting I would often feel hungry and not eat. I also know, I would often claim that I didn't feel hungry. Sometimes, I think that I *believed* I was not hungry, even when I was feeling physical hunger pangs. As if they were negated and denied by my brain before I even had a chance to think about it — which is weird, but that's anorexia for you.

There are, apparently, hormonal explanations for the lack of hunger phenomenon. People with anorexia have raised levels of a circulating hunger hormone called ghrelin — which is usually present to induce hunger — but seem to become less responsive to it after a prolonged

[90] Nothing tastes as good as skinny feels: the neurobiology of anorexia nervosa. Kaye et al Cell Trends in Neurosciences

[91] Hunger and satiety in anorexia nervosa: fMRI during cognitive processing of food pictures Santel et al. Brain Research

period of hunger.[92][93][94] (Incidentally, these increased levels of ghrelin may be why many people with anorexia experience insomnia and sleep difficulties.)

If you want to really get into the nitty gritty, then there are studies that look into the links between white matter reduction in people with anorexia in brain areas such as the hypothalamus that highlight the potential role of endocrine system dysfunction that contributes to the altered state of homeostasis.[95][96] I have read a lot of these studies, and every time I do, it strikes me how very complicated the physiological effects of long-term malnutrition are. It is like a domino effect, with so many different personalised variables per person, the possibilities and outcomes seem endless.

The good news is, that you don't have to understand what your ghrelin levels or your hypothalamus are doing in order to recover. You just need to eat.

Common sense

I think that there are some pretty common sense reasons why we often don't feel physical hunger cues. If your brain believes that you are in a famine environment, why would it waste energy generating

---

[92] Plasma obestatin, ghrelin, and ghrelin/obestatin ratio are increased in underweight patients with anorexia nervosa but not in symptomatic patients with bulimia nervosa. Monteleone et al Clin Endocrinol Metab. 2008

[93] Prog Neuropsychopharmacol Biol Psychiatry.Ghrelin and Eating Disorders, Atalayer

[94] Weight gain decreases elevated plasma ghrelin concentrations of patients with anorexia nervosa. Otto Eur J Endocrinol. 2001

[95] Gray Matter Decrease of the Anterior Cingulate Cortex in anorexia Nervosa. Mühlau et al.

[96] Anorexia nervosa is linked to reduced brain structure in reward and somatosensory regions: a meta-analysis of VBM studies. Titova et al

physical hunger cue? Physical hunger cues have an energy cost. When you are very low on fuel, you can't waste energy on signals that won't be responded to anyway. That's like trying to thumb a lift in Antarctica — all you're going to catch there is frostbite, so you might as well keep your hands in your pockets.

And what about your stomach? We've already noted that one of the effects of energy deficit is a delay in emptying of the stomach. Therefore, your tummy feels fuller for longer. Stands to reason this would lead to a reduction in hunger cues.

The *Adapted to Flee Famine Perspective* demonstrates that in other migratory animals, hunger cues cease for the duration of migration. A migrating bird can't very well just stop halfway across the ocean because he got hungry, can he? He also cannot stop just because he got tired. Hunger signals would act as a distraction when trying to migrate, hence it is of an evolutionary advantage if these are shut down when all focus has to be put on reaching a destination with abundant food present.

TL;DR: Anorexia messes with our physical hunger signals so you can't rely on them and will likely have to eat a lot more than you are physically hungry for in order to recover.

In recovery, most people find that physical hunger cues return at some point. In my coaching practice I have found that for many people, physical hunger cues do not return until intake is up and has stayed up.

Mental Hunger

When I refer to mental hunger, I am referring to the constant nagging thoughts around food, (and sometimes exercise or forms of restriction too).

In a warped way, my brain obsessed about exercise and restriction because that would allow me to fantasize about food and eating and planning to eat. Mental hunger is the focus on food that meant I spent hours a day flicking through cookbooks or watching cooking films. Mental hunger was me daydreaming of all the things I wanted to eat but never would. Mental hunger was even me planning on running the next morning so that I would be allowed to eat breakfast after. Mental hunger was me thinking about avoiding eating. There was barely a moment in my day where my mind was not planning what to eat, what not to eat, or when I was allowed to eat. It was a torturous, tedious way to spend the day and my own thoughts would drive me to the point of hysterics some evenings — but all the crying and pleading in the world would not make them stop.

Mental hunger can be exhausting. The nagging, prodding, relentless thoughts of food were the ultimate cruelty for a person who could not eat. I honestly think that for me, the mental hunger was the most painful part of my illness. The thoughts never let me be, and my sleepless nights seemed endless. I don't think I would have minded the insomnia as much had I been able to entertain myself with more interesting thoughts than food, but my brain had no interest in allowing me to contemplate anything other than the food I wouldn't eat.

Understanding mental hunger is often a real "aha" moment for people in recovery. When you click that all this food thinking is your brain trying to communicate hunger to you, you realise the extent of your malnutrition. You are really hungry!

Mental hunger counts as hunger!

Most of us tend to discount mental hunger, as if it is not as valid as physical hunger. I know I did. It didn't occur to me that I was thinking about food the whole time because I was hungry. I had little in the way of stomach growing or physical hunger pangs, and I didn't understand that my brain's inability to think of much other than food should be interpreted as a cue to eat.

Nothing that your body does is free. Physical hunger cues require a physical contraction of the stomach muscles, so delivering a physical hunger cue has an energetic cost to the body.[97] I imagine that mental hunger, on the other hand — thinking — is cheaper. When we are malnourished, the body is signaling to the brain that more food is needed. When incoming energy is so low that resources have to be sternly economised, mental hunger is your brain telling you that you need to eat.

Hunger is defined as "*a craving or need for food*" or "*an uneasy sensation occasioned by the lack of food*." Mental hunger is both of these things. Sure, there may be no physical signals, but it is certainly a craving and it is definitely uneasy. Mental hunger counts as hunger. If you are thinking about food, your body wants food.

[97] Walter Bradford Cannon - An Explanation of Hunger

This terrifies many people in recovery, as they say *"but I am thinking about food all the time, surely I don't need to eat all the time?"*

So be it. If you are thinking about food, you need to eat food. Unrestricted eating means just this: that you respond to mental hunger.

As you move into energy balance the mental hunger will lessen. Your desire to eat all the time should decrease. When your brain and body are in a state of energy balance, the signals that your brain is giving you to eat all the time will no longer be required. You will stop thinking about food all the time when you are no longer in energy deficit. Trust your body. It knows what you need. Your brain isn't making you hyper-focused on food for kicks and giggles. Mental hunger is there because you are in a state of malnutrition. Your body is screaming at you for food. Trust it and listen.

This can be a bit of a wake up call for people who have apparently "weight restored" but still have mental hunger and all the mental state indications that they are still in a weight-suppressed state. Presence of mental hunger indicates that you are either still in energy deficit, or you are still restricting food, or both. And while you may not be restricting in caloric terms, if you are adhering to orthorexic rules, then you are restricting in other ways and your brain knows it.

Mental hunger and unrestricted eating

When I talk about unrestricted eating, I am not only talking about not restricting in response to physical hunger. I am referring to listening to and eating in response to mental hunger too. Due to early satiation and digestive tract slowing, most of us feel physically full quite fast when we are malnourished. If you were to only eat to physical hunger you would unlikely eat enough to nutritionally rehabilitate. I have yet to meet a person with anorexia who can honestly say they don't have any mental hunger at all. (Many people can successfully ignore or suppress it, but that is not the same as it not being there.) If you are accountable about responding to mental hunger, you will eat enough food to nutritionally rehabilitate. That is the point of it being there in the first place.

And yes, you are thinking about food the whole time. That means your body wants you to eat food the whole time. Really!

All you have to do is actually eat the food. Oh, and not judge it.

The brain will obsess over what it wants but can't have

Picture a person alone in the desert, let's call her Jody. Jody is dying of thirst. Jody's mind is overrun by thoughts of water. Jody dreams about water. Jody sees mirages of water. Jody's brain would be singularly focused on water and not interested in much else. This is your brain on restriction.

Jody in the desert, on finding water, would go wild! She would drink it and drink it and want to do nothing other than be near that water for a while. She would have a little honeymoon period with that oasis where all she would want to do would be to lie next to it and take sips every now and then. However, if you put Jody in a house where water was on tap, over time she would cease to obsess about water because water is no longer scarce. When Jody knows that water is in the tap and there for her whenever she wants it, she would relax about it. Jody's brain would switch away from obsessing about water, and onto other things, like kittens and NASCAR.

When we restrict food, we turn food into a scarce commodity as far as our brains are concerned. If we stop restricting, and start allowing ourselves to eat what we want, sure, we may consume a lot of that previously forbidden food in the short run, but in the long run, it loses its "value." This was me with carrot cake. I love carrot cake. I didn't eat carrot cake for 12 years. I was obsessed with the thought of eating carrot cake. When I did allow myself to eat carrot cake again, I wanted the whole cake, not just a slice. However, over time, when I told myself I was allowed as much carrot cake as I wanted, the urge to eat massive amounts of it decreased. Now, I can buy a carrot cake and have it in the fridge and it doesn't burn a hole in my head like it used to. The mental hunger for it has gone. I can have it whenever I like. My brain doesn't have to keep telling me to eat it out of fear of scarcity.

Mental hunger hurts!

It feels wrong to admit this — as I should have been more concerned about the physical repercussions of being so underweight — but I will say it anyway: If it were not for the relentless mental hunger, I am not sure I would have been motivated to recover. It drove me insane. Constantly thinking about food. Building sandwiches in my head that I would never eat. Going to imaginary parties and eating birthday cake. Thoughts of hot chocolate with cream and marshmallows in daydreams that felt as realistic as the concept of the Lapland I would drink them in. It was this that got me in the end. I was driven into recovery by the mental hunger.

"Mental hunger is a kind of torture that is difficult to describe, it's unrelenting and drives you completely insane, you truly feel as though you are losing your mind. The only option you have is to eat, but you don't want to, if you do give in and eat then you open the floodgates and you cannot stop until there is nothing left to eat. The torture doesn't end there because now you have to purge, this is non-negotiable and then even after you have purged you still have to go for that run, and you don't want to stop running, you can't stop and then you restrict again and then you are right back where you started, it's a living hell" - LC, adult in recovery from anorexia.

Due to anosognosia, and the lack of egregious physical symptoms, many of us feel like we are getting by okay. Despite of all this, at some point most of us are driven to seek recovery due to this unrelenting mental hunger that drives us mad.

Your brain is allocating your attention to food and sometimes this is the only persistent indicator that we have that we are unwell.

Bottom line: If you are thinking about food, you are hungry.

Eating-Induced Hunger

Eating-induced hunger freaks a lot of us out! It is not uncommon when you are in recovery from anorexia to feel no physical hunger, only to get halfway through or finish a meal and suddenly feel starving. This phenomenon is not your hunger cues being broken and crazy. It actually makes sense if you think of it from the feast/famine perspective.

I think that your body is very smart, and in times of famine, it will not waste energy creating hunger cues because it wants you to migrate and not get all distracted on the way. Also, if you are in a famine, what is the point in sending out hunger signals? However, once you start eating, the body will assume that there is food in the environment again and want you to keep eating.

From a straight-up metabolism saving perspective, reflect that physical hunger cues are costly. If your body thinks there is no food in the environment, why would it generate a physical hunger cue? The return on investment of doing so would not look good. However, if you start eating, your brain twigs that there must be food around and therefore there is a higher chance that if it throws out a physical hunger cue that you can eat more. The investment in that hunger cue is more worthwhile.

For whatever reason, "inappropriate" hunger happens, and it is entirely appropriate, so if it happens to you don't be shocked by it.

When you are in recovery from anorexia, this eating-induced hunger can be painfully hard to respond to. It doesn't feel rational, it makes you nervous that you will develop an insatiable hunger and carry on eating forever, and it is all made even worse by the fact that you probably feel full at the same time due to having eaten. Oh, and not to mention feeling guilty.

So, many of us make the mistake of ignoring eating-induced hunger because we get scared by it. But think of it from a data-perspective from your brain's point of view. All your brain knows, is that it delivered a request for more food, but more food did not come. Therefore, by not responding to hunger, you just gave your brain data to support the perception that food is not available. You just reinforced the food scarcity notion.

The better course of action would be to drop your *judgement* of whether or not you should still be hungry, and eat more food. Simply respond to what your brain and body is asking for. Don't pretend that you know better. Don't wait until the next mealtime. Eat more food without judgement. I had to employ the "Stay Present" tool when I experienced eating-induced hunger and this helped me do the right thing and eat more if my body asked for it. Staying present forces you to focus on your current truth, and often my current truth was that I was hungry.

A hunger cue is a hunger cue regardless of how inappropriate you judge it to be. Hunger should be responded to.

Poststarvation Hyperphagia

"An increase in the sensation of hunger and overeating after a period of chronic energy deprivation can be part of an autoregulatory phenomenon attempting to restore body weight" - Dulloo, Poststarvation hyperphagia and body fat overshooting in humans: a role for feedback signals from lean and fat tissues.

Hyperphagia means an abnormally increased appetite.

Poststarvation hyperphagia, (also known as extreme hunger or intense hunger, but I always thought of it as my "bottomless pit" hunger) is an abnormally increased appetite following starvation.

It's like the mental hunger — always thinking about food — turns into physical hunger. Not everyone experiences this crippling sort of physical hunger in recovery, but many of us do. (Actually, if you think of poststarvation hyperphagia as the physicalisation of mental hunger, we all do get extreme hunger in the form of mental hunger.) It is as if your brain catches on that you are out of the famine now and it wants you to really go for it and feast.

" ... some of the men found it difficult to stop eating. Their daily intake commonly ranged between 8,000 and 10,000 calories ... " - Garner. *The effects of starvation on behaviour; Implications for dieting and eating disorders.*

This is the bottomless pit hunger that was first described by the men in the Minnesota Starvation Experiment in the rehabilitation process, and is often felt by people in recovery from anorexia. It is an alarming hunger — often disconcerting and you can feel like you are going slightly mad, but you're not.

"No 108 would eat and eat until he could hardly swallow any more and then he felt like eating half an hour later" - Garner. *The effects of starvation on behaviour; Implications for dieting and eating disorders.*

It seems that the degree of intense hunger that a person feels is somewhat dependent on their state of fat-free mass (muscle and tissue etc) deficit. Re-analysis of the good old Minnesota Starvation Experiment found that poststarvation hyperphagia persisted until a individual's fat-free mass was restored to the level that it was before weight loss, indicating that the body is giving feedback for more food until some vital skeletal and tissue levels are reached.[98][99]

"Subject No. 20 stuffs himself until he is bursting at the seams, to the point of being nearly sick and still feels hungry." - Garner. *The effects of starvation on behaviour; Implications for dieting and eating disorders.*

This all-powerful hunger will go away when your body is good and ready. Until then there is absolutely no point in fighting it. It is there to help you recover.

Imagine that you are holding your breath underwater. What happens when you at last come up for air? You gasp. Big, ugly, air gasps. I feel

[98] Keys A, Brozek J, Henschel A, Mickelsen O, Taylor HL. The Biology of Human Starvation. University of Minnesota Press: Minnesota, 1950.

[99] Dulloo AG, Jacquet J, Girardier L. Poststarvation hyperphagia and body fat overshooting in humans: a role for feedback signals from lean and fat tissues. Am J Clin Nutr 1997

like poststarvation hyperphagia is rather like this. You have not had enough food for a while, and your body is gasping for food. I often felt like I was inhaling food when I was eating — not even tasting it.

Believe me I tried to fight it when the black-hole hunger hit, but it was practically impossible. If you have not experienced it, it is the type of hunger that feels like a horse kicked you in the stomach. It will not be ignored. For me, it felt like ten years of absent physical hunger signals all at once.

Not everyone gets poststarvation hyperphagia in recovery. I didn't get it until I had increased my intake up considerably. Then it were as if my body decided that I had finally landed wherever I was migrating to and the famine was over. My body started screaming at me to eat. *Time to feast … the famine is over. We have arrived in the abundant lands, and thou shalt now scoff!*

You will likely feel utterly unable to do anything other than eat. That will scare you, but you will do it anyway because you won't feel like you have any choice. That's okay. That is what it is designed to do. An evolved feast response after famine. It will not last forever and it serves a purpose.

The bottomless pit

Sometimes I think that my ability to recover was strengthened by my ignorance around traditional eating disorder treatment. Other than the FEAST website, I had not even so much as read a blog post or article on anorexia recovery, so I really was very ignorant to all these things until I lived them. I am sure that if I had been to a treatment centre or eating to a strict meal plan, I would have felt even more conflicted about my unrelenting physical *need* to eat.

I had nobody to tell me that this was "binge" eating. I had nobody to tell me that this was emotional eating. I had nobody to tell me that I should only eat as per my meal plan. I responded to hunger by doing what felt like common sense: eating an extremely large amount of food.

That is not to say I was not scared, or forever doubting that I was doing the right thing. However, that common sense statement that my mother had told me so many times over the years rang true in the foreground: *"It doesn't matter how much you are currently eating, if you are underweight, it is not enough."*

Because she was right. Because that was common sense. An underweight body needs more food. It didn't matter if I was already eating 5000 calories a day. I was still in energy deficit. It didn't matter that I currently ate more than anyone else I knew — nobody else was in a state of starvation from anorexia. It didn't matter that I was already eating 10 times what I had been previously. I needed more.
I ate more. And what happened is that I ate even more than I felt was humanly possible for what seemed like forever. And then slowly the urge to eat reduced. Waned. Normalised.

"Serious binge eating developed in a subgroup of men, and this tendency persisted in some cases for months after free access to food was reintroduced; however, the majority of men reported gradually returning to eating normal amounts of food after about 5 months of refeeding.' - Garner. *The effects of starvation on behaviour; Implications for dieting and eating disorders.*

What I particularly like about Garner's reports on the Minnesota Starvation Experiment is that he points out that this binge eating behaviour was produced in "normal" young men, and thus is evident that the primary cause of binge eating may not be "psychological disturbances".

Quite right. Maybe it's just due to being really, really hungry.

Hunger FAQs

Here are some answers to common hunger questions that I get asked:

I am mentally hungry all the time, surely this is not normal?
Being mentally hungry the whole time is perfectly normal and appropriate if you are in a state of malnutrition or dietary restriction. Your body is in energy deficit and it is naturally wanting to consume as much food as possible in order to achieve a state of balance again.

I am only hungry for "junk" foods, surely it is not okay to eat these types of food?
"Junk" foods are most easily utilised by your body in recovery. Your body wants fat and sugar and nutrient density. Your body is smart — you should listen to it more often.

I never seem to be able to eat to fullness. Is there anything wrong with me?

No, other than you are in energy deficit. Wanting to eat all the time and wanting to eat to the point of being past physical comfort are common and documented effects of starvation. But we are all different, and some people feel quite the opposite and are overly full the whole time. Either way, if you are underweight you need to eat more than enough food to gain weight.

Surely it is wrong to keep eating if I have already eaten what was on my plan and I am still hungry?

Hunger is your body communicating with you that it needs food. If you are hungry you should eat more food regardless of what you have already eaten.

Is it possible to get mental hunger without physical hunger?

Absolutely yes. Mental hunger, or preoccupation with food and thinking about food is often present in the absence of physical hunger due to the suppression of hunger hormones that many of us experience when in a state of malnutrition. If you are thinking of food you should count that as hunger and eat.

What about when I am recovered or weight restored, do I still respond to thinking about food as a sign I need to eat?

Remember, recovery is about your mental state, not just your weight. If you are still obsessing about food that is a sign that you are in energy deficit, or restricting — regardless of what BMI you are.

What about when I am in full recovery and not in energy deficit, will I still have to eat every time I think about food? Won't that just lead to boredom eating?

When I was really in full recovery, a) I stopped obsessing about food, b) if I did think of food it was in a much more relaxed manner. I could think something like "I feel like lasagna for lunch," and decide to have that, and then the thought would leave me rather than keep prodding at me as it did when I was in energy deficit. I guess that my body removed the urgency of having to eat all the time. This heavily contrasts with how I was when I was in malnutrition and unable to think of anything other than the food I was thinking of. Now food is more of a passing thought. Like my brain trusts me if I think "I'll have that for lunch" and it doesn't need to keep bugging me. When you are in full recovery, you don't obsess about food all the time because your body is nutritionally stable.

On a more science-based answer: your levels of appetite hormones such as ghrelin are elevated when you are in energy deficit and this causes the hunger cues and desire to eat a lot.[100] As you come out of energy deficit, ghrelin levels normalise, and so does your hunger.[101]

I think obsessively about exercise, and my other routines, as well as food. If thinking of food is mental hunger and means I should eat, does thinking of exercise mean I should exercise?
Nice try. No. Thinking of exercise and any of the other conditions that allow you to eat means that you are hungry and need to eat more. Because exercise is a condition that allows you to eat, you are thinking about doing more exercise so that you can eat ... so even that in a

---

[100] Plasma levels of active form of ghrelin during oral glucose tolerance test in patients with anorexia nervosa. Nakai et al. Eur J Endocrinol. 2003

[101] Weight gain decreases elevated plasma ghrelin concentrations of patients with anorexia nervosa B Otto, et al. *EJE* (2001)

sense is the mental hunger as you are trying to work out how you can eat more.

I'm often lying awake at night trying to decide what to eat the next day. I don't feel hungry, but do think about what to eat a lot. What is going on here?

That is mental hunger. It can show up in many ways but if you are thinking about food you need to be eating food.

How do you get over that feeling that you won't be able to stop eating?

Often it is restriction and energy deficit that cause or brains to continually ask us to eat more and more. When you have truly let go of all restrictive thoughts and behaviours, and have given yourself freedom to eat whatever you want, and when you are out of energy deficit, your body won't desire food continually as it does whilst in a state of malnutrition.

Hunger summary

Anorexia affects hunger signals therefore physical hunger signals cannot be relied on. Your minimum intake should be set independently of any physical hunger cues, however, if hunger cues are present, you should always eat. This is true regardless of the time, and regardless of how much you have already eaten. If you are blessed with a hunger cue you must respond to it. If you do not, this constitutes restriction.

Hunger rules:
1. You do not have to be physically hungry in order to eat.

2. Mental hunger counts as hunger and should be responded to by eating.
3. If your body generates a hunger cue, you have to eat.

Feeling Full

Often in recovery I would feel very physically full and bloated after eating (despite often mentally wanting more food at the same time). My clients tell me the same is true for them often also, and research confirms that feeling satiated is a common struggle for people who go from not eating much to eating more.[102] I have to admit I think that a proportion of this was psychosomatic in my case, but it has been shown that anorexic rats (this is a real thing!) are also quickly satiated, and seem to lack appetite.[103] They leave food bowls full and opt instead to run in their running wheels. Doesn't that sound familiar?

So, is this lack of appetite all in our heads? Maybe not. Apparently a number of biochemical signals could lead to this "anorexic phenomenology." As your body stores more fat, the hormone leptin regulates these fat stores by making you feel less physically hungry (mental hunger can still be there, remember). Researchers have found that leptin levels increase back to normal in people with anorexia too early — so before you get to full nutritional restoration.[104] This complicated and seemingly counterproductive neuroendocrine state could contribute to the reasons (other than the blatantly obvious fear of weight gain) that are stopping you from reaching eating enough.[105] And as mentioned before, that delayed gastric emptying that your tummy does to economise is also a reason that you could feel full before you should do.

---

[102] Increased suppression of serum ghrelin concentration by hyperinsulinemia in women with anorexia nervosa.

[103] Self-starvation: A problem of overriding the satiety signal? Robin B.Kanarek1. .George H.Collier

[104] Adapted to Flee Famine: Adding an Evolutionary Perspective on anorexia Nervosa, Shan Guisinger

[105] Adapted to Flee Famine: Adding an Evolutionary Perspective on anorexia Nervosa, Shan Guisinger

The good news is, that all of these out-of-whack appetite suppression mechanisms go back to doing what they should do when you come out of energy deficit. The even better news is that you *can* still eat even when you are feeling full. I know this because I have done it many times — and I didn't pop yet!

I have known a couple of people who have experienced more than what I would call a normal level of resistance to eating when feeling full than most people with anorexia feel. They had more like what I would consider to be a phobia-level response to eating when full. There are therapies that can help with this, one of these people I know worked with a therapist and he said that helped. I also know another who bulldozed through on her own. There is always more than one way to flip a burger.

At least at the beginning as you are starting to eat more, you're going to have to eat more food than your stomach is used to handling. You have to put pressure on the stomach in order for it to change things up and for your digestion to gear up. Think of it as training. You are training your tummy to be able to digest faster. This can be uncomfortable, and can take a while to normalise, but it is something that you are going to have to be prepared to do.

Chapter 7: Nutritional Rehabilitation

I said it at the start of this book, but I am going to say it again now: you will have your own unique recovery process. This book is my opinion based on my experience. If my opinion conflicts with what you know about your body, then trust yourself to know what is right for you. Take what you need, leave what you don't.

(If you are at the risk of refeeding syndrome, or medically unstable, you should be working with a medical doctor to determine a safe refeeding route. This chapter is only relevant to people not at risk from refeeding syndrome.)

Why is it so hard for me to eat more?

Even for those of us who dislike being underweight and logically want to gain weight, eating more can feel close to impossible. Let's break this down:

Your brain thinks that you are in a hostile, famine environment. And on top of that, you have the anorexia response that makes your brain think that food is a threat to survival. So, eating small amounts feels safer. Your brain starts to associate eating small amounts with your ability to survive this hostile place it is in. And therefore, it gets all habitual about it. Your brain wants you to keep doing the things that it thinks have kept you alive. Now of course, your logical-thinking brain knows that you are not in a hostile place, and hopefully knows that food is not a threat, and that you need to gain weight. But your brain-stem reptile brain doesn't give two hoots for what logical thinking would assume. So logically you know you need to eat more, but when it actually comes down to doing it, you get stuck.

So this is why someone like me — someone who knows they need to gain weight, and wants to gain weight — can walk into the kitchen determined to have pizza for dinner, and come out with a salad, again. Logical thinking is being overridden by fear. If you are reading this book, you probably know this feeling.

Time and time again I would psych myself up to eating more food. I would feel determined, scared, and also excited to eat more. Then, by the time I had walked into the kitchen, it was gone. It was as if outside of a mealtime I could be full of intention, but when I got to making a meal, it followed the exact same protocol that had been keeping me underweight. It was always a case of *"next meal, my next meal will be bigger, I'll just play it safe with this one, and then after this I am going to eat more."*

For years, it didn't occur to me that I would have to force feed myself. The reason that I didn't make this realisation quickly, was because I love eating. I have always loved eating. But when it came to eating, the fear would convince me *I didn't really want that burger after all, thank you very much, and I'm actually happier with my usual salad.*

It felt absurd that someone who loves food, enjoys eating, and wants to gain weight would have to force feed herself when it came down to the actual *action* of eating more food. But this is what I had to do. It was never going to feel like the right time to have that burger. I had to force myself to make it happen. Crying and shaking, I refed myself with sheer bloody mindedness in order to get myself in the momentum of gaining weight. Chew. Swallow. Repeat. Of course it wasn't *all* bad. I do enjoy eating. I love eating. But I was terrified. A cruel duality.

I am happy to report that after the first week or so, it got much easier — my brain was learning that eating more was not a threat to me. The enjoyment stuck, but the fear waned.

"I love food. I love eating. But I had to pack my bags and go and live with my sister to get refed by her because I couldn't do it myself, alone. I am so thankful now that I did that, because in order to kick start recovery, I needed help to eat." SC - adult in recovery from anorexia.

Hopefully you are much smarter than I, and you will do what "SC" did above, and ask for help and support in getting through the hard phases or initial refeeding.

How much food do I need to eat?

Great question! Sadly I cannot give you a personalised answer in a book. It would be ludicrous to try and do so, as we are all different. That's why I am not going to give you a caloric minimum, or any blanket-statement numbers.

If you need to gain weight, you need to eat more calories than you expend for a prolonged period of time. This doesn't have to be exact, because your body doesn't expend exactly the same amount of energy each day. You don't even have to calculate your BMR, in fact the less you overthink how much you are eating, the better in terms of rewiring that anorexia desire for calorie exactness. Here is as complicated as it needs to be: If you are underweight, eat more than enough food to gain weight. And don't dither about doing so.

"When I started recovery I thought we were talking like a couple of cookies a day more. Now I get it -- it took way more than that!" - Mike, adult in recovery from anorexia.

In my opinion, the more food you eat during the nutritional rehabilitation phase, the better. This is not a math calculation and you can't get it wrong by eating "too much." Remember, you gotta lose the Goldilocks complex. You are feeding an intelligent organism — your body — not following a souffle recipe. What matters is that your body is being given an energy surplus each day in order to help it address the long-term energy deficit it has been in and you are eating without restrictive rules or judgements. Rehabilitation, plus rewiring.

One of the things I read on the FEAST[106] website is that *"food is medicine."* I think I will take that one step further and say that when you are underweight and in recovery from anorexia, food is the medicine that you cannot overdose on. The more you eat the more fuel your body has available to it in order to do what it needs to do.

So you'll be wondering what science I have to back my claims that you need to eat a lot of food. Other than my own experience of doing so, and straightforward common sense that malnutrition should be

---

[106] http://www.feast-ed.org

treated with nutrition ... oh, and the hardly insignificant fact that your brain likely spends most of the time thinking about food, of course.

I have to say I find the literature disappointing. The more liberal eating disorder research has refeeding intakes trending toward "higher" intakes of around 3000 calories a day for a person with anorexia in order to gain weight, which is far below what I needed to eat in order to nutritionally rehabilitate.[107] To be fair, it has been shown that some people need a lot more than that due to metabolic inefficiencies, and these are the people who usually lose weight in the first week of an inpatient stay due to the traditionally cautious nature of refeeding initially.[108]While it seems to me that there are tons of research papers published every year on the psychological theories of anorexia recovery, there is a real dearth in terms of biological aspects of nutritional rehabilitation. I know plenty of good dietitians who don't hesitate to have clients eat unrestricted amounts of food yet there is no consensus on higher caloric intakes.[109] However, 85 percent of studies between 2010 and 2015 recommended higher refeeding intakes are needed — so that's a good sign that things are changing to favour a more food first attitude.[110] While safety has to be priority, it is also shown that studies into higher refeeding intakes report no incidences of refeeding syndrome.[111]

---

[107] Outcomes of a rapid refeeding protocol in Adolescent anorexia Nervosa. Madden et al.

[108] Garber AK, Michihata N, Hetnal K, Shafer M, Mosicki A. A prospective examination of weight gain in hospitalized adolescents with anorexia nervosa on a recommended refeeding protocol. J Adolesc Health. 2012

[109] Garber, A. K. (2017). A few steps closer to answering the unanswered questions about higher calorie refeeding. *Journal of Eating Disorders, 5.*

[110] A systematic review of approaches to refeeding in patients with anorexia nervosa. *Garber AK, Sawyer SM, Golden NH, Guarda AS, Katzman DK, Kohn MR, Le Grange D, Madden S, Whitelaw M, Redgrave GW*

[111] Garber, A. K. (2017). A few steps closer to answering the unanswered questions about higher calorie refeeding. *Journal of Eating Disorders, 5.*

The thing is, I think that most of us when we are in malnutrition from anorexia — not all, but most — know deep down that we want to eat Willy Wonka's entire Chocolate Factory. But that's scary. So we baulk, and scrabble around looking for science to give us permission to do so. And the chances of finding large peer-reviewed studies on people like myself who simply surrendered to mental hunger and messily and freely ate their way into recovery aren't there, because we're outside of the system and, therefore, not counted. So ultimately you have to make a choice that is right for you, and on top of that you may find you have to defend your right to do so.

I chose food. I was bloody hungry. I had been resisting mental hunger for years. I was exhausted. I chose to stop fighting and to allow unrestricted food. Just because that is what I did, doesn't mean it is what you have to do. But I know that many of you reading this book, deep down want to do exactly that, and know it is the right path for you. And are desperate for permission to eat to mental hunger and really allow food in abundance without counting calories or exchanges.

It would not be right for me to *tell* you anything other than that you have permission to recover the way that you want to recover.

A note here from Therese Waterhaus, someone I consider to be a "really good" RDN:

"As an RDN, I start with maybe 3000 kcal. In someone who needs to gain weight, then regularly take their weight to gauge whether this kcal

amount is adequate, and often adjust upward as we go. It is pretty simple and more individualized to just keep adding 500 kcal per week until you see the scale start to move. It is fairly difficult, even with sophisticated equations, to predict what kcal level will do this for an individual."

I think that Therese nails it with "simple and individualized." You have to do what is right for you. And that is very different from what feels safe, or what feels right by your anorexia brain. Healthy brain "right" and anorexia brain "right" are often polar opposites. Choose the healthy brain option.

Coming at this from a place of experience, and common sense: Your body is starving and you need to feed it. You risk never reaching full recovery if you feed it too little. The more we eat the more our bodies have fuel to heal. The more we eat the more we are forced out of OCD-ED ritualised eating patterns. The more we eat, the more data our brain receives countering the existing notion that food is a threat.

In a famine environment, eating a lot of food would signal to your brain that you had arrived. The incoming food would be data to support that you had successfully made it to the lands of abundant food. Feast marks the end of famine. Hence, I believe that the more you eat in recovery the more your brain will assume it is safe to stop migrating.

Treat malnutrition with nutrition

Personally, I think that treatment centres can be the worst offenders when it comes to underfeeding people in recovery. I am often told that they do this because people with anorexia could "freak out" if given the option of more food. In terms of the notion that patients will pitch a fit about being fed more food ... erm, hello? That's anorexia!

You don't tell a cancer patient that it is okay not to have treatment because treatment is scary. Of course anorexia patients may be scared of more food. Pandering to this fear only confirms it in our heads and gives it more power over us. We need treatment providers to have compassion, and work with us through the fear. My clients are the most courageous people I know. And ... they can really eat when they are empowered to do so!

I don't think that the wonderful dedicated people who run treatment centres are doing anything other than their very best. I think that they believe what they have been taught. But I think that what they have been taught is still riddled with psychoanalysis. Because of this, nutrition has not been of focus in the way that it should have been when treatment programs were designed. Rather, the food aspect is systemised, and calculated. While it's fair enough to put minimums in place to help people eat more, there should never be maximums in anorexia recovery.

Malnutrition has to be treated with food first and foremost, and I still feel like the field is confused about what this really means in practice. It's like even though the marketing mouthpieces talk about the focus on nutrition, the underlying beliefs are still rife with psychoanalysis and fat phobia.

"The last treatment centre I was in (In Canada) I was given quite a small meal plan. When I asked what would happen if I wanted more food, I

was told something like that maybe I could have an extra piece of fruit, but no more than that otherwise I might be binge eating." - Anon, adult in recovery from anorexia.

I feel like the world has gone bonkers when people in a state of malnutrition who are (appropriately) hungry are told that anything more than an apple above their meal plan is a "binge." This serves nothing other than anorexia. In my opinion it is a cruelty to tell a person in a state of malnutrition that they should be afraid of their hunger.

Refeeding syndrome

Refeeding syndrome is what can happen when a person goes from a very malnourished state to eating more. If the body immediately starts to make more energy as you eat more food and doesn't have the nutrients required to meet the demand of processing more energy, you can get in big trouble. Refeeding syndrome has been known to be deadly, thus we must take it seriously.

There is no consensus on how common refeeding syndrome is, some studies say as low as 0.4 percent of patients get it, others say as high as 34 percent.[112][113] I say err on the side of caution, but be rational too — after a couple weeks of slowly increasing intake, the risk of refeeding syndrome is massively diminished.

---

[112] Severe hypophosphatemia following the institution of enteral feedings. Hayek ME, Eisenberg PGm Arch Surg. 1989

[113] Refeeding hypophosphatemia in critically ill patients in an intensive care unit. A prospective study. Marik PE, Bedigian, Arch Surg. 1996

There have been a number of studies in recent years that have experimented with feeding patients in hospital settings higher intakes. There is data to support a higher caloric intake in refeeding now.[114] Some have shown that this results in a shorter hospital stay, and no increase in the rate of refeeding syndrome.[115] Furthermore, for people who are at a point where they no longer meet the criteria for refeeding syndrome — and this can be reached in a matter of weeks of systematic increases in intake regardless — this cannot be used as an excuse not to eat more food.

Conservative intake guidelines can cause stagnation

I believe that when you are past the risk of refeeding syndrome, being conservative with your intake can do you more harm than good. If we put aside the physiological reasons, and look at the nature of the restriction that we all know so well, we see the outstanding truth: the more you eat, the more you are forced into breaking all the anorexia rules — and it is doing this that is an important part of the neural rewiring process. As you are forced to face your fears, higher intakes are the exposure and response control that will help you overcome the restrictions that plague you. What better time to eat all your most feared foods in high quantities than in the nutritional rehabilitation phase. Two birds; One stone.

For some of us, throwing caution to the wind and pressing ourselves to run into the fear that we feel around food works wonders. Pushing

[114] Int J Eat Disord. 2015 Refeeding and weight restoration outcomes in anorexia nervosa: Challenging current guidelines. Redgrave

[115] Higher calorie diets increase rate of weight gain and shorten hospital stay in hospitalized adolescents with anorexia nervosa.Garber AK, Mauldin K, Michihata N, Buckelew SM, Shafer MA, Moscicki AB. J Adolesc Health. 2013

and allowing myself to eat large quantities of the foods that I was most afraid of meant that I was rewiring those neural pathways that wanted me to stick to safe foods and small quantities.

I had to allow myself to slather mayonnaise on everything — if it wasn't dense nutrition it was not worth the time and effort. It was a game changer for me to think in this way. And yes, I was petrified. But I have always been one to run at things I am afraid of, and for anorexia recovery that tendency worked well in my favor. As Dr. Laura Hill[116] would say, I was using my character traits in my favor when I channeled my inner John McClane in recovery.

Eating a large quantity of food also began to signal to my brain that I no longer needed to migrate. The famine was over. My brain therefore gradually began to stop punishing me for feeding with those negative emotions. My movement compulsions eased. Eating more gradually became less stressful the more I ate. Resting more gradually became easier the more I ate. In short, feasting began to shut down the migration response.

Lessons on refeeding from Minnesota

I'm going to go back to the Minnesota Starvation Study for a moment. To recap, 36 healthy men without mental health problems were put on a semistarvation diet where they were fed an average of 1570 calories a day (note, this semistarvation diet is akin to what many treatment centres feed patients during the refeeding stage of anorexia — doesn't

---

[116] http://tabithafarrar.com/2018/01/dr-laura-hill-motivation-change-anorexia-recovery/

that ring alarm bells for anyone else?[117] That people in a "starvation experiment" were fed more than people in treatment for anorexia might be getting?)

Now I want to focus on the latter part of the study, where the recovery and refeeding part of the experiment is documented. In this phase, the men — who had only faced a very short period of semi-starvation (nothing like as long as most people with anorexia endure) were put through systematic daily calorie increases over three months. A subgroup was then followed for a further six months when the experiment was considered over, and the men were allowed to eat whatever they wanted.

In this time, many of the men reportedly ate between 5,200 and 10,000 calories a day in order to nutritionally rehabilitate.[118] Those of us who go into poststarvation hyperphagia find that we can easily consume this much or more in recovery.

Different people have different reactions to refeeding. Some of us go into hypermetabolism and can actually lose weight even when on medium or high intakes as a result of this. If that happens the answer is to eat even more. We have to be agile in our approach to intake amount too. If weight gain is not happening fast enough or stagnating, or if you are feeling hungry (mentally or physically), then food intake has to go up regardless of what it is already. If you are underweight and already eating 6,000 calories a day and not gaining weight,

---

[117] Adaptation to caloric restriction. Henry Longstreet Taylor and Ancel Keys The Laboratory of Physiological Hygiene, University of Minnesota, Minneapolis

[118] D.M Garner. The Effects of Starvation on Behavior Implication for Dieting and Eating Disorders.

regardless of your own or anyone else's judgement of that number, it has to increase.

An interesting computer simulation of the Minnesota Starvation Experiment[119] found that while the participant's resting metabolic rate fell steadily during semistarvation, it increased rapidly during refeeding. It seems that resting metabolism rises proportionally faster in refeeding. In plain English, you need more calories on the way up than you did on the way down.

The Important Role Of "Feasting"

I know that some people reading this will be thinking "*what about 'going the other way' and developing binge eating disorder, or bulimia?*" I will come back to feast eating in more detail in the following chapters, but a brief mention here is needed also.

Another interesting observation of the Minnesota Starvation Experiment is that those men technically "binge" ate (5,200 - 10,000 calories a day) in the unrestricted eating part at the end of the study. Eating large amounts of food in response to starvation is a normal mechanism.

Feast follows famine

I believe that what we are so quick to label as a "binge" is actually the feast that should naturally follow the famine. I will refer to anorexia

---

[119] Am J Physiol Endocrinol Metab. 2006 Computational model of in vivo human energy metabolism during semi-starvation and re-feeding

recovery binge eating as "feasting" from now on because I don't like the negative connotations that the word "binge" holds.

The fear of developing Binge Eating Disorder in recovery is very common among people with anorexia. Treatment professionals should not indulge this fear by telling patients that their desire to eat abnormally large amounts of food in recovery is wrong. In my experience, in the short term, feasting helps with nutritional rehabilitation. In the long term it tends to dissipate as the body recovers physically and no longer requires such large amounts of food.

The way I see it, eating abnormally large amounts of food is a natural balancing response to eating abnormally small amounts of food. I'm not saying feast eating should be forced, but it should not be avoided or wronged if it happens, and is nothing to be afraid of. For some of us, feast eating is such a strong response in reaction to restriction that it is impossible to refrain. I felt like my feasts were non-negotiable. I was a passenger on that train. And good for my body for insisting on them, because feast eating likely saved my life.

I am a mammal. You are a mammal. Mammals respond to periods of famine via feasting. This is why the desire to eat once we start eating is so intense. You cannot and should not try and override this basic biological desire to eat a lot of food.

Rather than discouraging feasting, which doesn't work anyway, it is the restriction, purging, exercise, and any other post-feast compensation behaviours that should be discouraged.

The way that the human body has evolved to protect itself from famine is incredible. I imagine that having the ability and capacity to eat a lot of food in one go would have been an evolutionary advantage in times where food was scarce. To feast after a time of famine should not be considered wrong or undesirable — it's actually a highly appropriate response!

Migrating and hibernating animals feast at various times of the cycle. Remember that humans are mammals too! I think we sometimes get so caught up in ourselves that we forget that humbling fact. Well, there is nothing like recovery feasting to remind you that beneath the Burberry hats and the Jimmy Choos, we ain't nothin but mammals.

Advantages of lots of food

Here are some advantages of unrestricted eating that I think are relevant:

1. The cue to end the famine response would have likely been feasting when lands of abundant food were reached, hence lower intakes run the risk of the body not coming out of the migration response.
2. The more you eat, the more you restore your natural metabolism and get your body out of energy deficit.
3. The more you eat, the more energy is available to your body to use to make physical and mental repairs.
4. Higher intakes mean you are forced to obliterate restrictive rules and tendencies therefore start the process of rewiring the brain.

5. For the same reason as #4, higher intakes force you to face the more common nutrient dense fear foods.

6. People who leave treatment with a higher BMI have a higher chance of sustaining recovery.[120]

Rewiring *as* you rehabilitate

A lot of people can and do gain weight on a small increase in calories. When your metabolism is in go-slow mode and your body knows it is underweight, it will do all it can to put on weight with even the smallest intake in food. However, gaining weight on a low intake often can mean gaining weight whilst still restricting — or gaining weight to a bunch of food rules. If you are still restricting as you gain weight you are still giving your body signals that there is not yet abundant food in the environment and it will continue to believe that food is scarce. So, scarcity mode prevails.

For example: When I was underweight, I could have been eating 3000 calories a day in a very prescriptive and controlled manner and I would have gained weight initially because my metabolism was so slow. But, that would have allowed me to keep most of my food rules while doing so, therefore there would have been a missed opportunity in terms of neural rewiring if I was unable to challenge myself out of eating my "safe" foods. In a sense, I would have been weight restoring under anorexia's conditions. Thus, I am keeping the anorexia 's neural pathways alive and strong as I gain weight.

[120] Higher Caloric Intake in Hospitalized Adolescents With Anorexia Nervosa Is Associated With Reduced Length of Stay and No Increased Rate of Refeeding Syndrome Neville H. Golden, M.D. (2013) Journal of Adolescent health.

Looking at this from your survival brain's point of view, here are some potential signals that you brain could use to conclude that food is scarce and therefore the scarcity response (anorexia) is still required:

- Not eating when hungry (mentally or physically).
- Not eating nutrient dense (high calorie) foods.
- Going long periods without eating.
- Maintaining behaviours that were put in place to serve migration.

If your brain asks you to eat food by giving you a hunger signal and you do not eat food, you just gave your brain data to support the notion that there is not enough food in your environment. Food was requested: no food came. Your brain knows if you restricted food. Your dietitian might not be able to tell. Your therapist may not see it. Your partner might not know. But your brain knows — and that is what matters.

I believe that all restriction has to stop in order for your body and brain to be confident that you no longer are in a famine environment. That's not to say you have to be perfect straight away, as nobody is and recovery is a messy process. But if your intentions are solid you will get there in the end.

How would a person *without* anorexia eat after starvation?

"During the refeeding phase of the experiment, many of the men ... 'ate more or less continuously.' " — D.M Garner. The Effects of Starvation on Behavior Implication for Dieting and Eating Disorders.

Another interesting aspect of the Minnesota Starvation Experiment comes from the part of the experiment that happened after the structural refeeding stage and when the subjects were let loose to eat whatever they wanted. They were literally given the green flag to eat unrestricted. And they did!

They ate! They feasted. They ate between 5,000 and 10,000 calories a day.[121]

Now, how would you be eating if you were not scared?

Probably constantly, right?

Eat smart

When I started eating more and went cold turkey on the exercise, this felt like a huge change, and relative to what I had been doing before, it was. But even then, the foods that I ate, the way that I ate — even the way that I shopped were very different from the way all those things were further down the line when I was closer to energy balance. I learned a lot about how to eat for recovery in that time.

Initially, restriction infested everything. My world was seen through the lens of a person trying to eat as little as possible and move as much

---

[121] D.M Garner. The Effects of Starvation on Behavior Implication for Dieting and Eating Disorders.

as possible. I ate diet foods, used artificial sweeteners, crammed my plate with vegetables. This didn't work out so well for me.

I had to change my lens to one seeking energy surplus. I had to focus on nutrient density. I stopped wasting my time with low-calorie foods, and filled my shopping trolley and my stomach with highly nutrient dense foods. That is eating smart in recovery. These caloric foods probably signaled to my brain that famine must be over for such nutrients to be available, but also were a lot easier and more available source of ready energy for my body to process. Cheese is a much easier source of ready-calories for my body to digest and use than carrots.

High nutrient density often means high in fat. This is much easier on a rehabilitating digestive system than high-fibre. My stomach was happier.

As I needed a high intake in order to weight restore fully, I found that lower-density foods added to my stomach discomfort, but didn't serve me in terms of the restoration that I was desperate for. I discovered that I had to eat a lot of things that were easy to eat and impactful. Cheese, full fat dairy, fast-food, ice cream, and my all time favorite: cheeseburgers. These foods were so feared to me that it took me a lot of mental preparation to work up to them, setting myself high daily calorie goals helped keep me accountable and forced me into seeing nutrient density as an aid — albeit a terrifying one at first.

Not only did eating a very high amount of these smart foods help me nutritionally rehabilitate, they packed the double punch of also forcing me to choose and eat my most feared foods every day.

Anorexia recovery requires running into fear. I used my fear to indicate to me the best food choices for me. If the thought of eating it scared me, then I ate it.

Orthorexia

Orthorexia is an obsessive preoccupation with eating healthy food.

Hands up if you have or have had this! Yes, me too! I see orthorexia as a facet of anorexia.

As I explained earlier, the brain may interpret fatty foods as a threat in a famine environment due to the energetic cost and risk associated with acquiring them. With the societal labelling of fatty or caloric foods as "bad," the modern-day interpretation of this feeling of threat caused by caloric foods is a desire to eat clean or eat "healthily."

I had a huge fear of fat, but what I learned in recovery was that it wasn't just about eating fat, so much as about eating the type of fat that anorexia had a problem with. I initially got myself to a place where I was eating more fat but it was all fats that my brain interpreted as "healthy fats." I could eat unlimited amounts of avocado in a day, but ask me to put butter on my bread and all hell would break loose. The real deal for me in recovery was challenging my fear of saturated fats — mainly animal fats. Recovery eating for me meant eating saturated fats in an unrestricted manner.

Orthorexia expresses itself in so many ways. Not only in the type of food you allow yourself to eat, but even within "types" of food. For example, when I was starting recovery I would allow myself peanut butter, but the, organic, no GMO, no added sugar, no fun, tastes-like-dirt, made by hippies, peanut butter. Do you know what my favourite actual peanut butter is? Skippy. And not even "Skippy Natural" at that. I like Superchuck Skippy. So another life lesson for me was to allow myself Skippy.

I understand that if you have gone from eating very little, to eating more, you will probably argue that because you are eating more, it doesn't matter that you are eating mostly "healthy" foods. I beg to differ. This is exactly why orthorexia is so pernicious.

In my anorexia recovery, "healthy" was a bit of a cop out. It is far harder, and far braver, to eat the foods that don't have that nice, safe, "healthy" label attached. Don't be fooled by the way that orthorexia presents itself so innocently. It will keep the scarcity neural pathways of restrictive eating and anxiety around food strong if you adhere to it. Remember, the clues to recovery are in the resistance that you feel. Run into the fear.

In a sense, it was incredibly liberating to be able to pick up a Mars bar for a snack rather than the granola bar that touted promises of "healthy fruits, nuts, and grains." I had to prove I could eat anything I wanted. I had to prove to my brain that no food is unhealthy. I had to accumulate data to oppose my orthorexia.

Plus, chocolate bars are delicious. I stopped pretending to myself and the world that I didn't like them. Outright lies. Who the hell doesn't like chocolate bars?

"Changing my mindset around what I considered to be healthy food was a real challenge, I had been brought up on a low fat diet as my mother had always been overweight since childhood and was continually on

one diet or another as an adult. When I left home I consequently gained a significant amount of weight, I then spent the rest of my adult life dieting and attending slimming clubs who reinforced that low fat foods were good. It has taken a lot of relearning to break away from this belief but I am getting there. Interestingly my mother who now has dementia and just eats whatever she wants whenever she wants is no longer overweight. - anon, adult in recovery from anorexia.

Overly "healthy" eating can be a difficult grey-seeming area to navigate in recovery, as a part of your brain will argue that "everyone knows it is wise to eat plenty of fruit and vegetables etc." But another part of your brain will know it is far more than that for you.

It doesn't matter what the general recommendations for the general public are in terms of nutrition. You are different. You are special. You have anorexia — it could kill you should you allow food rules and energy deficit to take over. You simply cannot afford to allow your brain to go there. All food is equal. No scrap that, in fact, for someone like you, chocolate cake is healthier than kale because chocolate cake is far more likely to keep anorexia at bay. Kale isn't. In that sense, too much kale might kill you.

But surely nutritional science says that eating processed foods is bad?
Nutritional science is in its infancy. Compared to medical science, the field hasn't even been around that long. Macronutrients were not discovered until somewhere in the middle of the 1800s. Vitamins even later in the 1900s. As far as I am aware, humans have been eating food

for a good while longer than that. Arguably we did a better job of doing so when we knew less …

Individuals process food differently

In one study not so long ago in Israel, it was found that two people can eat the exact same food and have wildly different blood sugar levels when tested afterwards.[122] Now tell me, how can we possible conclude that any one type of food is good or bad for every person? The study measured post-meal glycemic responses (PPGRs) for 800 people eating the same meals over a week.

"This high interpersonal variability suggests that at least with regard to PPGRs, approaches that grade dietary ingredients as universally "good" or "bad" based on their average PPGR in the population may have limited utility for an individual."[123]

Basically, different people process food differently. That feels like common sense, does it not? So let's stop pretending that we know what "healthy eating" even is. For every study proving one food is good for you, there is another proving just the opposite.

Let go of the idea of a "balanced diet"

In recovery from anorexia, many people find that they crave certain types of food. I went through stages when I only wanted to eat sweets for example. Days when I only wanted bread and bagels. Some days when I woke up thinking about steak and knew that day was going to

---

[122] Personalized Nutrition by Prediction of Glycemic Response David Zeevi et al (2015) Cell

[123] Personalized Nutrition by Prediction of Glycemic Response David Zeevi et al (2015) Cell

feature heavily in red meat. For me, not restricting meant allowing myself to eat chocolate cake with pop tarts for breakfast if that is what I was craving. Or unlimited amounts of steak and cheese if that was the food of my thoughts that day. Of course, that was incredibly hard for me to do mentally as anorexia was screaming at me that I was not eating a balanced diet and I was going to get scurvy if I ate less than 20 serving of vegetables a day etc, etc. However, by allowing myself to be brave and curious, I followed my mental hunger and it all balanced out in the end.

I believe that when a body has been deprived of certain food groups for years, it is out of balance, and in order to get back into balance it may need to go buck-wild on these certain food groups for a time. I ate my way through many food phases in recovery and the end result was that I naturally shifted into eating what would now be considered a balanced diet. But to get there, I had to be brave enough to trust that if I let go of restriction and ate the foods I was secretly obsessing about in large quantities that it would all circle around in the end. And it did.

"Last week I was all about the cereal, this week I feel like I want to eat a cow." - Gabs, adult in recovery from anorexia.

Don't judge your hunger

Many of us are terrified by the amount and type foods that we crave and want to eat in recovery. Do not be scared of your hunger, and do not judge what your body asks you to give it. Your body wants yummy, easy to digest, nutrient dense foods. Trust that it knows what it is doing.

For many of us our paranoid thought processes tell us that if we stop eating "healthily" now we will become addicted to processed foods. Don't give energy to these thoughts. Your body is asking for what it needs. But that anorexia judgement will try and make you second guess yourself. I found it helpful to imagine that I didn't know anything about the nutritional value of any foods. And what would I choose if I perceived that all foods were equal? Not vegetables!

All foods are good. All foods should be seen as equal. No foods are bad. Do not judge what you want to eat. Do not judge the amount that you want to eat. Do not judge when or how frequently you want to eat. The way that you want to eat in recovery is indicative only of the way that you eat when you are coming out of starvation.

The Emotional Side To Recovery Eating

Emotions are biologically based reactions that evolved with a function.[124] When you have anorexia eating becomes highly emotional as the brain uses emotions to both disincentivize eating (anorexia response) and to incentivize eating (malnutrition response).

The anorexia response also generates positive emotions, such as feeling calm, and reductions in anxiety, when we eat less and move more.

Anorexia response emotions:

Negative (to disincentivize eating):
- Fear
- Threat
- Disgust
- Shame
- Regret
- Anxiety
- Wrongdoing

Positive (when you restrict):
- Calmness
- Peacefulness
- Wellbeing
- Correctness

---

[124] Steimer, T. (2002). The biology of fear- and anxiety-related behaviors. *Dialogues in Clinical Neuroscience, 4*(3), 231–249.

- Success
- Contentment

As you eat more food in recovery and strive to satisfy your mental hunger, your anorexia brain is going to hurl negative emotions at you. Be ready for them! You are going to feel disgust, fear, regret and anxiety. When you recognise these emotions it is important that you breathe, then allow them to pass. Stay in the present moment and watch as the emotion fades in strength and then washes away.

Remember, you do not have to attach to your emotions. Practice functional detachment.

I feel guilt, but I am not guilty
I feel disgust, but I am not disgusting
I feel regret, but I have no reason to be regretful
I feel anxiety, but I do not need to be anxious.

When you do this, you are acknowledging the emotion you feel, and also acknowledging that it doesn't define you and that it is not truth.

It is not normal to feel a slew of negative emotions just because you ate an extra slice of cake. Truly, it's not. Your brain is generating these negative emotions because it believes you need to eat less and move more to migrate. One of the joys of full recovery is that when you are there, your brain no longer generates negative emotions to eating.

Unrestricted Eating

As you may have gathered by now, I am an advocate for unrestricted eating in anorexia recovery. Furthermore, I think that in order to amend long term energy deficit, one doesn't just have to eat a normal amount of food, one has to eat an abnormally large amount of food. Due to the extensive damage that malnutrition does to the body, I believe that giving the body abundant fuel so that it can restore is a more holistic and compassionate approach than playing by restrictive rules in refeeding.

I also believe that feasting cues the end of the famine, and hence helps turn off the migratory response.

I think that any person in recovery from anorexia, regardless of body size, should be encouraged to eat without restriction. The closest that you will ever get me to a blanket statement here, is that if you are underweight, in energy deficit, physically or mentally hungry, or restricting at all, you need to eat more food and stop restricting.

So what does eating without restriction actually mean?

Eating without restriction means that you eat what you want when you want it — in the quantity that you want it. For a body in a state of malnutrition, highly caloric foods are often desired. This is because your body is smart, and it knows it needs these types of foods. (Note: you do not have to be clinically underweight in order to be in malnutrition. Restriction can lead to malnutrition in any size body.)

Taking malnutrition out of the picture, the same applies for many people who do not allow themselves to eat what they want: they want it more. Ironically, when we restrict a food and we do not allow ourselves to have that food as often as we would really like, the brain starts to overly focus on that food. The brain wants that food more. We desire what is forbidden. It's a bit like if someone tells you not to push the red button, then all you can think about is the red button. So if one restricts chocolate, one is more likely to want to eat chocolate. If one restricts sugar, one is more likely to want to eat a lot of sugary food when faced with it. Therefore, it is restriction that results in an upset of the natural balance. Because you have interfered with the body's ability to self-regulate, it reacts by going into a scarcity mindset. When you restrict a food, and create scarcity, you give it power over you.

Thankfully, studies are beginning to find evidence to support what to my mind is common sense: that it is actually restriction that influences a tendency to "binge" on "highly palatable" foods. A 2017 study highlights that sugar addiction may not actually be addiction at all.[125] Rather, that the problem is not allowing access to sugary foods creates a very strong desire to eat sugary foods in high quantities.

I spoke to Maggie Westwater, one of the researchers of the study "Sugar addiction: the state of science," and she explained to me in a conversation — that I later published in a podcast — that it appears restriction of sugary foods seems to correlate with a higher intake of these foods.[126]

---

[125] Westwater, M.L., Fletcher, P.C. & Ziauddeen, H. Eur J Nutr (2016)

[126] http://tabithafarrar.com/2017/12/state-science-sugar-addiction-podcast/

"We find little evidence to support sugar addiction in humans, and findings from the animal literature suggest that addiction-like behaviours, such as bingeing, occur only in the context of intermittent access to sugar. These behaviours likely arise from intermittent access to sweet tasting or highly palatable foods, not the neurochemical effects of sugar." - Sugar addiction: the state of the science. Westwater, M.L., Fletcher, P.C. & Ziauddeen,

Yes, if you restrict something, you are more likely to binge on it. The restriction is the problem, not the food.

Eating without restriction once fully recovered

The notion is the same. I am fully recovered, and my body is no longer in malnutrition, but still eat what I want, when I want it, in the quantity that I want. However, because my body is no longer in a state of malnutrition, it doesn't need to be telling me to eat as much food as possible, constantly, all day, any more. My body asks me to eat the amount it needs to sustain my current state, and I do. I'd say I still eat more than most people, but that is only because — let's face it — most people have fallen into the restriction trap. Our culture makes it seem normal to suppress one's bodyweight and be on a diet.

Because I have, for years, allowed myself to eat "unhealthy" foods without restriction, because they are not "forbidden" or restricted, my brain doesn't crave them every second of the day. So, the notion of unrestricted eating is still the same, but as you move through recovery you will find that eating without restriction looks different depending on where your body is at and what it needs.

Now, for me, unrestricted eating looks like a very varied diet. Sure, I eat a fair amount of burgers (because I love them) but I enjoy fruit and vegetables too. Nothing is off limits. I never eat anything out of obligation either.

I found that when I kept my judgement out of the way, and stopped trying to suppress what I ate, my body got out of malnutrition and then it self-regulated. My diet naturally balanced itself in the long run. My metabolism normalised, and my desire to eat leveled out at what I need in order to sustain my natural, healthy, body weight.

Here is a question I know a lot of people reading this will have:
How do I know when to stop eating all the time?

Here's the deal with that as I experienced it:
Remember that you are dealing with a very intelligent organism: your body. For the most part, if you stay out the way and just do as it tells you (i.e. feed it), it will sort everything out for you. If you are underweight your body is sending signals to your brain saying "*Need to eat all the time!*" That is the mental hunger.

When your body is no longer in malnutrition your body will stop sending signals to your brain asking you to eat the whole time. It will simply go back to asking for food when it needs to — like a normal person. Therefore, if you eat to mental and physical hunger now, when you no longer need to eat all the time, your mental hunger will go and you won't even *want* to eat all the time anymore. Clause: if for any reason you should feel that the mental hunger is gone but you are still underweight (this happens to some people) then you have to keep making yourself eat high amounts until you get to a healthy weight range for your body.

Another important point is this: You eat without restriction for life! Not just for recovery. It is not like you get to a certain weight and then you start restricting again. That is not recovery, that is restriction and weight suppression. That is just anorexia at a slightly higher weight.

Eating FAQs

What if I eat too much food?

I do not believe there is such thing as "too much" food in recovery from anorexia. You are in energy deficit, and therefore will have to eat a lot in order to reach energy balance. Your body uses energy to repair and restore. The more you eat the more you give it so that it can do that. Your body simply wants to get you to your healthy, unsuppressed, natural, bodyweight. It has no "agenda" other than health.

What if I gain weight too fast?

Everyone has a different and individual weight gain trajectory. It has been shown that people who gain weight fast in treatment have positive treatment outcomes.[127] Trust your body to know what it is doing and don't allow the rate at which you gain weight to scare you — your body will end up at the weight it is supposed to be.

---

[127] Int J Eat Disord. 2017 Weight gain trajectories in hospital-based treatment of anorexia nervosa. Makhzoumi et al

I want to eat constantly and I am in the nutritional rehabilitation stage, how will I know when it is time to eat a more normal amount? Will I keep eating this much and gaining weight forever?

As you move into a place of energy balance, and your body is at its unsuppressed, healthy, natural weight, your mental hunger will decrease naturally and accordingly. Your desire for food will diminish as your body requires less in order to heal. Hence, you will still eat unrestricted amounts of food, but "unrestricted" will look like different levels of intake as you move though recovery. You will still eat to desire, but your desire will naturally alter as your body comes out of a state of nutritional emergency. If for any reason you are worried that this is not happening, you should work with a good eating disorder dietitian to help you move through this process.

Meal Plans

What works for you, right now?

The subject of meal plans can be a tricky one. Some people swear they are a necessity. Others say that they reinforce restrictive eating principles. There is not a blanket right or wrong answer here. What works for you is what is important. I should also disclose that because I never went through traditional anorexia treatment I never used a meal plan so have not personally experienced being on one, but the majority of my clients have at some point at least.

If you are risk from refeeding syndrome, or are medically unstable, you should be working with a registered dietitian or other treatment professional as you begin increasing what you are eating. If in doubt it is always better to err on the side of caution and work with someone specialised in eating disorders and recovery from malnutrition. Once past these risks, however, to follow a meal plan or not is a matter of personal preference.

You may find that at one stage of recovery a meal plan works for you, and at a later stage it is restricting you. So it is more a case of what is working for you right now. Assess your current situation in a detached manner so that you are not continuing to do something that is no longer effective, or overlooking something that could work now because it didn't work in the past. When you treat your recovery like a living, breathing, project, rather than a math equation, you realise that you have to be agile in your response to approaches to suit the current situation.

My overall opinion is that if there is a meal plan in place — once past the risk of refeeding syndrome — it should be seen as a minimum, and it should be flexible in terms of the specific food on it. Above all, unrestricted eating has to be encouraged. If a meal plan is too specific, it doesn't allow for neural rewiring as you cannot challenge your tendency to stick to safe foods.

For example, if a meal plan says have cereal and eggs and toast for breakfast but you wake up wanting pop tarts and pancakes, then you should eat pop tarts and pancakes — so long as you eat enough pop tarts and pancakes to more than cover the cereal, eggs and toast that you would have had. Or have the cereal, eggs and toast as well as the pop tarts and pancakes.

I don't believe we need to try and control what we eat via overly-balanced meal plans. A "balanced diet" and strict meal plan is appeasing the eating disorder if it is sticking to food rules. In order to rewire we need to disobey these rules. Many eating disorder professionals are guilty of appeasing eating disorders by responding to their client's fears by putting caps on intake in place. When we appease the eating disorder rules in nutritional rehabilitation we do not serve the individual because it has the effect of weight restoring them with restriction still present.

"Having previously weight restored the 'slow & steady' route, I can say that while it cured the outward physical signs of my ED it certainly did nothing to combat the mental issues that exist. My mind was still living in strict/set routines, the old habits of restriction and demanding control

*would come to the fore the minute the world around my started to shake.
So much so, I ended up having to leave university, and 2 years on my
weight is now lower than it ever got to before.*

*Since going taking a simple when my mind screams for food 'just eat'
approach my world has totally changed. I've put on weight, but mentally
I'm ok with that. My mood is through the roof in a positive way, my mind
& that inner food obsessed voice is silent" - C, adult in recovery from
anorexia*

Being overly exact and calculating recovery intake down to the last
calorie not only overcomplicates the whole process, but is rather
ignorant to the complexity of the human body. The body is not a
calculator. Treating it as if it were one is futile anyway because no two
people process food identically. It's another false sense of security
that keeps the scarcity mindset neural pathways active and reinforces
the eating disorder mindset.

The vast majority of us don't need to dissect our intake into
micronutrients. That is not how humans eat. If you are eating enough
food, you will be eating enough of each food group by default. It is
only people with eating disorders who want to recover from a state of
starvation on a carefully scrutinised diet. People who need to gain
weight and don't have an eating disorder don't care. They just eat. That
is as much most of us need to know.

*"I've been following a meal plan for 17 years. I think it's time to take the
plunge and just eat." - T, adult in recovery from anorexia*

That said, not everyone can jump straight in to unrestricted eating. If what is working for you right now is a prescriptive meal plan down to the last dollop of ketchup, then stick with what works for now! You have to do what is right for you. Many people find that initially in recovery they need the prescription until they have the confidence to move away from that. Meet yourself where you are at without judgement.

Meal plan summary
- If you are at risk of refeeding syndrome you should be working with an RDN in the beginning stages of refeeding.
- Meal plans can work initially to get us to commit to eating more. They can also become restrictive. Only you know if you are restricting or not. Being honest and accountable to your recovery will mean that you speak up and challenge anything that feels restrictive.
- If a meal plan is in place it has to be treated as a minimum, with the goal of eating over and above.
- If a meal plan is in place, it should not be restrictive in terms of type of food, more like a guide to the minimum that one has to try and exceed.

The "Safety Net" Eating Approach

I tend to prefer a "Safety Net" approach. Remember, there is no "one right way" of getting to unrestricted eating, and you will work out the right way for you. This is just one concept that I found helpful.

The Safety Net Eating approach means that you develop an idea of a minimum amount of food and as long as you eat above this and in an unrestrictive manner, you can eat what you want.

I never had a meal plan, but I had a mental picture in my head of what was an adequate amount of food at any one meal. I found that unless I did this, I would tend to undereat at mealtimes. I'm not talking a mental picture like "two carbs, two proteins and two fats per meal." No, that's not how humans eat. I'm talking a mental picture like a big plate of fish and chips or spaghetti bolognaise. Humans eat meals, not collections of macronutrients.

In my late teens and early twenties, I spent a lot of my time at weekends and evenings serving in English pubs. When I was in recovery, I pictured that all my meals would have to pass for something that would be served in a pub. The super-sized version, because if you are eating to gain weight you have to eat abnormally large amounts of food. Consistently, not just for one meal. Whatever I made myself had to be fit to be served as an oversized hearty pub meal. Needless to say, none of the pitiful orthorexic lunches I had been making myself wouldn't cut the mustard. I kept that mental picture of "would this be served in the pub" to guide me as to what was the least amount of food I could eat at any mealtime. The pub menu was my Safety Net in terms of meals. Snacks were as much as I could eat between meals, and I would often have things like fast-food burgers and fries as a snack. Doing this sort of thing was important for me, as it was breaking the rules. My anorexia brain didn't think it appropriate to eat a burger as a snack — so I did just that. I also tried as hard as I could to mindlessly devour chocolate bars, cheese, crisps, sandwiches etc. between my meals. I had a Safety Net in terms of the minimum amount of snacks I would eat in a day, but ate to mental hunger which often meant I was constantly snacking — especially in the primary stages of nutritional rehabilitation. I was really very hungry!

There were some days, when both my physical and mental hunger seemed less present. On these days I would still make myself eat a lot — because I needed to gain weight. When you are underweight, you have to eat to gain weight, not just when you feel like it. But most of us find that the majority of the time, we do feel like it! (If we are honest about that mental hunger.)

One of the biggest spanners that my anorexia brain kept throwing at me was the worry that I would get used to eating more than three meals a day and constantly snacking, and that I would want to do this forever. That it would turn into a habit. That was a huge fear for me. It probably is for you too. Well, I can tell you that as my body recovered, my hunger settled down to levels that are normal for my body to maintain its healthy weight. My desire to eat all the time (mental hunger) dissipated, and because I was at a healthy weight I no longer had to force myself to eat "weight gain" amounts. It all seemed to sort itself out quite naturally.

Breaking the rules around what sort of food you can eat is an important part of rewiring. For example, if you want chocolate ice cream for breakfast you have chocolate ice cream for breakfast — so long as you eat enough of it, you can eat what you want when you want. This, after all, is what unrestricted eating is.

A Safety Net is not a meal plan. There are no specific foods written on it. There are no prescriptions of macronutrients allocated to specific mealtimes. A Safety Net is a commitment to eating in a certain manner — one which will help you nutritionally rehabilitate. It is a commitment that you keep even on days when you don't feel like it. You don't need to count calories to do this. You don't have to be accurate. (Not that counting calories is accurate anyway.) You know that you can eat pizza, or burritos, or a burger or whatever you want for lunch, so long as it is at least equivalent of that mental picture you have in your mind of what a big lunch is.

What you do have to be is realistic, and adaptive. If your goal is weight gain, and you are not achieving this, then you have to eat more food. Don't be shy about it. Don't get wound up about how to do it. Don't overthink it. Don't waste time. Add more food.

Eating in full recovery

As your recovered weight stabilizes, and you maintain energy balance, your physical hunger cues should start to become more reliable and guide you towards naturally eating as your metabolism requires.

When you move out of energy deficit, the appetite hormones that ask you to eat the whole time will return back down from the high levels that they hold in malnutrition, to normal levels.[128] This means that mental hunger diminishes and finally you will realize one day that while you had eaten adequately and without stress, you hadn't been thinking of food all day. Yes, the mental hunger and thinking about food and other anorexia-related thoughts will go. This is not an overnight thing, it usually seems to happen slowly over months. For that first year or and evermore, make sure that you keep responding to hunger, be it mental or physical, and your natural eating ability will return to you fully functional.

I often get asked if I feel "intuitive eating" is possible for a person with anorexia. I don't like that term as it sounds pretentious to me. I tend to just call it "eating."

Yes, there will totally be a time when you will eat what you want without much fuss and you'll feel done when you are done without much fuss either. But you can't do this while you are underweight, as hunger cues can be unreliable and you feel full sooner than you should. As I mentioned above, I had random "non-hungry" days in recovery and you can't afford to not eat as much on those days if you are still underweight. It took me a good while to get to this point where I eat what I want, when I want it, with robust physical hunger cues — which is fine because there is no rush. It's not a race. Just stay present with yourself. Live in the moment that you are in, and eat for the moment you are in also. Be honest and true to yourself and don't judge your unique recovery process by anybody else's. Certainly don't

---

[128] Weight gain decreases elevated plasma ghrelin concentrations of patients with anorexia nervosa. Otto et al. (2001) EJE

judge your recovery process by the clean-and-green-intuitive-eating-raw-vegan-goddess on Instagram.

Hypermetabolism

Hypermetabolism is when your metabolism goes hyper. It happens to some of us in recovery — our metabolism skyrockets suddenly. This means that you need even more food in order to continue to gain weight, or even to protect yourself against losing weight. Hypermetabolism happened to me when I started eating proper recovery amounts, and I didn't have a clue what was happening until I did some research, but I was happy that I was not freezing cold all the time any more.

One thing I like about hypermetabolism is that it is so very physiological that the psychoanalysts generally leave it alone. (Unlike things such as lack of hunger cues — which can be turned into all sort of psychobabble like lack of nipple time as an infant, or suppression of desire.)

In hypermetabolism I felt … hot. Hot and hungry. I had such bad night sweats that I had to sleep on a towel. For 12 years I had felt cold, even in the heights of summer (which admittedly in England are not all that high). Now, all of a sudden, I was a furnace. I felt like everything I was eating was being converted directly into heat energy the second I swallowed it. I had to eat a lot more food in order to maintain weight gain. I didn't sit down and calculate this, as it felt like common sense. I could tell something funky was going on, but it felt like it was a positive change in that something was happening. I was intrigued, and as I was committed to weight gain already, decided that no harm could come of eating even more. Plus I felt very hungry.

"Target" Weights

We do not need to micro-manage the rate at which your body gains weight, nor do we need interfere with the weight your body deems optimal to settle at.

I think a target weight is rather a ridiculous concept. It implies that the correct weight for your body can be calculated by using a general height/weight equation. The word "target" further implies that going past the target is less than optimal. Maybe the way that I feel about the concept of a target weight is due to consistently meeting people in recovery from anorexia who have been given a target weight that is, in my opinion, too low. I honestly cannot fathom why it is consistently the case that people in recovery are given a target weight of a BMI 19 — the lowest weight at the end of the "healthy" weight range. (I cannot stand BMI as a measure of health either, but I'm not going to rant about it here, if you want rants, you can visit my blog.)

When I reached a BMI 19 my body looked a little better. But my mind was a mess. For me, it was not until a higher weight that I felt a huge shift in my mindset. I didn't know my recovery weight until I was there. Had I been given a target weight and stopped gaining weight when I reached said target, I would have never gained enough weight to get me out of energy deficit. When a person is out of energy deficit is something you cannot calculate or predict from a chart — the body gets to decide.

Your recovered weight should be about your mental state, not just the number on the scale.

Be brave and curious

Your body is an organism, not a calculator. And you are a unique human being, so we cannot group you into charts and statistics. No person, book, or chart is more qualified than your own body is to know what your body needs. Additionally, challenging that fear response over not planning and controlling what your bodyweight will be is part of the rewiring process.

A stressed brain hates gray areas, mystery, and ambiguity. You will hate not having a set number to aim for. I get that. Yes, you have to get into at least a healthy weight range, but don't expect to stop at a BMI of 19 if that is not where your body needs to be. If you want recovery and will do whatever it takes; often that will mean accepting a higher weight than anorexia deems okay.

Do not fall into the anorexia trap of allowing weight gain "what ifs" into your head. Don't allow anyone else to unwittingly pull you into this trap either. Get yourself into the healthy weight range and continue to gain weight until your mental state changes. That's as extensive as weight planning needs to get in my opinion.

One of the biggest tests in recovery is being prepared to not just get marginally weight restored, but get completely weight restored. Another is dealing with not knowing what your final weight will be. Funnily enough, many of us who get there look back and laugh about how worried we were about gaining a little weight. That is testimony of how incredible the mental shift is when your body and mind recover. Nowadays, I simply cannot fathom why I had sleepless nights fretting about gaining weight. It was fine. It is fine. You will be fine too.

(Commence onslaught of unicorn thoughts detailing why you are uniquely different from me and anyone else who recovered from anorexia and why eating and trusting simply won't work out for you. Drop them)

Recovery weight

In the same way it seems pretty standard to be extra hungry after a period of starvation, gaining and storing some additional weight as a temporary reserve is a natural bodily response to a period of malnutrition for some of us. This is commonly known as "overshoot," and is even termed as this in the scientific literature, but prefer to call it "recovery weight" as overshoot implies that you have gone over.[129] You haven't. You got it just right.

Your body should be allowed to increase weight to wherever it deems necessary for recovery operations to take place. Remember energy debt? Well, imagine that little extra fat storage is for the energy debt.

Think about the way that babies grow. First, they grow outwards, becoming chubby and lovely and fat. Then, when the time is right, they grow upwards. Then, they get chubby again, and they grow upwards again. Resource accumulation precedes growth. While a person in recovery from an eating disorder may not be growing in height still, they are growing and rebuilding the body in other ways. When it stores fat, the body is preparing for repair and growth. This fat storage is optimal and important.

Babies aren't psychoanalysed for eating a lot and growing, and neither should you be. It is not emotional eating or emotional weight gain or a rebellion against your mother. It is a physiological protective measure

---

[129]. Poststarvation hyperphagia and body fat overshooting in humans: a role for feedback signals from lean and fat tissues. Dulloo et al (1997) The American Society for Clinical Nutrition

in reaction to a state of starvation.

I like analogies for this sort of thing, so here is one: Imagine you want to buy a house. Unless you are a trust fund kid, you need to save money in the bank before you have any hope of putting down a deposit. Also, if you waltz into the bank with a one-off wad of cash, after having spent the last 10 years in the red, your bank manager is probably going to raise an eyebrow. If he has any sense, he is going to want to see that you have a reliable form of income (a job) and that you didn't just rob a bank. He wants to know that you have enough money for the deposit, sure, but he also wants to know you will have money every month for the mortgage payments.

I like to think of the body as a smart bank manager. It likes to know it has enough in resources before it commits to a growth or repair effort. It wants to store fat before it goes ahead and invests in repair work in the same way you would save money before a big purchase. It mostly wants to do this by storing fat around your stomach, because this also has the effect of further protecting your most vital internal organs. It will "spend" that fat in good time, and it will re-distribute to other parts of your body. Unless, of course, you start restricting, or going back into energy deficit via other behaviours such as exercise or purging. Your body isn't dumb. If it begins to get data that indicates famine again, it isn't going to be fooled into spending fat dollars on things like a menstrual cycle or stronger hair follicles. Just the same way you're not going to go and buy a house today if your boss gave you your two weeks' notice yesterday.

If calories were money, your body has been on the poverty line for however long you have had your eating disorder. Just because calories have started coming in finally doesn't mean it can use them all up immediately. Nope, your body needs to do some saving first.

In the Minnesota Starvation Experiment, the subjects, when allowed to eat again, "overshot" their pre-study weight by around 10 percent.[130] They returned to their pre-study weight after that, mostly between 12 and 16 months.

If you are looking for reassurance and are unable to trust your body this is more difficult. I cannot give you a guarantee about how your recovery path will be, and neither can anyone else. What I can tell you is that I have known many people with anorexia, and nowadays I am happy to say I know many people who recovered. I do not know any fully recovered people who are unhappy about being recovered! The process requires you to be brave and curious and trust that if you give it enough fuel, your body will get you where you need to be.

Target weight summary
- Target weights are generally set too low, and are thus often problematic.
- Recovery weight may be higher than your final resting weight due to your body initially storing resources in order to make repairs.
- Think about mental state rather than weight. If you are supposedly weight restored but are still on anorexia's scarcity mindset, you should experiment with gaining more weight, or looking for where you are still restricting food.

[130] D.M Garner. The Effects of Starvation on Behavior Implication for Dieting and Eating Disorders.

- Be brave and curious. Trust and allow your body to do what it needs to do in order to reach a place of full health.

Your body is not a calculator

All our bodies react to food differently. Some people go into hypermetabolism. Others do not. Some experience bottomless-pit hunger. Others don't. Some "weight restore" slowly. Others faster. The human body is an organism and, therefore, we cannot treat it like a calculator.

Calories in doesn't equal calories out. Not all the calories that we consume are available for the body to use. Two people can eat the exact same food and have a different metabolic response.[131] Also, what you read on a nutrition label is generally inaccurate — estimates show nutrition labels are up to 25 percent out of whack.[132] Even if nutrition labels were accurate, they only measure calories that present in the forms of the macronutrients as presented by Wilber Atwater over a hundred years ago. Macronutrients are based on a system of averages and no food is "average," so even the most precise system that we currently have for assessing food is arguably only a fraction of the whole picture.

Even the exact same food can vary one day from the next as to how it is absorbed. Some foods are also good at escaping digestion. Certain foods are not digested in a way that makes all the calories available so

---

[131] Personalized Nutrition by Prediction of Glycemic Response David Zeevi et al

[132] Obesity (Silver Spring). 2013 Food Label Accuracy of Common Snack Foods Reiner Jumpertz

who really knows how much of them your body can actually use.[133] Additionally, some foods require that your immune system has to get involved in digesting them, and running your immune system is expensive in terms of calories. Hence, some foods use more energy than others in the process of digestion. We are not machines, our bodies don't all work identically.

[133] Am J Clin Nutr. 2012. Discrepancy between the Atwater factor predicted and empirically measured energy values of almonds in human diets.Novotny

Chapter 8: Post-Famine Feasting

I have already explained that I see recovery feasting as a natural bodily response to starvation or semi-starvation. It turns out this is the case for many animals — not just humans. Animal studies show that animals that have been given restricted access to food consequently increase their intake of food dramatically once allowed to eat again.[134] Laboratory animals deprived of food for as few as two hours will consume significantly more calories upon the return of the food than animals that were not deprived.[135]

Nobody looks at a bear who is feasting before a period of torpor and accuses him of emotional eating. Nobody tells the little groundhog, which is rumored to be able to eat the equivalent of a 15-pound steak in preparation for a 150-day hibernation, that it is comfort eating.[136]

In humans, strict dietary restraint and/or abstinence from eating forbidden, highly palatable foods has been shown to contribute to feasting in response to the restriction.[137] If you don't allow yourself to have something, you want it all the more.

When we understand that eating large quantities of food is a normal response to starvation — and not one that is limited to humans either

---

[134] Opioid-dependent anticipatory negative contrast and binge-like eating in rats with limited access to highly preferred food, Cotton, Neuropsychopharmacology, 2008

[135] The role of palatable food and hunger as trigger factors in an animal model of stress induced binge eating Hagan. Int J Eat Disord. 2003

[136] Source: National Wildlife Federation

[137] Appetite. 2009 .The Biology of Binge Eating. Mathes et al

— we can stop psychologising it. We can stop talking about recovery feasting as "emotional eating." I know that we cannot ask the laboratory rat; *"Are you binge eating because Mrs Rat is mean to you at the weekends, or is it because you are just really hungry?"* But I'm going to go out on a limb here and assume that Mr. Rat is eating a ton because his body is telling him to make up for the starvation, not due to a deep-rooted need for food to make up for the lack of real love and understanding in his life.

Why would feasting have evolved as a starvation response?

While it may not seem obvious now that there is a Starbucks on every corner. If you imagine a time without grocery stores or chain restaurants, the evolution of the feast response to starvation may seem more plausible. If you didn't have the capacity to eat a lot of food when it became available to you, you would likely die.

Imagine Jenny and Joe Caveman living thousands of years ago in a cave. There have been no buffalo for months, and neither of them have eaten in three weeks. Finally, the buffalo come, and Jenny Caveman kills one. Suddenly there is a ton of food available. Their cave does not have a freezer, or a refrigerator. They do not know when the next herd of buffalo will come. In order to have the greatest chance of survival, Joe and Jenny Caveman need to have the capacity to eat the heck out of that buffalo.

This response is not just useful in times of feast/famine environments. It has been shown that feast eating is present in veterans who were prisoners of war in German camps.[138] And before you jump to the conclusion that they were eating as a way to cope with the horrors of war, it has been shown that this was not an emotional response to war trauma. Comparisons were made between war veterans who had suffered starvation in these camps and combat veterans who had lived through the war without significant weight loss. The soldiers who had not suffered significant weight loss did not report feast eating.

I can't help but think how much easier it would be to feast eat after a period of malnutrition in situations where everyone around you was also feast eating. Imagine a tribe of humans successfully migrated and got to the land of abundant food, and everyone would be stuffing their faces. There would be so much less shame and guilt about doing so. If you are in recovery you will already know that it's really bloody hard to be feasting when everyone around you is not doing the same. But you just have to remember that not everyone else around is in malnutrition. You are. So you do what you need to do.

Furthermore, we could speculate that the humans in famine situations who survived to pass on genes, would have been those with the capacity to feast eat as soon as food was present. The ability to feast after a period of starvation would have been a super skill in times of famine.

This also ties in somewhat with theories around the hibernation-like metabolic changes that anorexia induces, as animals feast when in the hypophagia stage of the hibernation and when food is abundant — interestingly many of us with anorexia notice that we hoard, or

---

[138] J Abnorm Psychol. 1994 Food restriction and binge eating: a study of former prisoners of war. Polivy

stockpile food despite our inability to eat it, in the same way a hibernating animal would do. Those animal instincts to gather and protect food surface when our brains detect we are not eating enough of it.

Feast eating is not wrong

I don't expect everyone reading this book to agree with me on this. That's okay. Ultimately you have to do what it right for you.

One of the reasons that some people in anorexia recovery get scared when they feast or "binge" is due to the notion that they have done something wrong or bad in doing so — most of us get an overwhelming and utterly inappropriate guilt reaction to eating. Gratifying such a reaction by indicating that feast eating is indeed "bad" only appeases the feelings of guilt already generated by anorexia and strengthens the conviction that it is bad to eat a lot of food. I have found that when I explain to clients that "binges" happen in recovery, and that its normal and not a big deal, they are more accepting of them, and can have compassion for why their bodies are doing that.

"For years I have been terrified of binge eating. I always was told it was to be avoided at all costs in recovery. I could throttle every person who told me that now. When I stopped freaking out and restricting after eating a lot, things gradually evened out" - JC, adult in recovery from anorexia.

The appropriate reaction to an underweight person eating a lot after a period of restriction is one of nonchalance. There is certainly no need to compensate by reducing intake, exercising, or purging. These compensatory behaviours are a problem, the feasting behaviour as a natural reaction to restriction is not.

Post-eating guilt

I have known children with anorexia (too young to really understand why they might feel guilty after eating) report experiencing intense post-eating guilt, so we cannot blame it entirely on society having indicated that eating a lot is wrong. However, when it happens, we tend to look externally to help us either confirm or reject the emotion we are having. This is when we start to ask things like "*do you think I ate too much?*" or even seemingly casual non-question statements such as "*Boy, that was a big meal ...*" to clock the reactions of others. We are testing the waters, so to speak. The last thing we need is to be told we ate too much.

"I know I am driving my partner mad but I can't seem to help asking after every meal if she thought I ate a lot. Even if it is not driving her mad, it is driving me mad!" - Anna, adult in recovery from anorexia.

When a treatment provider reduces a person's meal plan or suggest that they "back off eating" because they freaked out after eating a lot of food, they confirm that person's fears that they somehow ate too much. If you do that, you are meeting an inappropriate and irrational fear and confirming it to be true. The appropriate response should be to promote confidence. Tell them that there is no such thing as too much food in recovery and explain that they by no means did anything wrong.

Bulimia development

Bulimia is a cycle of binge and purge activity. I think of anything that is a binge/purge cycle as bulimia, and whilst I never purged via vomiting, I purged via exercise. I was in this binge/restrict/exercise cycle for a good four years.

This binge/purge cycle is formed with repetition of binge/purge behaviours. Our brains are excellent at developing habitual behaviour around eating and other survival dependent activities. With the absence of purging, I have observed in myself and others that binge episodes in anorexia recovery tend to generally fizzle out as the body reaches nutritional rehabilitation. When we restrict food for long periods of time, I think that we train our bodies to be very good at starvation mode. One could even say that we prime them to go into anorexia mode at the very hint of inadequate or restrictive intake. Hence, some of us find that even a couple hours longer between meals, or any sort of restriction results in eating or wanting to eat a lot more when we do eat than we really feel comfortable with.

If purging becomes a default behavior after eating a lot of food, it doesn't take long for the cycle to become behavioural. In order to avoid this, I believe that intake has to be adequate for your body, and restriction and all compensatory behaviours eliminated. That is what the goal chapters following this one will focus on. I understand that bulimia can be developed in different ways, and for this reason I think that individual situations need to be assessed.

"Since I have had anorexia, it feels like a reflex action to compulsively move straight after eating. I'm finally managing to overcome this." - RB, adult in recovery from anorexia.

Exercise was my purging behaviour of choice. Any behaviour that attempts to negate food eaten as a response to the guilt reaction to eating more than considered normal I consider to be purging.

Nighttime eating

I used to eat a huge amount of food every night between 11pm and 1am then restrict all day. This cycle went on for over 4 years. I finally worked out I needed to make myself to eat more during the day — regardless of how much I had eaten at night.

There are studies that point to a link between a tendency to eat at night and stress.[139] The evolution of such a response interests me. I think that there must be an evolutionary reason for it. Maybe in dangerous environments, or in times of famine when humans had to use daylight hours to migrate, it would have been safer to eat at night. I don't have any research to back that up, I'm just trying to put some pieces together to make sense out the observation that so many people with anorexia find it easier to eat at night.

"At night it feels easier to eat. Like my ED sleeps a little!" - EJ, adult in recovery from anorexia.

---

[139] American Physiological Society. (2002, February 18). "Night Eating Syndrome" May Be Related To The Performance Of The Body -- Not The Mind.

Many of us find that it is easier for us to eat at night, and when we do the floodgates open. This scares us, and we compensate by purging, exercising or restricting the next day. All this does, is set one up for another night feast.

Over time, because I set myself up for this cycle of binge then restrict, I was systematically feast eating every single night. No matter where I was at 11pm, it was like every cell in my body ordered me to feast. This wrecked my social life, as I could not fathom not being at home all night. It also meant that my restriction during the day was extreme, as were the OCD rituals.

I tried without success for years to get myself out of this mess by restricting food and fighting the urge to eat at night. I hope to save you some time by telling you not to do that.

I had to make myself eat lots during the day. And that was mentally very hard. To wake up the morning after eating so much food, and force myself to eat breakfast despite all those anorexia-generated fears screaming at me. But over time it worked. Additionally, I had to eat during the day the same sorts of food that I was eating at night. I found at night I was much more able to eat the foods that I really wanted, and during the day my orthorexia was stronger. So I had to bring those night foods into the day.

Most importantly, I had to still allow those night feasts. I reframed them in my mind and thanked them from keeping me alive over the years. I stopped trying to focus on stopping the nighttime eating, and instead focused on starting real daytime eating too. Over the course of the next year, the nighttime eating dissipated. What that felt like, was a gradual disinterest in eating at night. The more my brain learned to trust that I would not restrict during the day, the less it needed to focus on eating at night. Plus, as I become more nutritionally rehabilitated, my body began to prioritise sleep again. Of course, this only works if you are eating adequate amounts of food during the day.

Turns out I wasn't a chronic binge eater after all. I was just hungry.

Feast foods

I tended to feast on the foods that I was most restrictive about. This lead to a wealth of anorexia-generated grief, self judgement, and guilt. I never lusted after broccoli at 11pm. It was chocolate cake, ice cream, Heinz Golden Syrup puddings, peanut butter, Snickers bars etc, etc.

The feelings of guilt and regret that I felt after eating huge quantities of these foods were intense. You probably know what I mean. There was a lot of judgement around these foods. That turned inwards to judgement about me — the sort of person who ate a lot of these foods. Oh, how anorexia can be so very dramatic about something as natural and innate as eating food.

The desire to eat these foods in high quantities was starvation-generated. The grief for doing so was anorexia-generated.

For me, the key to breaking my binge-restrict cycle, was to allow/force myself to eat these types of foods during the day. It didn't work just to eat safe foods during the day — although that was a start — as I was still restricting by not eating the scary foods that I really desired. Even if during the daytime I could convince myself that I didn't really want these foods at all, my nighttime eating told a different story. I did really want those foods.

It was interesting to me how I was able to eat a jar of peanut butter at night, but would freak out about the thought of spreading it on crumpets during the day. If you had asked me, therefore, if I ate peanut butter, I would not have been telling fibs if I had told you I did. The difference, was the way in which I could eat, and the conditions placed on eating peanut butter. Those were what I had to work to remove. I had to be able to eat all foods at all times — without conditions.

The foods that you eat, the way that you feel about them, indeed any of these judgements and emotions say nothing about you as a person. The foods that you eat when coming out of starvation say nothing about the foods you will like post-recovery. I ate tons of those red shoelace sweets in recovery, you know, the ones that grown ups used to tell you will dye your intestines red due to all the food colouring in them — I haven't wanted anything like that for ages now. The very thought of eating those now makes my back teeth ache. The fact that I wanted them in recovery means nothing more than I wanted them. It doesn't matter. You don't need to over-analyze any of this.

Recovery feasting summary

Your body doesn't care what your reasons behind not eating enough are. Your body doesn't care if your weight loss was intentional or if it was inflicted on you in a concentration camp. Your body wants to rectify what it considers to be a bad situation of inadequate intake. It has evolved to do this by motivating you to eat a lot of food when food is available.

There is no point in fighting the urge to feast after a period of restriction. It is your body trying to keep you alive.

- Do not freak out if you eat a lot of food in recovery.
- Do not judge the foods that you eat. No food is bad. All food is beneficial.
- Do not restrict or try and compensate for feast eating by purging, exercise or other compensatory behaviours — this will result in more determined binges and potentially a habitual behaviour development.
- The best way to remedy excessive night eating is to eat more food over the course of the day and not to leave long gaps between eating. Teach your body that food is abundant.
- Some people feast regularly all the way into optimal nutritional rehabilitation. Don't stress about it.
- Feast eating can happen at any time. Many of us experience it at night, but it happens in the day too.

Section Three:

Rewiring

I want to thank my numerous meditation teachers for giving me the tools to understand neural rewiring. I was the person sitting at the back fidgeting and yawning a lot, and you probably wrote me off as a lost cause.

In terms of recovery, it helped me to let go of all the soul searching and come down to earth with the humbling truth that humans are mammals. Of course, we love to think that we are so superior, and blessed, and chosen, but in reality, we're probably just mammals that got lucky. And that my human body was a hungry mammal desperate for food. And like all of the other down-and-dirty animal instincts that we like to pretend we are better than, there was an urgency to my need to eat. And that I should respect and trust that. So I did.

Anorexia creates neural pathways leading to thoughts and behaviours that support restriction. Unfortunately, even if you eat more and gain weight, those neural pathways can still persist. So even when you are trying your best not to support restriction anymore, you will be unwittingly pushed towards it as your thoughts and energy will still run along those neural pathways. Hence, we need to rewire those pathways and give your thoughts and energy a different path.

Rewiring neural pathways is hard! It will sometimes feel as frustrating as doing something like trying to write with your non-dominant hand — so your left hand if you are right handed or vice versa. It will feel wrong, and weird, and uncoordinated. You'll want to revert to the easy option of doing what you usually do. But just like if you are trying to train yourself to write a different way, you have to persist to make any progress.

Chapter 9: Finding and eliminating restriction

Restriction is like an onion. It has many layers. The most obvious layer is total restriction of food. When we don't eat. This is unsustainable, so most people with anorexia are not in "total" restriction, or if we are, it is not for a long time. The body cannot survive on no food at all. Then, there is caloric restriction, which is when we do eat, but not enough — or with conditions. This is where most people with anorexia sit for the majority of their illness. Eating food but not enough. Having limits on the amount or type of food eaten in a day, or a mealtime, or both.

At the start of my struggle with anorexia, I was in heavy dietary restriction for around six months and then the urge to move and exercise started. In this time, I started eating slightly more but making sure that was negated by working out. After a couple of years of this the exercise compulsion had grown to ridiculous levels, and I began binge eating at night as my body's response to this. I managed to stay alive in a binge-restrict and exercise cycle for around eight years. The exercise then became unsustainable, and I finally went cold turkey, but moved onto compulsive lower-level movement (this will be covered in the following chapters).

During a person's life with anorexia, restriction can take many forms, but it all comes down to fear of eating too much and moving too little negotiating with the desire to eat a lot and get out of malnutrition.

How to rewire restriction

"Where your attention goes, energy flows." I don't know where this expression first came from, but yoga and meditation people use it a lot. That's one of the more sage mutterings I have heard from yoga teachers. They also say rather silly things like *"open your heart,"* and *"reach for your higher power,"* a lot too.

Even when you cannot control your thoughts, you can control your reaction to your thoughts. You do this, by stopping energy flow to unhelpful thoughts, and redirecting it to helpful ones.

Neuroplasticity means that you can change the way your brain operates. I know it sounds terribly new-agey, but the concept has been around since at least the late sixties when research showed that the brain is alterable, like plastic.[140][141] Your behaviours and reactions may seem spontaneous and out of your control, but that is not true. In a sense, your behaviours and reactions are products of how your experiences have already trained your brain to react and think.

Say someone offers you a donut. You feel anxious, because you have anorexia, and this fires a series of neurons together leading to thoughts telling you that you should not eat the donut. The reason that these neurons are so quick to fire, is because you have had this same response many times before on seeing this type of food. Your past experiences on seeing a donut have taught your brain that

[140] Pascual-Leone A.; Amedi A.; Fregni F.; Merabet L. B. (2005). "The plastic human brain cortex". Annual Review of Neuroscience. 28: 377–401.

[141] Livingston R.B. (1966). "Brain mechanisms in conditioning and learning". Neurosciences Research Program Bulletin. 4 (3): 349–354.

thoughts telling you not to eat it are the appropriate thoughts to send out. Those neural pathways are very strong. You see the donut and bam! You've already decided *"Hell no!"*. Sometimes you don't even have to actually see that donut to feel anxiety and decide you are not going to eat it, you only have to imagine seeing it! That is how primed that reaction is. It is a hard-wired response that we have to un-wire and re-wire in order for you to have the control to actually make a conscious decision about eating a donut or not.

In a sense, every time you don't eat the donut you further teach your brain that anxiety and avoidance is the appropriate response to seeing a donut because you have reacted in a way that confirms that anxiety — and you avoided eating the donut!

Had you eaten that donut, you would have indicated to your brain that anxiety and avoidance was not the correct response. If you repeat eating donuts over and over again, you will create a new neural pathway. One that doesn't associate donuts with anxiety. One that associates donuts with pleasure.

Every time you react to hunger with restriction, you strengthen the neural pathways telling you that hunger is to be feared.

Every time you don't eat something you are scared of, you strengthen the neural pathways telling you to be afraid.

Every time you workout in order to "allow" yourself to eat, you confirm the notion in your brain that you have to workout in order to eat.

As you might be starting to realise now, you probably have a lot of neural rewiring to do in recovery. And we are going to start by outlining some of the most common restriction behaviours, as these are the perfect place to start.

Common Types Of Restriction

In this section I will list out some of the more common types of restriction that people with anorexia fall into. I will also make a toolkit suggestion for each one just to demonstrate how to use the tools in the toolkit in real life examples.

Dietary restriction

This is the most common, least complicated type of restriction. Straight out dietary restriction. *"I don't eat xxx"*

Dietary restriction is the foundation for the vast majority of these other common types of restriction. It can be as simple as eating less than you want, but can also get quite complex. Cutting out food groups, only eating certain types of food, gluten-free, paleo, sugar-free etc, is all dietary restriction.

Orthorexia is a form of dietary restriction. Only allowing oneself to eat foods that one judges to be healthy enough is a very socially acceptable form of restriction — which makes it all the more dangerous and harder to overcome. You have to go against the grain and be the person who can eat anything.

Of course the rewiring action here is to introduce foods that you feel resistant to eating due to them not sitting in accordance with your anorexia dietary rules.

Toolkit suggestions:

Break the rules with DRR: Detect your resistance to eating certain types of foods. Reject it. Redirect it by eating the foods that scare you! Repeat over and over until you feel no emotional reaction to these foods.

24-hour period rules

"Honestly I could eat yoghurt all day, but I it feels wrong to have more than one pot in 24 hours …" - Mike, adult in recovery from anorexia.

This is a type of restriction where you are allowed to eat all sorts of foods, but only a certain amount of a specific type of food in any given period. For example, I would be allowed to eat bread, but only one slice of bread a day.

The 24-hour period operates so that in any given 24-hour day, you are only allowed to eat X amount of anything. Most common by far that I have seen is bread/wheat products. Many people with anorexia really struggle with things like eating toast with breakfast and then a sandwich at lunch and pizza for dinner.

Any type of food can be subjected to time period restriction. I had rules that I was only allowed X Jelly Beans in a 24-hour period. It is more often than not that every single food that you eat in a day has a quantity limit over a 24-hour period.

It is also common to have rules such as only being allowed to eat pasta once a week, or a banana on 3 days a week, or a cookie only on Saturdays, or having to have vegetables with every meal etc.

If you notice that your brain goes to these types of restriction, make sure that you ignore those thoughts and rebel against them. Break the rules. For me, this looked like weeks of ensuring that I was eating bread with every meal and ice cream multiple times a day.

Toolkit suggestions:
DRR: Detect the rule. Reject the rule. Redirect your energy by eating multiples of whatever it is that the rule doesn't want you to eat.

"Day of week" rules

"Day of week" food rules work like this: "*I ate porridge for breakfast last Tuesday, therefore I will do it this Tuesday.*" Or "*I worked out last Thursday morning before breakfast, so I have to work out this Thursday morning in order to be allowed to eat breakfast.*"

When your brain feels like it is in a threatening environment it forms habitual behaviours very quickly. Whatever you did last Tuesday resulted in you still being alive at the end of the day, hence a desire to repeat. It is a survival response. Many of us really struggle with change because our brains are very fearful that doing anything differently will have a bad result.

I really struggled with this sort of restriction. Regardless of what I wanted to eat, I had to eat the same foods on the same days of the week. This sort of thing turns into OCD-ED really quickly. Over the years I was eating what I ate each day entirely out of habit. Even after the desire to restrict or follow the anorexia rules diminished I had intense fear about changing these habitual behaviours.

"I would eat exactly the same foods in the same quantities everyday, I would only deviate from those foods on the rare occasion I went out to eat with friends and family but would then use ED behaviours to compensate. I followed these rules for 13 years!" - LC, adult in recovery from anorexia.

Toolkit suggestion:
"Fuck It! Attitude" helped me out a lot with this sort of thing. What is the worst that can happen if I don't eat today whatever it is that I usually eat on a Monday?

The good news about this one is that it can work in your favour in recovery. If you rest and eat unrestricted for a week, the next week will be a lot easier.

"Next day" rules

"I didn't allow myself to eat the chocolate bar after dinner last night, and it already feels impossible to add it back in today." - Anon, adult in recovery from anorexia

"Next day" rules happen when you are only allowed to have equal or less than what you had the day before. So if I ate less one day, be it intentional or unintentional, I would feel compelled to match that by eating less the next day too.

Eating less one day is associated with having done better that day, hence it is very hard to add more food the next day and doing so feels threatening. I think that this is possibly due to your brain being in such a state of stress due to malnutrition that it sees adding more food than the day before as a threat, hence builds mental walls around doing so. For whatever reasons this happens, it happens.

Toolkit suggestions:
"Eat and Forget" rule: I was not allowed to go over and relive what I had eaten one day to the next. To reinforce this positive rule, I backed it up with a clause that if I were to start comparing today's food to yesterday's food, I would have to use this awareness for good by eating more today.

Stay present: Focus on eating for the moment that you are in.

"Saving for later" rules

"I'm still hungry...My ED wants to 'save' calories for tonight bc I like having a grilled cheese and ice cream sandwich when I get home on fridays" - J, adult in recovery from anorexia

This is restriction now in anticipation of eating later. It can look like pushing back breakfast as late as possible. It can look like skimping on meals and snacks earlier on in the day in favor of being able to eat more later. It is creating a "buffer" of energy deficit in anticipation of eating more than usual later. It can look like many different things, but the main thing you will notice is that you are having thoughts about not eating now as you are already thinking about what you want to eat later.

I broke this rule by putting minimum intake brackets at certain times in the day. For example, I had to have eaten at least xxxx before 10am. So no saving. Plus, I had to constantly remind myself that there is no such thing as too much food in recovery, so the more I ate later the better anyway. That worked for me, but it is important to remember we are all individuals, so find what works for you.

I also used to "save" eating until someone else could (unwittingly) witness it. So if it was lunchtime but there was nobody else in the house I would save eating lunch until someone was there. Because people were always telling me to eat more, I had got it in my head that if people saw me eating they would leave me alone and not try and make me eat more food. I call this "exhibition eating." Funnily enough, nobody was fooled.

I want to mention alcohol in here because I know so many of us find that if we know we have a night out looming we "safe" calories for drinking. When I had anorexia, I would always eat less before going out. Before I had anorexia, it would never have occurred to me to not eat as much if I were going out later. I'd eat as usual, then go out and drink cider all night, and follow it all up with a 2am burger and chips with curry sauce on the way home.

Toolkit suggestions:
Stay present: Eat for the moment you are in.
DRR: Detect the urge to save for later. Reject it. Redirect by eating now. Also, "Back to Black" meditation as a general thought detection and dismissal skill will help you squash your overthinking brain when you notice yourself getting hectic thoughts about saving.

Meal plan restriction

Meal plans can help you get back into regular eating initially. They can give you structure and reassurance if you need it in order to start eating more. While I am not a fan of meal plans myself for the long term I would never tell you not to use one if you think it is a help to you. However, you have to see any meal plan as a minimum not a maximum. This is very important, otherwise you can use your meal plan as a form of restriction.

Say, for example, if a dietitian gives you a meal plan of 3000 calories. If you eat exactly 3000 calories, but could have easily eaten and were hungry for more, then you have restricted. If you were hungry at any prescribed meal and you did not eat more than your meal plan suggested, then you have restricted. If you really wanted a burger but you ate a chicken sandwich because your meal plan said so, then you have restricted. If you wanted pop tarts for breakfast but didn't because your meal plan said you have to have "two proteins and a carbohydrate," you have restricted.

Any time you eat something less than what you truly desired, you have restricted.

This can be really difficult because if your meal plan was given to you by someone in a professional position of authority, your anorexia brain will use that to justify why you should not eat anything additional. Furthermore, there are still treatment centres that label eating anything more than the meal plan that they set as "binge eating." This sort of attitude only feeds the eating disorder, and is an aid to restriction. Remember that no matter what anyone else says, you are in control of what you eat. If you can eat more than what is on your meal plan, you go!

To eat to a prescribed meal plan is one thing. To eat over and above it is another — that's courageous. That's taking control of your own recovery. As mentioned in the previous chapters, hunger can be allusive, inappropriate, and raging. If hunger is nonexistent then you still eat anyway. However, if hunger presents, and it doesn't matter when or how, it is important that you react to hunger by eating. Don't feel that you have to wait until a mealtime or a snack time to eat. You can eat now and then eat again.

Toolkit suggestions:
Breathing: If you start to consider going above your meal plan, your brain will likely start panicking and overthinking. Keep yourself calm

and stay present (eat for the moment you are in) with long slow deep breathing to help you stay clear and take positive action.

Also, "Black to Black" meditation will help you get better at shutting down those restrictive thoughts.

Compensatory behaviours

"Oh sure, I can eat just about anything. So long as I run my socks off beforehand!" - Anna, adult in recovery from anorexia.

Behaviors such as purging, use of laxatives, exercise, and compulsive movement, all count as restriction in my book because the purpose is to negate intake. You are restricting the amount of net energy available to your body. These are behaviours that very quickly develop into OCD-ED, and are hard to challenge when they become that entrenched.

You do not have to earn your food. If you nutritionally rehabilitate while participating in compensatory behaviours, you will nutritionally rehabilitate under anorexia's terms and conditions. The whole next chapter is dedicated to this type of restriction.

Toolkit suggestions:
Urge Surf: When you feel the urge to compensate, do nothing.

Event restriction

I noticed today that mentally I am already preparing for Thanksgiving by wanting to eat less. It's only October!! I have to make myself stop doing that, don't I? Why is this so hard!! It's not like I have ever over-eaten at Thanksgiving anyway. I restrict that day just like any other. So why don't I learn? This year I'm learning. - Monny, Adult in recovery from anorexia

"Event restriction" is when you start creating energy deficit in preparation for an event on the horizon in which you perceive you will eat more or do less. This is usually something involving food, and many people typically restrict or exercise a lot more leading up to Christmas or Thanksgiving, but I would event restrict for even the smallest alteration in my routine. For example, taking the cat to the vet for an annual check up on Friday would mean even on Monday I was restricting even more in case I had to sit in the waiting room. This sort of event anxiety is one of the reasons I became so opposed to doing anything that was out of my daily routine. Sitting was a huge problem for me as I had standing rules during the day. In order to prepare for having to sit for any appointment I would event restrict.

Event restriction can also take the form of exercising more. Anything that creates more energy deficit now in preparation for a perceived increase in eating or rest in the future. Many people in recovery describe event restriction as trying to create a "buffer." Don't be scared of letting go of that buffer. It feels safe but it isn't safe.

Seeing as I would event restrict for a trip to the vet, you can imagine how bad it was for larger family events. Clients have also told me that they would event restrict before family reunions in order to lose weight and look sicker. Why? Due to fear that unless they presented underweight they would not have their illness taken seriously.

I need to starve before I see someone so that they can see what's going on. Mostly doctors, I went on a MASSIVE bender (starvation bender? in a way the opposite of a bender) as soon as I started the process of intake to inpatient in early March. Just to be really sick when I got there. I think its like, tidy-up-house-for-inspection kind of thinking. - Anon, adult in recovery from anorexia

I have definitely "event restricted" over the years and did so most often at my sickest. The nerves I felt before a particular event made me lose my appetite further. Ironically I would not eat and not eat and then sometimes during the event I was so nervous about my stomach would growl embarrassingly. I still find myself wanting to do this sometimes, but that tendency has faded as I eat my high minimums on a regular basis. - "E", adult in recovery from anorexia.

I have been event restricting for as long as I can remember! The thing that makes me want to restrict most these days is when I have to go to the eating disorder unit to be weighed, I didn't mind all the time I was losing weight, but now I am gaining I have a huge fear they will discharge me now I'm supposedly weight restored when I know my ED is still very active, so I really want to weigh less when I go there so they don't say I'm now recovered when I know I am not! - LC, adult in recovery from anorexia.

The biggest irony with event restriction is that it doesn't work. Most of us event restrict ahead of a meal out with friends because we think that if we don't eat as much or exercise more before then we will feel more able to eat more later. It rarely works that way. Many of us find that restriction actually makes us feel even more anxious about eating. Restriction is like a drug, and the more you restrict the more you want to restrict. The more you restrict the harder it is to relax and eat. This is likely because any increase in energy deficit indicates to your brain that the famine is worse, and therefore the urges to move more and eat less increase.

The same is true for exercise. The more that you exercise, the greater your anxiety around eating becomes, and the more you feel you have to move. This is because the more you restrict and the more you move the greater your energy deficit. The greater your energy deficit, the more urgency your brain feels to migrate.

Toolkit suggestions:
Stay present: Eat for the moment you are in.
Urge surf: When you notice thoughts about event restricting, do nothing. Stay present and focus on your recovery goals.

Calorie rules

I think that many of us start counting calories as it helps us to gauge our success at not eating as much. Then all these calorie rules and ceilings show up, and you can get yourself in quite a tangle with it all.

In recovery I used my calorie counting to my advantage initially by giving myself caloric goals in order to get myself up and over 3000, then up and over 4000, then 5000 and so on. I also used calorie brackets to help me distribute my food better over the day and not save all my food for later. So saying don't count calories isn't a particularly helpful blanket statement. Everything depends on your attitude and intention, and some people can use calorie counting to their advantage in preliminary stages of recovery.

For other people, calorie counting is not helpful as it opens a mental can of worms. Work out what is right for you, right now. But the long-term goal has to be to stop calorie counting.

Another problem, even when counting calories in order to eat more, is that people with anorexia tend to round up. So 540 cals is rounded up to 600 cals. Switch this around in your head so that you round down. This is a pro-recovery calorie rule that you can make for yourself.

Many people in recovery, including myself, claim that they calorie count in order to make sure that they eat enough. I'm going to call bullshit on you about this. You calorie count to make sure you don't eat "too much." So if your dietitian says to eat 3000 calories, you are calorie counting to ensure that you don't go over this. Hence, this is restriction. If you truly understand that there is no such thing as "too much" food in recovery, you would not need to calorie count — if you were in any doubt about having eaten enough, you would simply eat more. It is your fear of going "over" that leads you to want to check out the calories.

Counting calories plays into the scarcity mindset. Unrestricted eating will likely lead to a reduction in the urge to count calories. Also, as your brain comes out of malnutrition and your hyper-awareness around food decreases, you will find you lose interest in calorie counting.

For some of us, myself included, calorie counting can get utterly out of control. It moves from being a restriction tool, to mindless OCD-ED. I would constantly be counting (and recounting calories) in my head. It was tedious and tiresome, and took a lot of my mental energy. In the end I realised my obsessive calorie accounting was actually a form of mental hunger — my brain trying to work out ways allow me to eat more and stay within my ration allowance. So I determined that if I was counting calories then I was obviously hungry and needed to eat more food.

I the long run, if you are truly eating without restriction you don't need to count calories. In the same way a billionaire doesn't need to count dollar bills to make sure she has enough money to cover the perfume she just bought on Amazon Prime. If calories are unlimited in your brain, you don't need to count them. You are only counting calories when you are rationing them mentally. If there is no ceiling, you don't need to check what you have had. If you are eating unrestricted and in accordance to your mental hunger, you will eat enough. Yes, this will likely be far more than any meal plan would prescribe and far more than you feel comfortable with, but if you are brave and curious, your mental hunger will lead you to exactly the right amount to eat … no counting or adding up required. Eat like a billionaire!

Toolkit suggestion: Eat and Forget and Distraction. Don't allow yourself to go over and over what you have eaten, but if you find that you are, reject the urge to count calories and distract yourself!

Timing rules

"I'm so hungry but it's not 'time' to eat for another 45 min"- J, adult in recovery from anorexia

An example of restrictive timing rules would be having a rule that says you cannot eat breakfast before 9am. Regardless of how hungry you may feel before 9am, you cannot eat before 9am.

I had a timing rule for everything. I was not allowed to eat before 9am regardless of how early I woke up. I had similar timing rules for lunch and dinner and any snacks in between.

One of my clients had a timing rule that said she can only eat X calories in X hours. This meant that if she pushed back eating until later in the day, she couldn't eat her entire meal plan because that would be "too many calories in too short a space of time." Ironically, she actually picked this idea up from a treatment centre. We worked through it by both setting her up for a lot of support in the mornings so that she would not save food for later, and also using DRR for the timing rule where the redirect was texting me and asking for support if the thought to not allow herself to eat that much in whatever time window came up.

Toolkit suggestion:
PNSP: Mentally rehearse eating before your set times, and then do it!

Drag-it-out eating

"I have to make dinner last 30 mins because that's how long the show I like to watch is. I guess I am scared that if I eat it all before the show is over then I will want to eat more." - Anon, Adult in recovery from anorexia.

"Drag-it-out eating" is when you portion food out and eat it very slowly in order to make it last longer. This is restriction because usually when we do this we believe that doing so will lead to eating less. I used to do it whenever eating with others as I was worried if I finished my meal first I would be offered more food. I also started to do this when eating alone just because the longer I could make food last the less time I would have between meals — and less time means less temptation to eat. One of my clients ate slowly because she read somewhere that the slower you eat the less of the food you absorb (which is total nonsense). Another of my clients ate slowly as he had read something that said if you eat slowly you end up eating less as you become more satiated towards the end of the meal. It could also be that we eat slowly in order to savour the limited amount of food that we have.

I did this for years. It could take me a day to eat a bag of peanuts because I would eat them one by one and savour every second rather than shovelling a handful in my mouth at a time as I do now. I did this because I was scared to finish the food. I was scared to finish the food because I knew I would still be hungry after it had gone. Or because I was so deprived of eating and enjoyed it so much I didn't want it to end.

It doesn't have to end. I can have as many bags of peanuts as I want.

Toolkit suggestion:
"Fuck It" Attitude: So what if you finish before anyone else? So what if you want to eat more? You can eat more!

Portion control restriction

"I can eat absolutely anything for dinner … so long as it fits into my stupid bowl."

Most of us control our allowed portion sizes for meals. I used to buy ready-made frozen versions of meals that I could quite easily have made myself just so that I could control the portion size. The thought of having leftovers available and having the ability to go back for seconds was scary.

It was a huge challenge for me in recovery to cook a large family-sized packet of pasta, pour a load of pesto and grated cheese over it, mix it up, and allow myself to eat unlimited amounts. But doing this was the start of me learning how to stop restricting my portion sizes.

I also had to learn to allow myself to eat over the pre-packaged portion. So multiple chocolate bars at a time etc. In doing so I was able to teach myself to eat the amount that actually I wanted, not stop at the amount that I thought I should have.

I include anything that limits portion size in this category of restriction. Using small plates and bowls, and eating with teaspoons are common examples of portion size restriction.

Toolkit suggestion:
PNSP: I used to mentally rehearse eating larger portions and then go and do it.

Food waste restriction

"I burnt my toast this morning so I had to throw it away. My ED is screaming at me that I am not allowed to have toast again tomorrow because I wasted food today." - Anon, Adult in recovery from anorexia

"I realised after lunch I accidentally ate the wrong hummus - the one I ate was out of date. I have a massive urge to restrict later or make up for this by doing more exercise. I know that you will tell me I have to let it go and not restrict or walk more. It feels so wrong. I feel like I need to make it right." - CL, adult in recovery from anorexia.

Frugality is another behavior that is normally considered an admirable trait in a person but that can get a bit ... unhealthy ... in a person who has anorexia.

Food waste restriction is a prime example of a type of restriction I didn't think anyone in the world would understand until I started talking to other people in recovery. Should I waste food — or even worse waste food that I had spent money on — I would feel that I had done something "wrong" and would have to make up for it by skipping eating that food the next day. Or I would skip eating something later that day in lieu. Or I would feel the urge to exercise more.

I speculate that this is because the malnourished survival brain doesn't want us to waste our precious time pursuing food that is not worthwhile, and also interprets food waste as a threat to survival. Or it could just be that in a famine, wasting food would indeed be a travesty. The default response to guilt for most of us is to move more and eat less — hence the urge to compensate for any food mistakes by restricting or exercising.

Those of us with a higher OCD-ED element to our anorexia tend to struggle with this sort of restriction a lot more.

Toolkit suggestion:
DRR: When you detect these thoughts telling you to miss eating something tomorrow due to something that you did "wrong" today: reject them.

Monetary restriction

"If it isn't on sale I can't buy it. And yeah, of course that limits me to the shitty fruit and veg that is in the bargain bin at the end of the day." - CP, adult in recovery from anorexia.

This may seem out of place as it is not strictly food related, but anorexia doesn't just affect our caloric energy relationships. Many of us find that as much as we are rewarded for caloric energy deficit, we are rewarded for monetary surplus. That also means that in the same way we see anything that threatens our state of energy deficit as something to be feared, we interpret spending money as threatening.

"It made me cry with relief when you told me about your inability to spend money. I have felt like this at various points in my life, I could spend money on my daughter, but not on myself." - Anon, adult in recovery from anorexia.

My resistance to spending money was as strong as my resistance to stopping exercise. My inability to spend money was actually stronger than my inability to eat more. For me, spending money was a huge fear point. Of course at the time I didn't realise that this was due to anorexia — I just assumed I was a tight person. But it turned out that as I got my body into a state of energy surplus my aversion to spending money abated. And further down the line as a recovery coach it dawned on me that the majority of my clients had a fear-based reaction to spending money also.

When I was in energy deficit, I would walk into a shop and experience a fight, flight or freeze response. Most often this meant that I left without having bought anything. This bled into my food restriction as I gradually spent less and less on food and became obsessed with saving money in the bank. As money saving is another culturally applaudable behaviour, nobody ever thought that my frugality was anything more than good economic habits.

My monetary restriction was heavily affecting my ability to recover. Even when I wanted to be able to eat more I couldn't buy food. Anything I did buy had to be the most economical version, on sale, or marked down for quick sale at the end of the day.

Not everyone with anorexia deals with monetary restriction but those who do have to take it very seriously and approach it in the same manner that they approach food restriction. Run into that fear by spending money.

Toolkit suggestion:
PNSP: I practiced going into a store and spending money ahead of time in a quick meditation to train my brain out of the fear response.

Throwing away food

Throwing away food: breaking part of whatever you are eating off and binning it. Or throwing out foods that feel threatening. Many people with anorexia are terrified of having fear foods in their house as they feel the urge to feast on them and that feels unsafe.

"Husband came home with a week's worth of Taco Bell last night. I took a bite of a burrito and then panicked and threw the entire lot in the trash after he had gone to bed." - TC, adult in recovery from anorexia.

Ironically, those of us who have "food waste restriction" often still throw away food — and the guilt of doing so often leads to further restriction.

I found that throwing out pieces of food or parts of my meals sometimes seemed to happen so quickly it was as if I wasn't really in control of doing so. More like a reflex reaction to a thought that I was eating too much. Woosh, before I knew it something was in the bin! I remedied this by getting myself more food to replace anything I had thrown out. So basically, I did not allow myself to get away with it.

Toolkit suggestion:
Urge Surf: Let the urge to chuck it out pass.

Food avoidance

Food avoidance is when you outright avoid food. This can be avoiding social situations that food may be present at. It can also be avoiding food by not buying it and having it available to you.

"I refuse to buy cereal. I cannot have it in the house." - TC, adult in recovery from anorexia

Avoiding food because you are afraid you will want to eat a lot of it is very common. However, studies show that it is likely intermittent access to food that causes people to want to eat large amounts of that food.[142] Not allowing yourself access to the foods that you desire is running away from fear and this likely increases your fear of these foods. Run towards fear by allowing yourself to be surrounded with abundance.

Toolkit suggestion:
"Fuck It!" Attitude: Stop the avoidance and see where it takes you. Have an honest think about the ways in which you avoid food. Write them down, then plan to make yourself go and do/buy/eat the things you have been avoiding.

Post-feasting restriction

"My ED tells me I am nuts. You are seriously expecting to eat breakfast this morning after all you ate last night? OMG it feels so wrong!" - Anon, adult in recovery from anorexia.

It is very normal to eat a lot of food in recovery. Eating a lot of food is not the problem. It is the restriction that might follow it that is the problem.

What we refer to as a "binge" must be seen as a measure taken by the body to rectify restriction. Therefore we should not focus on reducing

---

[142] Westwater, M.L., Fletcher, P.C. & Ziauddeen, H. Eur J Nutr (2016) 55(Suppl 2): 55. https://doi.org/10.1007/s00394-016-1229-6

the symptom (feasting) but rather we should focus on the cause (restriction). Sadly, this holds many people back. Having come from a place of engrained restriction, any kind of eating can feel overwhelming and "out of control."

"For over a decade, I was stuck in maniacal restriction—not because I was afraid of food, but because I was afraid of binges. I only knew them to be a further step on the ladder of sickness, by social standards and conventional 'recovery' models, so I held tight to my restraint and believed crocodiles were waiting to devour me, the moment I opened my mouth. Eating anything, even drinking too much water, felt like dangerous territory. Moreover, I believed that certain foods, or certain categories, caused binges. So it perpetuated anorexia, as I was terrified of 'becoming' bulimic. It wasn't about control—it never is. For me, it was simply the deficit, using binges as lies to keep me running the cycle. I know now, by experience, that there is no such thing as a binge for someone who has been a starving zombie. Nor is it ever appropriate for the starving zombie to be concerned with too much food. Honestly, it is both heartbreaking, and revolutionary." - Stella, adult in recovery from anorexia

If you eat a lot of food — and there is no upper limit here — you should see that as a rectifying action. You should continue to eat for the rest of that day as soon as you feel able to.

Even if you have thrashed your intake goal for that whole day in one sitting, you have to employ the idea that everything you eat is an independent event (Eat and Forget). What you eat or how much you eat at one meal bears no influence on what you eat or how much you eat at another meal.

Toolkit suggestion: Eat and Forget!

"Safe choice" restriction

"Safe choice" restriction is when you choose a "safer" version of what you really want. So choosing the organic meat-free burger instead of the juicy cheeseburger that you really wanted. Or low-fat dairy instead of whole milk. Or the "healthy choice" ice cream instead of Ben and Jerry's.

Sadly, this is a form of restriction that is rife and accepted in society. As an adult in recovery from anorexia, I had to understand that I am different, and even if everyone around me is buying the low-fat ice cream, that I can't do that.

Toolkit suggestion:
DRR: Redirect the urge to stay safe by buying and eating the scarier option.

"Filler" food restriction

"Filler" foods are the non-nutrient dense foods that you eat to fill you up. Most commonly fruit and vegetables are used here. I used to fill my plate with vegetables, and I had to learn to fill my plate with the nutrient-dense foods that my body needed.

I was actually so reliant on vegetables for the bulk of my diet that I had to take some time off eating them to force myself to fill my plate with other foods. It's not just vegetables that are used as filler foods, you are doing this every time you eat something low in calories to fill you up so that you won't be hungry to eat other things. Water loading comes in here too — when you try and quench your hunger with water rather than food.

Other common examples are snacking on fruit rather than that big piece of cake that you want. I'm sure you will be able to think of all the ways that you restrict by eating filler foods.

Toolkit suggestion:
PNSP: Imagine yourself filling your plate, and your body, with the yummy nutrient dense foods that you really desire. Practice mentally, then get out there and do it for real.

Leisure time restriction

Most of us heavily restrict our leisure time. We often feel that we always have to be doing something productive. I was very afraid of free time. The reason that I feared time and space was because unoccupied time allowed my mental hunger to get stronger. Non-busy time was painful for me because deep down the urge to eat was so strong. I was scared of any free time or time that wasn't filled with activity that prevented me from being tempted to eat.

I filled every moment of the day with something. Over time this became very ritualised. Every second of my day was planned out. Running from one thing to the next with an intense fear of down time.

When I recognised this in recovery I had to force myself to allow free time. Doing so was every bit as terrifying as forcing myself to eat more was. And yes, my fears were true: I did want to eat in that time. Turns out, allowing myself to rest and eat without restriction was crucial.

Toolkit suggestion:
DRR: Detect and reject your busy urges. Redirect with rest!

Whatever the reason, restriction signals scarcity
You need to show your brain that you are no longer in an environment of scarcity. Regardless of the reason behind not eating all that you mentally want to, your brain will use the fact that your actual intake doesn't equal your desired intake as a signal that food is scarce. While it thinks that food is scarce, it will keep the anorexia active — regardless of any weight you are putting on. Hence the importance of eating unrestricted and without judgement.

Chapter 10: Determining Restriction

In the last chapter I outlined some of the more common forms of restriction. These are a handful of potentially thousands of ways that you might restrict. You may recognise some of the examples I provided in yourself, but you'll likely have many restrictive rules and behaviours that are specific to you. Only you ever really know if you are restricting or not. Hence, you are accountable for outing yourself.

What is restriction for one person isn't necessarily restriction for another. And this is where things get messy. It lies in the intention behind the action, and this is where we have to get brutally honest.

Nobody really knows if restriction is being acted on than the person involved. You.

I hear time and time again of people in treatment being told not to eat something because it is an "anorexic food." There is no such thing as an anorexic food. Food is food, and our intentions behind eating what we eat are where the clues to restriction lie.

For example: I was once told by a treatment provider that Marmite should not be allowed in recovery because it is an "anorexic food." I've loved Marmite my whole life, and I ate mountains of Marmite on hot buttered toast as a kid. Now, when I was restricting, I would eat Marmite, but on rice cakes and with no butter. It is not the Marmite that is the problem, it is the lack of butter, lack of toast, and both of those things are totally restriction driven. It would be wrong to tell me not to have Marmite. But I would have to be honest and look at that measly, dry, rice cake and admit that restriction was all over that choice.

No one else can determine your motivating factors. You have to be honest with yourself, and err on the side of caution by assuming that restriction is driving your choices. Any kind of lingering doubt signifies that restriction is pushing you along. I had been restricting for so long that sometimes I didn't honestly know if I liked a food or not, let alone if I was eating a certain way due to restriction. In such instances, I would ask myself what the ten-year-old version of Tabitha would eat. The answer was never dry rice cakes!

If you are eating a granola bar rather than a chocolate bar, can you be sure it is because you prefer the taste, or is it because you have some idea that it is healthier?

When you really begin to understand the nature of restriction, where and how it operates, you will start to question everything you do — in a good way.

Sometimes you honestly won't know the answer as to whether or not you are acting in favour of restriction. You can use some of the concepts below to help you make sure.

How to halt the restriction train of thought

I noticed that even the smallest restrictive decision made me feel like I had stepped right back into my eating disorder, or handed control back. As a consequence, the urges to restrict further or partake in any other anorexia behaviours such as exercise would become stronger again.

For example: Say I did something very pro-recovery and went out for a burger. But, when I get there, I allowed restriction to push me into ordering a plain burger rather than the cheeseburger I really wanted. I would find that the whole event felt like it had been handed over to my eating disorder, and the grief from having eaten at all would be larger, as would the urge to compensate. However, when I didn't allow the restriction to influence my choices, the eating experience was altogether easier, and I had less urge to compensate afterwards.

Neural pathways are like a domino effect. Acting on one restrictive thought sparks another restrictive thought or urge to fire.

You can stop and redirect that mental flow at any time. Yes, you have the control to do that. You do it either making a conscious decision to ignore all restrictive thoughts, or (even better) by acting on an anti-restrictive thought. When I realised the mistake I made by ordering the plain burger rather than the cheeseburger, I ate a chunk of cheese to make up for not having it with my burger as I had really wanted. This would shift me back out of the restrictive mindset.

Useful Anti-Restriction Concepts

Here are a couple of techniques that I found helpful in the process of rewiring my restrictive thoughts and behaviours.

Run into fear — choose the most challenging prospect

Anorexia's perception of food as a threat causes us to run away from that fear by restricting food, or compensating for eating. Highly caloric foods are usually the greatest threat. In order to give your brain enough data to oppose the notion that food is a threat, or that you have to compensate for eating, you need to stop running away from fear, and instead run into it.

The more you eat the foods that you are scared of, the more you oppose the notion that food is a threat. You are creating and storing memories to the contrary. You are proving to your suspicious brain that food is nothing to be afraid of, and that there will be no negative consequences to eating.

Running into fear, rather than away from it, is both terrifying and empowering. If you are faced with a choice, run into fear by choosing the "scariest" possible option.

For example, I remember the first time, at a BBQ, that I asked for, yes, asked for, a beef burger rather than my usual "safe" veggie burger. I felt enormous adrenaline at doing this, and was visibly shaking as I ate it. However, the next time, asking for and eating a proper burger was exponentially easier. In fact, I would have felt disappointed at the prospect of a veggie burger, as eating the real thing (and to my surprise, not spontaneously combusting afterwards) had given me so much confidence.

I did have thoughts of compensating via exercise or restriction after eating that burger, but I urged surfed by not responding to them. The next time I ate a burger, the thoughts of compensating for it were far reduced. This is an example of creating a neural reference for a situation in a positive light.

"Eat and Forget" Rule

Anorexia-generated guilt post-eating can lead to never-ending food post mortems. It can also lead to continual rehashing of meals in your head, and therefore panic and stress as you try and work out how you can compensate for having eaten and make it "okay."

The concept of "Eat and Forget" takes mental discipline, but you can do it. It means immediately shutting down thoughts that come in about the food you have eaten that day. It is selective amnesia.

You eat a food. Then you forget it ever happened. When you catch yourself reflecting back on what you ate you are strict with yourself and force yourself out of that train of thought. "Eat and Forget" will save you a lot of mental energy. There is no point in re-living every meal.

Treat all meals and snacks as independent

If every meal and snack is an independent event, you cannot play games with adjusting or compensating or saving. For example, if you planned to eat X at breakfast, but managed to eat more than that (well done!) then you will usually have thoughts of eating less at lunch to "make up" for the extra at breakfast. This rule stops you doing that. What you ate at breakfast is independent of what you will eat at any other time.

"No saving" rule

For years I "saved" my treat foods to eat just before bed. I would look forward to them all day. Pine for them. I was scared to eat them earlier in the day, assuming I would not be able to handle wanting more.

Do not save food for later. Do not hoard calories for later. Do not save calories on a Friday morning in anticipation of eating more on a Friday night. You can and should eat more now, and eat more later.

If you recognize that you are "saving" you should counter these urges by taking the opposite action — eating.

Unstick on "sticky" foods

"Sticky" foods are the foods that you get "stuck" on. A common example is bread. Many of us get stuck on having a certain bread allowance each day; you might get comfortable eating a few slices, but the anorexia places an imaginary boundary/ration on eating any more. Anything over this bread ration feels wrong and anxiety provoking. In order to overcome this boundary, you can set a minimum bread amount for every meal. If you really want to thrash the rule, you'll also eat your sticky foods between meals, and at any given opportunity. So, you'd go through as much bread in a single day as needed to dissolve the rulebook.

Eating disorder rules aren't always consistent, and they certainly don't have to make any logical sense. When we restrict the quantity of a type of food that we have, we increase our desire to have that food more often. We are also creating an imaginary cage for ourselves in which we cannot step outside of. There is no justification for restriction. There are infinite excuses as to why you should not eat more than X amount of X food in any one time period. Don't listen to any of them.

Force yourself out of this, and you will have the freedom to eat as much as you want when you want. When you mentally un-restrict foods, there may be a honeymoon period in which you eat a lot of that food (like the thirsty person in the desert finding water). However, after time, this desire to eat a lot of that food diminishes. Go with it, and know it's the best thing you can possibly do.

Ignore, don't fight

I don't want you to fight your restrictive tendencies. I want you to ignore them.

I have two younger sisters. When we were kids, the middle one used to be queen of being able to wind me up. I was an easy target as I always took the bait and we would end up bickering over ridiculous things like what colour of My Little Pony was best, or which one of us was better at building forts.

When someone is picking a fight with you it is incredibly hard to ignore them. It truly takes the high road, and I was always a sucker for the low road. However, getting into fights generally only wastes your own energy. That is true of little sisters, but it is also true for anorexia thoughts.

You can fight with the thought. But you are still giving it mental energy when you do so. Where your attention goes, energy flows! When you pay attention to anorexia thoughts, you are still giving them mental energy, and thus strengthening those neural pathways.

Mantra: "Talk to the hand!"

Ignore. Push those restrictive thoughts out your head, and don't even give them the time of day.

Non-Food Restriction

Restriction most commonly is evident in food behaviours, but there are other aspects of life that it can affect too. I've already touched on money and leisure time, but will go into more detail here.

The more weight I lost, and the less I ate, the greater my inability to spend money. To the point, where at university I would steal toilet rolls from the university loo and take them home in my bag. Toilet rolls are inexpensive. I had the money in the bank. It wasn't that I could not afford to buy told rolls, it was that I had odd money-saving rules preventing me from doing so.

A psychoanalyst (not mine) once told me that the reason I would not spend money on myself was because I didn't think I was worthy. This is an example of projecting meaning onto behaviour. I, personally, rarely had feelings of unworthiness. Anorexia, for me, brought out a supercilious attitude rather than a humble one. It was nothing to do with not being worthy and everything to do the same irrational fear that stopped me eating. There was no logic behind my inability to spend 50p on a toilet roll. Incidentally, it was harder for me to buy toilet roll than it was for me to buy a car. Smaller, everyday purchases felt impossible. Things that I needed on a basic human needs level were what I restricted. I got a reward from knowing I could survive without spending money on the things that most people buy regularly. In addition to the reward, I would get that feeling of blind resistance as soon as I even thought about buying anything. It was very disabling.

We can also restrict on the amount of help we will allow others to give us. One person I worked with lived at home with her parents and insisted that nobody in the house has to clean but her. Of course, she justified this to them as her way of making up for the fact that she doesn't have to pay rent. She later told me that in the same way it gave her that feeling of comfort to see people eat food that she wouldn't, she feels better when she is the person scrubbing dishes in the kitchen when everyone else is sitting eating dessert. It makes us feel good to expend energy when others are not. In the same way it makes us feel good to not consume energy when others are.

The next chapter will move more into energy expenditure and ritual, but it is relevant here too. You have to think of martyrdom as restriction. It all plays into and strengthens the same system.

Common, non-food areas of restriction:
- Money — fear of spending
- Rest — feelings of "wrongness" for resting
- Work — overworking
- Leisure — fear of doing anything unproductive

Those are the most common I have observed. You will likely have your own to add. These are important, and in the recovery process you will have to challenge restriction here too.

Action: Can you identify the non-obvious ways in which you restrict?

Chapter 11: Finding And Eliminating All Compensatory And OCD-ED Behaviors

OCD-ED = Compulsive behaviours that have evolved due to long term eating disordered behaviour leading to habit formation. The behaviors may or may not be directly related to food and exercise.

Rather like aspects such as body dysmorphia, the Obsessive Compulsive Disorder (OCD) element of eating disorders affects some of us a lot, some of us a little, and some of us not at all. I fell into the "a lot" category with OCD, which I refer to as OCD-ED because for me, it was all entirely tied into anorexia and full recovery ended my OCD tendencies. Genetic studies have recently revealed the genetic locus for anorexia lies very close to that of OCD.[143] I would say that in my experience, OCD-ED is usually more prevalent in adults that have been struggling with AN for many years. The teenagers and kids I have worked with don't tend to have developed quite as strong habitual aspects.

Because OCD-ED (especially the compulsive movement variety) affected me so incredibly, we're going to have a big ol' chapter on it here. I have worked with some people with anorexia who have not been affected by OCD-ED very much at all, and so a big focus on this area is not required. Only you know your truth when it comes to things like compulsive movement and other aspects of OCD-ED, so take or leave this chapter as you need to.

---

[143] http://tabithafarrar.com/podcast/cynthia-bulik

For some of us, our anorexia causes us to feel reward emotions when we move. For many of us, movement makes eating more permissible. Over time, movement and food can become linked in the brain. So you feel like in order to be allowed to eat, you have to have fulfilled certain movement criteria. If you recognise that this is true for you, and that movement and food are linked in your brain, I believe that you have to abstain from exercise until food and movement are no longer linked in your brain. Not forever, as when you are fully recovered, movement can be a wonderful part of life again, but just for the recovery process and neural rewiring.

I'd also like to point out that some of us seem to have our general productivity linked to eating. So unless we are being productive in a way that we judge to be valuable, we feel unable to eat as much. Hence some people find that unless they are studying or working they can't eat as much. Nutritional rehabilitation is crucial, but that just as important is finding and eliminating all obsessive thoughts and behaviors while nutritional rehabilitation is in progress.

"I find it much harder to eat when I am out of school -- like summer vac. I think it is because I am not studying, I feel like I am floating about without a purpose and it feels lazy and wrong" - MM, adult in recovery from anorexia.

OCD-ED
Something that startled me in recovery, is that restricting made the urge to restrict stronger; exercise and lower level movement made the

urge to restrict stronger; and following through with any OCD-ED made the urge to restrict and exercise stronger.

If I woke up and ate a big breakfast rather than going for a run, it was easier for me to eat a big lunch. However, if I woke up and went a run or a walk before breakfast, breakfast was harder, and so was every other meal that day. I found that in myself, and I have since found that in many of my clients. There is a domino effect to anorexia compliance. Restriction/exercise/OCD-ED leads to greater and more persistent restriction/exercise/OCD-ED. This makes sense with the famine theory of anorexia: if you consider that restriction or exercise puts your body further into energy deficit. It further pushes your brain into believing that famine is present and migration is the only option for survival. Restriction and exercise are giving your brain signals that your current environment is not one in which you can survive and that you have to move.

Migration catch-22

This is what I call the migration catch 22: The more you move the more your brain interprets that as you are migrating therefore the less it wants you to eat and the more it wants you to move. The less you eat the more your brain assumes a famine response and pushes you to move more and eat less. If you struggle to be hungry in the morning this is likely due to the long-period of not having eaten overnight. All the more reason to have a big breakfast.

"I have (finally) learned that my mood, state of mind, and ability to eat directly correlates with how much I have moved. As in, the more I move, the more rigid my mindset and the grumpier I feel and the less I want to

eat. It is fascinating (and by move. It is frustrating, but a very important realization." - SF, adult in recovery from anorexia

In this section I cover exercise, lower-level movement, and non-movement OCD-ED. All three categories are equally important. When I went cold turkey on running, I did feel a release of tension in terms of the urge to restrict, however I made the mistake of overlooking the walking I was doing and the other lower-level movement compulsions. What I found was that over the weeks of not running, the importance in my head of the 20 minute walk I did each morning grew until that was as much of a compulsion as running had been. Walking, even short distances, became compulsory for me and as almost as hard of a beast to tackle as my running compulsions had been.

Do not overlook the importance of tackling all forms of OCD-ED, no matter how small they seem.

OCD-ED behaviours

In order to fully recover from anorexia, we have to stop and rewire the compulsive behaviors associated with our own variant of the illness. For me there were many. Far too many for me to write here. The most obvious were the order and rigidity in which I did everything; the obsessive and compulsive and downright ludicrous amount of exercise I did; and the fact that I would and could not sit down during daylight hours.

"I'm only allowed to change my bedsheets once a week on a Thursday morning, I was never like this before my eating disorder, why are things like this so difficult for me now?" - Em, adult in recovery from anorexia.

Those were the obvious ones.

The less obvious ones are neither food nor exercise related. They would lie in things like a feeling that every time I put fuel in my car I had to fill up, then walk inside and walk to the bathroom — even if I was paying with credit card at the pump. This was not because I needed to go to the loo, but because I did this once and it felt good because it was a little extra walking and I had done it every time since. Often I would not actually use the toilet at all, but I would walk to it and walk right out again. After a while, it was just about the habit. I would feel anxiety about not doing this and so would just quickly do it for an easy life. That's negative state relief, by the way, rather than reward seeking. I would also do this if I was a passenger in someone else's car and they stopped to fuel up.

Or, another example would be whenever I came back home, I would have to walk upstairs and put my bag in my bedroom just because it is the furthest room away from the front door in the house. I did this for years. One of the considerations in my second year at university when I had to move out of digs and find my own flat, was finding a bedroom on at least a second floor so that I could continue to do this. I turned down a load of really nice flats just because they didn't have a second floor. The flat that I did end up taking was grotty and inconveniently located, but it had stairs.

"Every day is the same, like Groundhog day." - Em, adult in recovery from anorexia.

Then there were things like the order of my day. My morning routine of waking up, going into the kitchen and drinking a pint of water. Brushing my teeth. Walking outside to get the post from the postbox (often I had already seen one of my flatmates bring it in, but I would pretend I had not seen them do it just so I could walk into the courtyard and back.) I could have kept some water or juice by the side of my bed, but I would not allow myself. If I wanted water I had to walk into the kitchen for it.

These are just a couple of examples pulled from a matrix of rituals. I was very good at hiding them, but one of the reasons I struggled to get close to other people was due to wanting to keep these secrets.

My obsession with movement filtered into everything. When waitressing (not a job I think you should be doing if you are in recovery due to all the walking involved) I would choose to work the section farthest away from the kitchen so I had longer to walk every time I had to take an order in. We're talking a couple of metres, a tiny, insignificant distance, but it mattered incredibly in my brain. If had to go somewhere in the car (which was the only time I was allowed to sit down, but not without high levels of anxiety) then I would park in the parking space farthest away from the meter so that I would get to walk a couple steps more.

OCD-ED was in everything from the way that I used to make a cup of tea (ritualistic walking around the kitchen) to the way I emptied the dishwasher (one item at a time to ensure the most ground covered) to the way I would vacuum the house. I should stress here, that my anorexia was heavily weighted in OCD, much more than most other people experience, and that if you don't experience these behaviours it doesn't mean that you are any less ill than someone who does, we simply all express different elements of the illness more or less.

This ritualised day was one of the reasons I was so stressed all the time — I had so much to do! The smallest interruption would spark off a cascading storm of anxiety and a race against time to get all my rituals done by the end of the day. Because one never gets to simply not do something — I would do it all even if it meant I was up at 3am in the morning.

I do not have general OCD. Now in full recovery I am not ritualistic about anything much. I literally cannot think of anything that I feel I have to do in a certain way. (Oh, wait, yes I can: tea. Has to be strong PG tips or Tetley with whole milk.)

Many of my clients have noticed the same, that they become more relaxed as they move towards full recovery. While plenty of people with anorexia have pre-eating disorder OCD and other anxiety disorders, not all of us have co-morbid anxiety disorders. Many of us find that full recovery relieves many other anxiety-driven problems also.

"All my rituals had to be done before I could eat. If they were not I would feel anxious and in complete inner chaos." - RB, adult in recovery from anorexia.

Common OCD-ED Behaviours

Most of us have OCD-like rituals around all or some of the following:

- Buying food
- Preparing food
- Arranging food storage
- Arranging food on the plate
- Hoarding food
- Order of eating food
- Manner of eating food
- Timing of eating food
- Location of eating food
- Rate of eating food/number of bites to take
- Caloric value of any given meal or snack
- Amount of food consumed in a 24-hour period
- Amount of exercise done in a 24-hour period
- Quality or type of food eaten
- Money spent on food or other items
- Obsessiveness about "safe" foods
- Weighing oneself and body checking
- General daily rituals
- Grocery shopping rituals
- Chewing and spitting

Additionally, most of these rules and rituals play into one another so at any given time one might have to be satisfying a number of different rules. Most of us also have our other, specialized, individualistic rituals and routines that it takes a trained eye to spot. As with other types of OCD, these rituals can become so extensive that they interfere with everything else in our lives. The OCD-ED rituals become like weeds infesting a flowerbed. As we grow older with the illness they increase until we find every waking hour is consumed by ritual.

These rituals often start with some logic or reason attached to them (especially true of the larger and more obvious food and exercise ones) but after years they just become things that one has to do without even remembering why. Many of us never feel like we can talk about them, as they either seem too odd and embarrassing, or so insignificant that nobody would understand the problem.

"Okay, weirdo confession ... I have this certain ritual when I log on to my computer that I have to check all my emails in a certain order, then texts, then Facebook, Facebook messenger, then Twitter, then Instagram. I have to answer all messages and comments and only after I have done all this can I eat breakfast." - Mike, adult in recovery from anorexia.

Those of us who have had anorexia and not reached a point of full recovery for years and years pick up new OCD-ED behaviors along the way. We are less able to drop them, but sometimes we are able to substitute them out for other ones.

One of the main reasons we submit to the demands of the rituals, is because it marginally reduces anxiety to do so. Or at least it did at one point. Not doing so, even the thought of not doing so, creates overwhelming anxiety and stress. It is not enough to simply tell someone to stop their ritualistic behavior and leave them hanging. They need consistent and effective support and positive reinforcement to help them push through the anxiety that is created by disobedience to the rituals and compulsions.

"Hubby wouldn't let me clean the windowsills. I cried! Then he went out half an hour later and I cleaned the already clean windowsills!" - RB, adult in recovery from anorexia.

When I say support, I am not necessarily talking about high-brow, high-cost therapy.. Often peer support, family support, and compassion in a space where we can talk about our stress without fear of judgement is enough to help us get through it.

Action: Go over the list above and think about your own OCD-ED behaviours if you have any.

OCD-ED and your social life

OCD-ED wrecked my social life. It always makes me so sad to think about because I basically missed out on the majority of my twenties. I developed my compulsive exercise habit towards the end of my first year at university. Because I had to get up at 5am and run before lectures every day, it meant I forfeited going out and being social in the evenings.

Speaking of going out, many of us get obsessed with our safe foods, and therefore we won't go out with friends and try different foods because we want to stay at home and eat our safe foods. My remedy for this was to allow myself to eat my safe foods on top of going out and trying new things. That way I wouldn't feel like I was having something I enjoyed taken away from me. As I became more nutritionally rehabilitated, my brain became less dependent on my safe foods, and I didn't feel the need to eat them every day. I became more able to be relaxed and explore new foods.

"I often feel overwhealmed with how much I "have" to do. The reality is that I don't "have" to do anything other than eat and rest and recover." - RB, adult in recovery from anorexia.

The tragedy of many of the OCD-ED elements of anorexia is that the more of them we develop the more time they take out of our day. The more time we spend fulfilling OCD-ED demands the less time we spend doing other things. The less time we spend doing other things the less we socialise. The less we socialise the fewer friends we have. The fewer friends we have the less we get invited to do other things. The less we get invited to do other things the more time we have to fill with OCD-ED rituals.

And then, when you get to the point that you want it all to stop it is even harder because your OCD-ED rituals are all you have in your life and it is lonely and vast out there without them. There is also the time and space problem. The OCD-ED kept me busy enough not to feel hungry. I was so scared of that space opening up. I was so scared of space in case it allowed for hunger.

When you stop any OCD-ED rituals that you have, you will open up more space for other things. And while there will be a natural lag between opening up that space and having it filled with friends and people, if you make the space they will come.

"But can't I just focus on eating more food now, and tackle the other stuff later?" you may be thinking.

While we are attempting to create energy balance by eating more food, we need to plug the holes in the bucket — all of them. While some of the OCD behaviors that we have may seem so tiny that they cannot possibly lead to further energy deficit, they are still important and still have to be stopped because they keep the entire anorexia neural network alive. OCD behaviors have a domino effect for one, and one leads to another.

Plus, this stuff is exhausting. You don't want to keep doing it all. You don't have to. Time to stop.

How To Approach OCD And Compulsive Behaviours

You don't help a person with contamination OCD by giving them more soap. You don't help a person with anorexia by giving them food rules and rituals. We need to create mental freedom by breaking food rules and rituals. This requires running into fear rather than away from it. In this respect, while in the short term you may feel safer if given a "healthy and balanced" meal plan by a dietician, in the long term you should question whether this has simply redirected your ruleset rather than eliminating it.

Only you know where your rules, your OCD-ED thoughts and behaviours, and your compulsions lie. Ultimately it will be up to you to expose and reject them. Approach this like a bull in a china shop. Smash the rules. Allow it to be messy and allow it to feel out of control. Adopt the seat of the adventurer, and see what happens if you just don't do those OCD behaviours anymore. You will be rewarded in the long run with a mental freedom that distributes the true bliss of full recovery into every aspect of your life.

Strip search everything you do to expose compulsive behaviours.

Goal: eliminate all compulsive behaviors regardless of how logical, justifiable and seemingly "harmless" they are.

For example, for a person without anorexia, walking a short distance to the store rather than taking the car could be seen as logical, justifiable, sensible, harmless to self, and morally applaudable. For a person with anorexia who has a large element of compulsive movement, walking a short distance to the store may be a hidden movement compulsive action. For me any type of movement could become obsessive when I was underweight and in malnutrition.

It can be hard to pull apart less egregious compulsive behaviours from normal behaviours. One step to help you discriminate is to look for possible energy deficit creation (i.e eating less or moving more) as even if this was not an overt intention, anytime you have an urge to do something that could increase energy deficit it has to be suspect. Or, if the action is superfluous, then you can assume that it is one that you should challenge.

Your anxiety is another clue. If not doing a behavior makes you feel anxious, that is your cue to knowing it is compulsive and you have to stop.

Tip: The International OCD Foundation has support groups, and lots of very good facts and resources about OCD.

Anorexia And Exercise

For some of you, this chapter will be the most important part of this whole book. For others, it will not be relevant at all. Not all people with anorexia fall into compulsive exercise, but for those of us who do, moving less can be harder to overcome than eating more food.

One thing I want to make clear is that movement is not the enemy. The goal in recovery is to get you to a point again where you can have a healthy, joyful, uncomplicated, relationship with movement. There needs to be the freedom of choice in this relationship, and zero obligation. If movement feels compulsive, it is likely that you do not have a healthy relationship with movement, and that it feels like a burden rather than a choice. It is likely that movement and food are linked in your brain: you can eat so long as you moved enough. The key in recovery is to unlink these two things. Movement and food should be independent in your brain, not intertwined and dependent like they may feel now. We need to rewire this relationship.

Take it from someone who used to exercise for hours a day, every day: this is deadly important. Trying to cut down, or reduce the amount I was doing slowly didn't work. I had to go cold turkey for long enough for my brain to understand that I got to eat food every day even if I had not exercised that day. It doesn't matter if you are exercising for two hours a day or two minutes, if it feels compulsory, if you feel like you have to do it, you have to stop. Even if it is a five-minute walk around the block with the dog after dinner, if the thought of not doing it causes you anxiety, then that is your clue that you need to take a break. Not forever, just for long enough to rewire.

Compulsive exercise has been described in the literature since the 1970s, and it can exist as a standalone condition outside of eating disorders.[144] That said, the prevalence is much higher among people with eating disorders than it is among the non-eating disorder population.[145] More recently it is becoming a recognised symptom, which is fabulous. It used to boggle my mind, that I could walk into my doctor's office a bag of bones, and she would say nothing to discourage me from exercise when I admitted to her that I ran every day. Hopefully these days that is less likely to happen. I still think there is a lack of knowledge around movement in anorexia by treatment providers.

Problems with excessive exercise

Even for people who are not underweight, there is such a thing as too much exercise. It is called Overtraining Syndrome.[146] Common problems associated with doing too much exercise are a weaker immune system, loss of menstrual cycle, an increased incidence of upper respiratory tract infection, and iron deficiency — and these are common for competitors who still regularly take time off from training, not idiots like me who overtrain past the point of overtraining syndrome and never allow themselves to rest.

I was aware of these risks when I was excessively exercising, and that knowledge did little to convince me to stop running. It's like my brain

[144] Obsessive and Compulsive Traits in Athletes (1992) Sports Medicine

[145] Compulsive exercise to control shape or weight in eating disorders: prevalence, associated features, and treatment outcome. Grave et al. Elsevier (2008)

[146] Kreher, J. B., & Schwartz, J. B. (2012). Overtraining Syndrome: A Practical Guide. *Sports Health, 4*(2), 128–138.

had a blind spot for truths that went against my anorexia beliefs. This circles around to the part about "your perception creates your reality" at the start of this book. Watch out for that, and catch yourself when you dismiss arguments that don't agree with your anorexia-brain.

Exercise, restriction, and your heart

Exercising when underweight has serious implications. Putting greater physical demand on an already under-resourced body is rather like trying to drive a semi over a rope bridge. At some point, something is going to snap.

As described in Section One, when you restrict food and therefore deprive your body of energy, your body is forced to recruit energy from your fat stores, but also from organs such as the heart. Heart problems are common among people with anorexia due to malnutrition anyway, and this is true regardless of whether you exercise or not. I'm not going to beat around the bush with this: people with anorexia often die from cardiac complications. Restrictive behaviours are hard on the heart; they compromise it physically, but also create electrolyte imbalances and nerve damage.[147][148][149]

I have bradycardia as a result of my years over-exercising and under-eating. I want to note here that not a single cardiologist I saw understood the impact of malnutrition on the heart, and I had to push the importance of my history with anorexia. So you can't allow your

---

[147] MEYER, C. ... et al, 2011. Compulsive exercise and eating disorders. European Eating Disorders Review,

[148] Boyd, C., Abraham, S., & Luscombe, G. (2007). Exercise behaviours and feelings in eating disorder and non-eating disorder groups. European Eating Disorders Review,

[149] Psychol Res Behav Manag. 2017. Compulsive exercise: links, risks and challenges facedent. Lichtenstein et al

cardiologists lack of anorexia knowledge to give you permission to keep exercising. I would also like to note that even in electrocardiograms, the possible electrolyte imbalances that cause the heart rhythm to fluctuate may not be visible but the ongoing damage can still be present. I had to wear a holter monitor for 30 days to discover the abnormalities that I could feel but that were not coming up on the ECG.

Your bones and joints

Osteoporosis is another common effect of long-term malnutrition,[150] and this weakening of the bones coupled with exercise can lead to stress fractures and joint damage. Permanent damage can also occur to muscles, tendons, ligaments and joints due to the repetition of movement and lack of rest and recuperation. People with anorexia are typically pretty rubbish at taking days off.

Studies have shown that people with compulsive exercise tendencies often continue to exercise regardless of ... everything. So despite bad weather, physical injury, and illness.[151] And I thought that was just me! I used to go out running whatever the weather, and I can tell you, living in Scotland I ran in some pretty nasty conditions. My flatmates used to look at me as if I were nuts (and in a sense, I was) when I would pull on my trainers and run out into a thrashing winter storm.

---

[150] Osteoporosis and anorexia nervosa: Relative role of endocrine alterations and malnutrition Jacoangeli et al. (2013)

[151] Running and stress fractures. Colt EW, Spyropoulos E Br Med J. 1979

Overuse injuries are a problem that many of us don't actually feel until we take time off.[152][153] I certainly have some joint and muscular issues as a result of my many years spent running. It's quite common for a compulsive exerciser to keep exercising despite pain and injury. For example, I used to think that the best way to deal with an injury was to "run it out."

It turns out the best way to deal with an injury is to rest. Egregiously, people with anorexia tend to have a higher pain threshold than most.[154] A bird on the wing can't just stop and sit down if her wings start to ache. Anorexia places a buffer over pain.

It is rather concerning to me that most General Practitioners are unaware that exercise isn't "healthy" when a person is in a state of malnutrition. I have never been told by a doctor to exercise less, even when I was very obviously underweight. It bothers me to think that if this was my experience, people with anorexia in larger bodies must suffer even greater pressure to keep exercising. None of my doctors were ever trying to do me harm, they just seemed unaware that the blanket notion that all exercise is good for you doesn't work in every situation.

It is dangerous to exercise when underweight. Yet many of us (myself included) cannot see this or are able to apply some unicorn logic to ourselves that tells us we are different.

---

[152] Exercise dependence. Veale DM Br J Addict. 1987

[153] Stress fractures of the tibia: can personality traits help us detect the injury-prone athlete? Ekenman Scand J Med Sci Sports. 2001

[154] Elevated pain threshold in eating disorders: physiological and psychological factors (2005) Elsevier

I only really started running after losing weight. It hadn't greatly appealed to me before. I have always been an active person. But, it was always fun things, like horse riding. When I lost weight, suddenly recreational sport was not enough. I took up running. I stopped horse riding — a sport I had loved all my life — because it felt like a waste of time. Why do that when I could burn so much more by spending that time running? I gradually lost all interest in horses as my illness progressed. (Thankfully I gained it back with full recovery.)

I lost more weight, and I started to run more often. I lost more weight, and I started to run multiple times a day. I never took one single day off running for 6 years — which sometimes meant running through the night if I had been unable to do it in the daytime.

I'm not sure that I ever really liked running. In fact, I'm pretty sure I always hated it.

There is often no meaning behind the exercise for those of us who suffer with exercise compulsions. I was not running away from anything (I was asked that a number of times by people who had read too much pop-psychoanalysis). I was not training for anything in particular. I would never have admitted that I didn't even really like running. Sure, I liked the fact that it was the only time of the day in which I was not having guilty thoughts telling me that I *should* be running. I think I liked that it made me feel successful, but I couldn't say that I was enjoying myself while doing it. And yes, I liked that while I was running my hunger subsided. But the actual act of running? No.

Maybe you do like exercise. Maybe you don't. We won't know until you have been safely in full recovery for a while. Until then, detach yourself from the behaviour, and assume it is anorexia generated.

"I can remember telling my ED nurse that I couldn't possibly live without running, that it was my whole world and that when I was running this was the only time that I felt relaxed and free from the anxiety that had taken over my life. I then went cold turkey on running as instructed by Tabs and although it was one of the hardest things I've ever had to give up, im not even sure I would want to go back to it now. - LC, adult in recovery from anorexia.

Will you ever be able to exercise again?

The whole point of getting fully recovered is true freedom to do whatever the hell you want to do. Not what you feel obliged to do, and not being a slave to rituals and compulsions. For many people, skillfully moving their body is one of the things that makes them love and respect it. My example here is being able to get strong and well enough to do something I really love and am skilled at again — horse riding — in a 100 percent joyful and non-compulsive manner. Movement is not then enemy.

When you are fully recovered, movement and eating will not be linked in your brain. This means that you will base your decisions to exercise, or go for a walk, or whatever it is you do purely on your enjoyment of doing so. There is such a huge difference between moving because you want to, and moving because you feel like you have to, or because you are trying to suppress your bodyweight.

I've known some people fully recover, and get back into sport — in a fun and healthy way. I've also known some compulsive exercisers fully recover and never pick up exercise again. It is a choice. I love that I can do the things that I enjoy such as walk my dogs and ride horses, without it being about burning calories. My decisions about what I eat are never linked to how much I have moved. I can go for weeks if we have a snow storm not even doing as much as walking the dogs, and there are never those thoughts of eating less due to not moving as much like there would have been when I had anorexia. I am always so thankful to my recovery that I once again have a relationship with movement that feels wonderful and unobligated, just as it was before any of this started.

I don't have any remnants of feeling threatened by other people exercising like I did when I had anorexia either. I have friends who are runners and I couldn't care less about how much running they do. I have no desire to run. For me, running was purely anorexia influenced. But if other people want to go running they can be my guest. My brain doesn't process details about how much exercise other people do or don't do as important any more. I care as much about the exercise schedules of other people as I do about what type of toothpaste they buy.

In order to rewire my relationship with movement to this degree, I had to be honest and accountable to myself in terms of compulsive feelings around movement. It took a long time before I could truly say that I felt zero compulsions to move. Be vigilant, and only entertain exercise again once you are well in the clear physically, out of malnutrition, and confident that there is no compulsion driving you.

Chapter 12: Compulsive Exercise Theories

This first section outlines the theories behind compulsive exercise in anorexia. I'll point out that I only ever researched any of this after having recovered from compulsive exercise, when I was trying to piece together what had happened to me.

Animal studies

When starved in the laboratory, rats can develop anorexia-like tendencies such as ignoring their food and exercising excessively. In the same way I would go to the gym rather than eat, anorexic rats whose feeding time is restricted will opt to run in a wheel rather than eat. Isn't that fascinating?[155][156]

Laboratory rats normally run less than 1 km/day. But if they are starved to the point where they are 70 percent of their normal weight, they will increase their movement and run up to 20 km per day! These emaciated rats can maintain this extraordinary activity for up to 90 days. Greater weight loss leads to greater hyperactivity. As a group, female rats become hyperactive earlier than males, a sex difference mirrored in humans.

Let's get this straight, rats who are starved and then given inadequate amounts of food start running more than usual. Additionally, the more

---

[155] J. L. Treasure, J. B. Owen, Intriguing links between animal behavior and anorexia nervosa. Int J Eat Disord 21, 307-311 (1997).

[156] W. F. Epling, W. B. Pierce, Activity based anorexia: A biobehavioral perspective. Int J Eat Disord 5, 475-485 (1988).

weight they lose, the more that they run. Rats too switch into migration mode when in energy deficit, just like me!

Migration Theory

In Section One I wrote about the migratory effect of starvation. This can mean that we actually get more energy to our limbs because the body wants us to use that energy to walk ourselves to somewhere that food is present.

Since it was first described medically. This report by William Gull in 1874 is typical: "The patient complained of no pain, but was restless and active. This was in fact a striking expression of the nervous state, for it seemed hardly possible that a body so wasted could undergo the exercise which seemed agreeable"

If you, like me, exercised more obsessively the more weight you lost, this will sound familiar. As Key's noted after the Minnesota Starvation Experiment, while starvation affects the body in drastic ways, the individual is somewhat shielded from the severity of the situation. I was adamant that I was fine, and that all the exercise I was compelled to do was fine too.

Behavioral psychologists have theorised that hyperactivity in rodents in response to starvation is an evolutionary adaptation to famine.[157] The proposition is that when food is scarce organisms do one of two things: They can stay put and conserve as much energy as possible (hibernation) or get moving and hot foot it somewhere else to find

---

[157] Activity-based anorexia: A biobehavioral perspective Epling & Pierce. Inlt Jour. Eating Disorders (1998)

food — migration. So not everyone feels the urge to move when they are in energy deficit as I did.

Increased physical activity is said to be a problem in up to 80 percent of anorexia nervosa patients.[158] There are theories that propose this increased physical activity combined with food restriction activates the brain's reward circuits and is addictive. Alternatively, the *Adapted to Flee Famine Perspective* explains that refusing to eat food when food is scarce, and compulsion to move is what facilitates upping sticks and traveling to areas where there is more food. Humans would have had to have been good hunters, and likely have decimated complete areas before moving on.[159] This also explains why eating small amounts of food — enough to keep one alive, but not enough to weight restore and reach full recovery — doesn't turn the want to exercise and the want to restrict off.

Shan Guisinger explained to me that the urge to migrate to areas of more food wouldn't do much good if that migratory response turned off again with the first handful of berries one found.[160] No, the body and brain want to know that this is not just a one off. They want to know that you hit the jackpot. In order to turn of this migratory response, food has to be abundant. Your body and brain know food is abundant when you eat a lot of it, and frequently.

---

[158] Problematic Exercise in anorexia Nervosa: Testing Potential Risk Factors against Different Definitions Rizk et al 2015

[159] *Nature* (2002) Review article Evolution, consequences and future of plant and animal domestication. Jared Diamond

[160] http://tabithafarrar.com/2017/08/shan-guisinger-adapt-flee-famine-perspective-anorexia-evolution/

In circumstances of scarcity, it is not wise to stop and set up camp when food is initially present again, as the grass might be even greener further along. It has been hypothesised that when migrating, travel should not stop when food first met, as stopping to eat may come at the cost of finding a richer food patch.[161] Food has to be abundant. Food also has to be real — it has been shown that saccharin did not make rats come out of the excessive exercise, but that sugar did.[162] I found that foods high in fat and calories were more effective at reducing the compulsion to exercise. When I was eating mostly vegetables my compulsions were through the roof, but when I resisted my orthorexic tendencies and ate foods with ample fat in, I began to relax more. I didn't know it at the time, but apparently highly palatable foods have been shown reduce hyperactivity in rats too [163]

Depression

Researchers have looked into the differences between levels of depression in "high level" and "low level" exercisers in people with anorexia.[164] Several studies on mental health have shown that exercise has a positive impact on a variety of psychological disorders — but can that be said in the case of anorexia?

Maybe. Maybe not. One study showed that the increased amount of daily activity in the individuals with anorexia who were also exercisers

---

[161] Activity-based anorexia: A biobehavioral perspective Epling & Pierce. Inlt Jour. Eating Disorders (1998)

[162] Food restriction-induced hyperactivity: Addiction or adaptation to famine? Duclos

[163] Int J Eat Disord. 2008 A High-Fat Diet Prevents and Reverses the Development of Activity-Based anorexia in Rats, Brown et al.

[164] Impact of exercise on energy metabolism in anorexia nervosa Zipfel et al.

was not sufficient to suppress their levels of depression.[165] I certainly felt no happier for having exercised overall. Only a sense of relief marred with the dread that I would have to do it all again tomorrow. Conversely, it has been found that levels of depression are typically higher among anorexia patients with high-level activity compared to those with low level activity.

The notion that we exercise in order to increase positive mood is a sticking point many of us use to justify why we were sucked into exercising. It was an excuse I myself clung on to for years. If I were asked why I ran so much, I would answer that it made me feel better. In truth, I don't know that this is the case and I suspect that this answer came from something I had heard somewhere about exercise being an antidepressant. Let's be clear: I exercised because I felt I had to. I could kid myself that it was because I wanted to, but that doesn't make it true.

Self-reporting on these sorts of things can be problematic. For example, even if I did know that deep down I was exercising because I didn't have the option or control not to, rather than because it lifted my mood, it would still have been truthful for me to give the answer that I exercised because it made me feel better. That was arguably true either way, but *"making me feel better because it lifts my mood,"* is different from *"making me feel better because even the thought of not exercising makes me feel anxious."* It turns out that people with

---

[165] Impact of exercise on energy metabolism in anorexia nervosa Zipfel et al.

anorexia tend to exercise because it feels bad not to, rather than because it feels good.[166]

When compulsive exercise is looked at in non-eating disorder populations of students, it has been shown that students with exercise compulsions more commonly struggled with lower self-satisfaction, negative mood, and reduced social behavior than students without.[167] Levels of anxiety were a lot higher too, as were levels of depression.

Incidentally, of people diagnosed with eating disorders in the military, 66 percent of these are in the Marines.[168] Why doesn't that surprise me? I applied to join the army in 2002, got accepted, but then left my induction weekend early because I couldn't handle the "rest day" on the Sunday after physical test out on the Saturday. I realised that being in the army was not for me because there were times I would have to sit down and read about operating weapons. I had no interest in weapons or fighting, I was there for the log runs and obstacle courses.

Compulsive Exercise And You

"After I weaned my son when he was around age 3, I for some reason decided to take up running (I now see that this was a result of the energy deficit state I'd entered into after losing weight while nursing). I am type A, very competitive and driven and I approached running with the goal of being faster, better, more efficient. So I looked for ways to improve my

[166] Martinsen, Marianne, Solfrid Bratland-Sanda, Audun Kristian Eriksson, and Jorunn Sundgot-Borgen. "Dieting to win or to be thin? A study of dieting and disordered eating among adolescent elite athletes and non-athlete controls." British Journal of Sports Medicine 44, no. 1 (2010): 70-76.

[167] Li M, Nie J, Ren Y. [Effects of exercise dependence on psychological health of Chinese college students]. Psychiatria Danubina. 2015;27(4):413–419. Polish.

[168] Diagnosed Eating Disorders in the U.S. Military: A Nine Year Review Antczak, Amanda J. ; Brininger, Teresa L.. ARMY RESEARCH INST OF ENVIRONMENTAL MEDICINE NATICK MA MILITARY PERFORMANCE DIV

performance and found the diet that really led me down the ED rabbit hole. I lost even more weight and the compulsion to move really ramped up. I felt like I was on a hamster wheel." - E, adult in recovery from anorexia

Compulsive movement in children too young to understand the idea that exercise is "good for you" is very telling, and really shows how the disorder generates the compulsion even when the higher brain doesn't have a logical explanation for it. I know of children with anorexia under the age of 8 years old who compulsively jogged, and if asked why they were doing it, answered that they didn't know. Younger children with this illness who have not yet had ideas projected onto their actions and behaviours innocently display the true and pure compulsivity behind needing to move.

The paths to compulsive movement may be different, but the devastating and exhausting result is the same: we become utterly dependent on it.

I hated exercise and I didn't want to do it, but I HAD to. Because if I skipped a day, or a single compulsion, then I feared I would never do it again. (I'm all or nothing, baby!!) That I would all of a sudden stop moving at all, never want to work out or do anything active, - J, adult in recovery from anorexia

How do I know if it is compulsive?

If the thought of not exercising makes you feel anxious and panicked, then consider it is compulsive. If you are underweight yet feel compelled that you need to work out, there is a problem. Nobody in a state of physical compromise should exercise.

"The only time I felt calm and free of anxiety was when I was moving. I found myself not only running many miles a week but also lifting weights at the gym and squeezing in walks whenever I could. Any excuse to move, I would take it. I started to feel like there was a problem when, for my son's 5th birthday which was held at the big fancy gym we belonged to, I snuck upstairs to the machines to get in an extra workout while waiting for everyone to arrive. At the time I thought I was being "fit." But I missed out on these small moments with my family because I could not stop myself from moving. I would do squats and push-ups and planks and dips whenever I had the chance. Sometimes I would wake up in the middle of the night (I had insomnia and would wake up with a stomach growling loudly) and I would do exercise then too. I could NOT stop" - Anon, adult in recovery from anorexia

Cold Turkey

"Giving up the excessive exercise for me was much harder than getting over the fear of eating." - L, adult in recovery from anorexia

I think that if people really "got" the compulsive element of anorexia, then they would understand that the compulsive exercise should be treated in the same way any other OCD behaviour should be treated. And how do you stop an OCD behaviour? You stop or redirect the behavior. For me this meant going cold turkey on the exercise, which was utterly terrifying.

The prospect of not exercising would make me physically shake with dread. However, the actual action of not exercising was not nearly as bad as the thought of it. Not having to exercise was actually a huge relief.

If the thought of stopping exercise utterly terrifies you, that is indicative of how out of control this compulsive exercise is.

Action: Answer the following questions:
1. Does the thought of not exercising make you feel anxious or stressed?
2. Do you find it hard to take a day off exercising?
3. Do you gear your life around being able to exercise?
4. Do you dislike public holidays because family time makes it harder to exercise?
5. Do you get irritated if a family member or spouse is exercising and you cannot?
6. Are you underweight?
7. Do movement and eating feel linked in your brain?

If the answer to any of these questions is "yes" then you should stop exercising.

"Giving up exercise has been so hard for me. I feel like I have to earn my food through exercise because I feel like it's the only "socially accepted" way to purge. So exhausting....it makes me irritable to exercise compulsively but it makes me anxious and irritable NOT to do it. So terrible." - Anne, adult in recovery from anorexia

And yes, I totally do understand how terrified that can make you feel. Your reptile brain thinks that your survival is dependent on your ability to move. It is going to pitch a fit and try and scare you into moving and exercising. You have to hold tight. Stay still, and rest.

Mentally accepting cold turkey is the hardest part

Here are some typical thoughts you might have around the concept of not exercising

- "Exercising is healthy, everyone knows that."
- "Exercising increases metabolism, therefore is good for me."
- "I feel like I have tons of energy, so why not exercise?"
- "It is normal to work out."
- "Not working out will make me lazy."
- "Not exercising will mean I lose all my hard-earned fitness."
- "Not exercising will mean I lose my athlete identity."
- "I enjoy the social aspect of exercise, and will lose out on that if I stop."
- "The only time I don't feel stressed is when I am exercising."
- "I need to exercise to tone the muscles as I weight restore."
- "I'm not sick enough to need to stop exercise."
- "I don't exercise long enough or hard enough to need to stop."

Here are my counters to those:

- Exercise is not healthy for an underweight person. It places additional strain on the heart and other organs.
- When your brain is detecting malnutrition, it is not going to increase your metabolism. Exercise won't increase your metabolism. Food will.

- The "energy" you feel is not healthy energy, it is not a sign that you have a lot of energy to spare. Rather, it is a sign that your body is under stress from malnutrition and is pushing you to migrate by making you feel like you want to move. This energy that is in your limbs has a high opportunity cost if you use it. Other parts of your body need that energy.
- It is not "normal" to work out. Gyms have only been a part of society for the last 50 years.
- It is not "lazy" to rest when you are in rehabilitation from illness or injury.
- Your body will benefit from rest and nutrition.
- If your identity is truly wrapped up in your ability to exercise, then this is not a sustainable identity anyway. It is not a healthy identity. It is an anorexia identity.
- If your social life is dependent on you exercising, then this is not sustainable and is not a "true" social life. Friends should be friends regardless of exercise.
- Any "stress" that you feel is likely generated by anorexia in some way or another. Much of the time, we find that without the illness, we do not have that much stress.
- It doesn't matter if you are only doing two minutes a day. If it feels compulsive you are not in control.
- It is not healthy to try and control your natural body shape via food restriction or compulsive exercise.

I tried initially to stop exercising myself while still working in a gym. That was a disaster and I failed miserably.

As I describe in detail in *Love Fat* I finally stopped suddenly one day.

That day was both the worst and best day of my life. Worst because of the place I had to go mentally in order to make the decision to stop exercising. Best because stopping running was the first day of my recovery.

There have been studies that show people with anorexia overestimate how much they actually enjoy all the exercise they do, but I don't really need data to tell me that about myself and likely you don't either.[169][170] All I needed to do was cut the nonsense and be honest. Stopping was traumatic, but it was a huge relief!

"Stopping cold turkey was so liberating! Now when I eat I eat cuz I want to, not because "I earned it" - wikd, adult in recovery from anorexia

Stop stalling

You can put on weight while still exercising. Of course you can. If you eat enough food, your body will gain weight regardless of how much exercise you do because that is the underweight body's priority. For this reason, many people argue that they don't need to stop exercise in order to "recover."

Although nutritional rehabilitation is key, full recovery is not just about gaining weight. Full recovery is the ability to eat without conditions and without fear. In order to be able to eat without conditions, you have to be able to stop exercising and not reduce your intake. You

[169] Martinsen, Marianne, Solfrid Bratland-Sanda, Audun Kristian Eriksson, and Jorunn Sundgot-Borgen. "Dieting to win or to be thin? A study of dieting and disordered eating among adolescent elite athletes and non-athlete controls." British Journal of Sports Medicine 44, no. 1 (2010): 70-76.

[170] Boyd, Catherine, Suzanne Abraham, and Georgina Luscombe. "Exercise behaviours and feelings in eating disorder and non-eating disorder groups." European Eating Disorders Review 15, no. 2 (2007): 112-118.

need to unlink this dependent relationship between movement and food in your brain.

And anyway, if an action is compulsive then you are not in control. If you were in control, stopping exercise would not make you want to cry and scream. Rather than allowing the panic to overwhelm you, look forward to the day when you can move for the sake of pure enjoyment rather than compulsion.

"I actually have found cold turkey much easier than trying to just reduce exercise which never really worked. I'm honestly only 8 days into cold turkey and every evening I go to bed thinking that tomorrow I will run but every morning I wake up and don't, the anxiety is getting easier each day, just got to stick with it!" - Anon adult in recovery from anorexia

Stopping exercise can help you eat more

This is another huge irony. Many of us find, that when we stop exercise, we are more relaxed about eating. Which, incidentally, is the opposite of what we think will happen. I noticed this profoundly. About five days after stopping exercise, something kicked in and I was able to eat more with relatively less anxiety about doing so. It makes sense if you think about that from a migration point of view. You stop moving so much, and nothing bad happens, so your body begins to think that maybe you are out of the famine zone. It stops disincentivizing eating as much. Both eating more and resting start to become less fearful.

Out of all the people whom I have worked with in coaching, the majority have found this happens also. For some, there are a couple days of initial anxiety increases, then after that they feel overall more enthusiastic about eating more and challenging fear foods. This always makes me so happy. The exuberant text messages and emails that I get between sessions from clients as they astound themselves by eating more — and feeling good about it.

"I was worried that if I stopped I wouldn't be able to do it again. I personally found it relatively easy once I COMPLETELY gave it up - I spent a long time just trying to ease off and this really didn't work. But to just have a rule of no exercise made it much much easier. I still miss it, but much easier to just have a ban - which is why I think the food issue is a lot more difficult for me... I can't just avoid it". - V, adult in recovery from anorexia

While this is true for many of us in recovery, for some the urge to restrict is greater the less that they do. There is no one-fits-all, but there are trends.

Cold turkey FAQs

How do I stop exercising?

You just stop. Then, you fill your time with distractions and eating, and support.

How long do I stop exercising for?

For the sake of your body, if you are underweight, in energy deficit, and in malnutrition, you should stop exercise and all superfluous movement until you are nutritionally rehabilitated.

If you are not underweight, but have a compulsive element to your movement. You need to stop long enough to unlink the connection between exercise and food in your brain. This took around a year for me. If you start up again be wary and look for feelings that indicate that your activity is becoming compulsive again. You should only ever do activities because they are fun.

Chapter 13: Lower-Level Movement Compulsions

"I tend to stand when waiting somewhere, shifting nervously back and forth. I jiggle my leg when I have to sit. I take the stairs instead of the elevator. I can FEEL the compulsion to do these things in the same way a smoker might get an intense craving to smoke that is so strong it overrides your best intentions to do what is best for yourself." - E, adult in recovery from anorexia

What I didn't realise when I initially gave up formal exercise was that doing this wasn't the whole deal. There was more to the movement/ food connection. My compulsion to move continued to exist in practically everything I did. Literally. Taking the longer route. Walking rather than taking the car. Getting up and down to fetch things when eating a meal. Never sitting. Always having to stand. Fidgeting.

When I stopped formal exercise these lower-level movement compulsions increased. Many of these had existed while I was exercising formally as well, but it became far more pronounced when I stopped running.

This is hideous to live through. A part of me was exhausted and wanted nothing more than to be able to stop moving. But that didn't feel like an option because so much felt dependent on my levels of movement. Mostly my ability to eat at all. It was all conditional. I got to eat only if I had moved enough that day.

While I could see that the amount of exercise I did was unreasonable. I could see how it may have been doing damage to my body. I could see how doing it worked against my goal to gain weight and recover. The same could not be said of that habitual dog walk every morning. The same could not be said about the frequent walks to the shops. I could not argue physical reasons as to why continuing to do these things were detrimental to my health. But I knew deep down they were.

These lower-level movement compulsions hide in plain sight and can be harder to uncover than the egregious abuses of excessive exercise. I want to be clear that I am not saying that movement is bad. It is not. But many of you reading this will know exactly what I am getting at. You do not feel in control. Movement feels compulsive. This is when it is a problem. When you are fully recovered, you will be able to do the housework and walk the dog without it being "clocked" in your brain as permission to eat.

"The only way to squash the desire and drive to move/exercise is to stop it completely. I find allowing myself just to do a little leads into more. It's like a person who has an alcohol problem sitting in a bar with alcohol around them. I find even to take a little walk drives me to want to do more. So for me avoidance is needed in the area of exercise. It's not easy but right now I'm seeing it as the only way to overcome those drives and compulsions that are result of eating disorder." - T, adult in recovery from anorexia.

Most of us find that as we move into nutritional rehabilitation, the drive to move decreases.

"I am more hungry these days, obviously exercise is an appetite suppressant for me." - Sfinn, adult in recovery from anorexia

Examples Of Lower-Level Movement

Walking

"My thing was always to go the really long way around to anywhere I had to go. And if there wasn't a long way round I would make one up! So walking in the opposite direction for a little while and then turning back. If I knew a journey would take 10 minutes directly, I would give myself an extra 30 minutes to get there. It worked because in that situation if I arrived "early", I would keep walking to "kill some time". It was all justified by it being really beautiful outside so I needed to take advantage of the lovely day, or if it was a bad weather day I was "getting some fresh air" because I had been home all day (which I generally hadn't)." - Sfinn, adult in recovery from anorexia.

Walking seems so innocent but can be the hardest anorexia behaviour to overcome for many of us. I had a number of daily walks that I had to do. Some of these had justification and an excuse attached to them such as walking to the store. However, much of the time I would just walk for walking's sake, so compulsive walking doesn't have to have a rhyme or reason.

Typical walking excuses include things like walking the dog; walking to the store; walking to do chores; and situational dependent walking rituals — so depending on if it is a workday or a weekday one changes one's walking compulsions depending on where one is.

Example: On days when I worked at the pub I had walking rituals around going about my business at work. i.e. as soon I got there, rather than walking in the front door next to the parking lot, I would have to walk around to the back door. This was approximately a 20-metre difference. A stone's throw of a distance. However, I had to do it.

In recovery I had to be very careful to rewire the walking compulsions by taking the shorter route rather than the longer one. So detecting the urge to walk farther, and rejecting it. And I also had to reject the urge to walk everywhere, and instead take the car as a redirect.

Thankfully I can report, that with full recovery and persistent mental and behavioural rewiring walking no longer has a compulsive aspect to it at all. For me, it took a long time to get to that point, but it is entirely achievable.

Housework

"I vacuum twice a day. I live alone. Most of the rooms I vacuum aren't even as much as sat in between being vacuumed! I have to do it at the exact same times too." - J, Adult in recovery from anorexia.

Vacuuming the house, laundry, cleaning the kitchen, cooking, emptying the dishwasher, doing the washing up, organizing the fridge etc. are all examples of housework that can be turned into OCD-ED.

I have heard this from people who have children too, that they like the excuse of having to cook to be on their feet all day. People report getting resistant to offers of help from spouse/partners and almost territorial about the cooking. While on the outside this looks like you simply enjoy cooking, I think most of us know deep down something more is going on.

To anyone on the outside, it may have looked like I was simply a very house-proud person, as I was always cleaning. That is not true. I am not house proud at all. It was all an excuse to move. I had to resist the urge to frantically clean every day, and in time, the compulsive element to housework diminished.

Shopping

"I must be the only person who goes to every shop in town daily but never buys anything. It's about the walking." - Gail, adult in recovery from anorexia.

Arguably shopping ties in with walking but disguises under another excuse. One very interesting entwinement of behaviours here, is for those of us who have a fear-based reaction to spending money we turn shopping trips into extended walking excuses as we walk from store to store to compare prices.

The reason that shopping crops up for so many of us and turns into an OCD-ED behaviour is, again, because we can hide it in plain sight. Shopping for grocery items is normal. Nobody is going to tell you not to go shopping for food — especially if you are underweight.

Shopping for food is fine. Take the car, and go to one store.

Standing

"I noticed that I have to have all machines and laptops at chest level to avoid sitting. I guess I need to stop doing that?"- A, adult in recovery from anorexia.

Well done for spotting that standing is not strictly movement. I'm going to tell you about it anyway. It is still a compulsive behaviour for many of us and needs to be outed.

Rules about having to stand rather than sit down can have devastating social consequences. It is more obvious that people with anorexia opt out of social situations involving food but not so understood is that many of us opt out of social situations that will require that we sit.

I personally struggled incredibly with standing, and it was one of the reasons I could not get on a plane or go on long car journeys. I had to force myself to sit during the day, and for some reason this was one of the very hardest aspects of recovery for me. Sitting down rather than standing used to make my skin crawl — that's not normal! I am so happy to report that I can happily sit all day now if I want to and not feel an ounce of guilt.

Fidgeting and pacing

Leg jigging, foot tapping etc. Having to get up and down a lot. Like most of these low-level movements it really irritates the person who has to do it, but they are engulfed in panic at the thought of not doing it. This one also gets overlooked as some people do jig naturally.

Pacing should be included here, as it is an escalated form of fidgeting. Some of my clients have been driven to pace when they eat, and this can be another reason that they insist that any eating they do is done in private.

Pacing certainly has to stop. You will likely need to apply a few breathing exercises when you want to pace in order to keep yourself calm and present enough to not do it. It is worth focusing on stopping pacing and fidgeting, as it is exhausting to maintain.

Favoring occupations that allow for movement

"I couldn't ever have a desk job. I would even struggle to stand at a till. Are my days always going to be spent as a server?" - Monny, Adult in recovery from anorexia.

This can mean a person's entire working career is influenced by anorexia. e.g choosing a lower paid waiting career even when you have the grades/qualifications for a much higher paid desk job. Choosing jobs that allow you to move.

349

This was me, fresh out of university, deciding that I wanted to work in the pub serving beers and running plates of steak and chips out to the beer garden all day and night instead of continuing with school and pursuing my masters degree. Why did I make that decision? Because one can move more when serving in a pub than when sitting in a lecture hall. It was that simple.

Not only has my recovery done me a favor, it has saved the rest of the world from enduring me serving them at the pub. I was a horrible waitress.

Action: Can you identify any lower-level movement compulsions that you might have?

Rewiring lower-level movement: Detect. Reject. Redirect.

When these compulsions exist as our little secrets, trying to overcome them is much harder. Naming them and talking about them can feel uncomfortable, but in the right environment can be empowering rather than embarrassing.

You don't need hours in therapy to stop these compulsions. You don't need to work up to the right time. You don't need to spend years talking about them and trying to figure out some hidden meaning. You can stop. Right now.

Name it, then stop it. Naming the compulsion as anorexia-generated will help you be able to dismiss it as an inappropriate and meaningless urge. Stop jumping through the hoops.

For years, walking to the store rather than taking the car might have been second nature to you. Even so, you have to rewire those habits and take the car.

Easy to say "do nothing," right? What about the flood of anxiety that hits when you disobey?

Do nothing there too. You do not have to participate in your emotions. You don't have to get involved. Emotions, like urges, come and go, and they only stay if you step into them and empower them. If you step out of the way, emotions will pass by.

The energy jolt

I noticed that often if I ate something that was more than I was used to, or if I ate a fear food, that I would sometimes have what I called an "energy jolt." This feels like a sudden urge to move, and may or may not be accompanied with thoughts of wanting to move (or purge in some other way) in order to negate the additional food eaten.

Of course, I never remember this happening before I got anorexia. It seemed to start with anorexia, and now, recovered, it no longer happens.

When I say a sudden urge to move, I mean as if I had been stung by a wasp. The urge to get up and walk would overwhelm my entire body and leave my head spinning. This is far more than a simple thought about moving, it is like an electric shock screaming at me to get up. But it was momentary, and I found that if I could stay still and ride it out — urge surf — it would dissipate.

I've worked with people who experienced this and it led to purging. I totally understand how in that brief moment of panic, the urge to purge is incredibly strong. You have to ride it out. It can be very uncomfortable but is usually short lived if you focus and stay calm and still. Urge surf, stay calm, breathe.

Non-Movement OCD-ED

Exercise and lower-level movement are the most obvious forms of OCD-ED. They are not the only forms.

When you have anorexia, gravitating towards eating less and moving more feels natural, and can be as thoughtless as the way that you naturally move to stand in the sun if you are feeling cold. In recovery half the work is understanding that many of the things you feel naturally inclined to do are slowly killing you.

Some of the OCD-ED is pure straightforward OCD — like having to eat in a certain order. But in a sense that can still be traced back to avoiding eating more. Anything that makes eating more complicated than it should be has the potential to reduce eating behaviour.

Calorie counting

"I lie awake at night going overandoverandoverandover. Well aware there are a million better things to think about. I hate that I do this" - Anon, adult in recovery from anorexia

Whilst it is widely accepted that most people with anorexia calorie count, I don't think that it is understood how horrifically engrossing this can be for some of us. I think that calorie counting starts as a restriction tool (hence it was already covered in the restriction chapters), but over time can move into a mindless compulsion over the years. I used to have persistent looping calorie counting thought patterns that I found incredibly hard to distract myself from. I wasn't just calorie counting at mealtimes, I was doing it constantly over and over again in my head every couple of minutes. I would count and recount straight away.

There was the aspect of looking at nutritional labels, and this was a behavioural habit that I had to use mindfulness and Urge Surf to overcome. But the mental totting up wasn't as easy to stop doing as it would happen almost unconsciously. I found that nutritional rehabilitation was the main aid to stopping the urge to calorie count, but I did use the thought redirection method DRR as outlined in the toolkit.

Toolkit suggestion:
DRR: When you notice that you are counting calories, reject and redirect the thoughts. If you are in any doubt that you have eaten enough food, you should simply eat more food! No need to count anything.

Weighing Food

"I need to stop weighing my cereal bars! I don't trust that they will weigh what the packet says so I have to weigh them at home before I am allowed to eat. OMG, am I crazy?" - June, adult in recovery from anorexia.

Luckily for me, I never got into weighing my food, but so many of my clients have struggled with this. Weighing food is common with the more obvious items such as cereal and grains, but also even with packaged foods to ensure that the item in the pack is the same weight as that specified on the package.

The urge to weigh food and constant food weight checking can mean that flexibility around what and where one can eat is compromised even further. In short, it really messes with your ability to challenge food restriction and also to be social and eat among other people.

While it will provide you with temporary anxiety reduction to get out the scales and check the weight of your food, every time you do it you reinforce the behavioural neural pathway in your brain. Weighing food has to stop.

1. Throw out the kitchen scales.
2. If you get thoughts or concerns that you might accidentally eat less if you don't weigh your food, simply add more food. Don't worry about going "over," there is no such thing as "too much" food in recovery.
3. When estimating food quantity by eye rather than weighing, err on the side of generosity. If in doubt add more.
4. When you get the urge to weigh food, urge surf it out.

Weighing food plays into the scarcity mindset. Nutritional rehabilitation and cessation of dietary restriction will likely reduce much of your desire to weigh food, but in the meantime, do your best to stop the behaviour.

Eating the same foods/food rotation

"As I eat exactly the same everyday, I can taste the subtle difference in food depending on it date of manufacture or place of production - so this means trawling supermarkets for specific use by dates or farm growers..." - Anon, adult in recovery from anorexia.

I would eat the same foods, at the same time, every day, with no desire to change. The mere thought of change was always met with a lot of mental resistance. Many of us find that we either have to eat the same food every day, or go by certain rotations of foods. One of my clients for example had a set lunchtime rotation of salad one day and crackers the next, with rotating toppings.

For those of us who eat the same foods every day, acquiring those foods can become OCD-ED in itself. I used to stockpile the foods that I could eat, and have rituals and routines about the day of the week that I was allowed to open a packet etc.

The food rotation part can become its own type of stressor as it can play into the OCD-ED that many of us have around food waste, best before dates, and economical cooking. This can lead us to feel like we are tripping over our own rules and forever chasing solutions to satisfy the OCD-ED urges.

We overcome this by riding the urges to eat the same thing and challenging ourselves to eat different foods. While a harm-reduction model of care for anorexia would say that so long as a person is eating it doesn't matter if they are rigid about it, I disagree. I have lived that life and I would not wish it on anyone. As so many of the OCD-ED elements of this illness were linked for me, I had to tackle all of them to find true mental freedom.

Kitchen/cooking space

"My husband is terrified to go into the kitchen. He has good reason to be!"
- Milly, adult in recovery from anorexia.

The kitchen is usually a place of greater significance than any other. It is, after all, where the food preparation takes place. I was incredibly territorial about my kitchen — to the point where nobody dare step foot inside.

Having another person in my kitchen caused me anxiety. I would hover and watch every move if anyone were to do so much as make themselves a coffee. While I couldn't rationalise it at the time, the only explanation that I have for this right now is the brain's possessiveness response to perceived scarcity. Everything involved with food and cooking and eating was so precious and important to me. My kitchen the centrepoint for it all.

I found that my kitchen possessiveness naturally subsided as my body came out of malnutrition. I had to do some mental work to rewire my stress response to another person entering the kitchen, but the main factor here was reaching full nutritional restoration. When your brain comes out of scarcity mindset, it no longer has to see the presence of other people in your food storage area as a threat.

"My mum tried to be helpful and wash up my few measly bits of crockery from my evening meal. As soon as I heard her start to attend to them I raced into the kitchen and my fierce side came out - insisting she leave them as I HAD to do them. The rise in anxiety at potentially not having that excuse to stand for that tiny amount of time to wash up demonstrated to me how powerful and compulsive it was." - Anon, adult in recovery from anorexia.

If someone got to washing the dishes first I would re-wash them!" - RB, adult in recovery from anorexia.

Money

"Unless it is in the markdown bin in the corner of the store, I'm not allowed it." - Anon, adult in recovery from anorexia.

Money spending can be restrictive, but an OCD-ED component can develop over the years for many of us too. In the same way that we can get OCD-ED about calorie counting, saving calories for later, never going over a certain amount of calories in a set time period, we can experience the same thought patterns relating to money. For example, if I were to get caught short and have to buy lunch out one day, then I would mentally feel very anxious unless I was able to work out how to "make up" for this extra expenditure by a) making more money that day, or b) spending less later that day.

Likewise, should I get told that I was not needed for a work shift one week, I would feel incredible weight of stress unless I could either work out how to pick up another shift elsewhere or make up for the lost money that week by spending less. This is the reason that I had two or three different jobs at one time. So that I could always ask for an extra shift somewhere else. Incidentally, I also counted hours worked in the same manner I counted calories.

The working obsession and the food restriction would play into one another in that I could somewhat mitigate the stress of one with the other. For example, if I had one less shift offered to me, I could "make up" for it by eating less that day. Bonkers, I know.

This is the sort of mental anguish and balancing energy ins and outs that I was doing all day long in my head. My ability to eat was dependent not only on my exercise levels, but on my income and the hours I had that day as well. My brain was constantly trying to work out how to balance the books.

If you recognise any of this monetary flow OCD-ED then I suggest you stop working totally for as long as savings will allow for in recovery. Your resistance to doing that, you will find is usually more due to anxiety caused by anorexia than it is due to not having enough savings to take some time off. You need to unlink money and food and exercise in your brain.

I want to stress that this tightness of wallet can seep into the most bizarre of areas. When I was writing this book a person in recovery told me of her paper saving obsession that developed with anorexia. She said that her resistance to buying paper for her schoolwork led to her handwriting getting smaller and smaller. This brought back my own memories of university and the lengths I would go to in order to save paper. Tiny handwriting so small I couldn't read it. I also outright refused to print anything, as this would use paper and paper costs money. If I had to print something I would not use the printer in my bedroom but instead walked into campus to use the one in the main hall for free.

Praying

"I'm so embarrassed because I am not at all religious but I have to go upstairs to the bedroom, probably because this is the farthest darn room away from the kitchen, and pray for my family before eating." - Anon, adult in recovery from anorexia.

This is so interesting to me that I wanted to give it a shout out here. I have had a few clients and other people in recovery tell me that praying behaviour developed after the onset of their anorexia. The relevance here, is that these were not religious people, and even while praying didn't hold any belief in "God," but felt compelled to do so. One person told me "I'm not slightly religious, but I have to pray every night using the same words in the same order."

The non-religious people whom I spoke to who had felt compelled to take up prayer after the onset of anorexia were all perturbed by this behaviour to some degree. I know I was annoyed with my nightly prayer ritual, as I have strong atheist beliefs.

In the middle ages, Anorexia Mirabilis was first documented, and those who went without food in the name of God were known as "The Starving Saints." So there is a clear religious link there. There have been studies that have looked into the religious themes in anorexia, but more from a cause and effect focus. .i.e. people who are religious are more likely to develop AN.[171][172] I am more interested in looking at it the other way around, not that religious beliefs lead to a greater incidence of anorexia, but that anorexia's mindset leads to a favoring of doctrine.

Hoarding food

"I have 43 iced lemon cake portions in the freezer" - Anon, adult in recovery from anorexia.

When I was a kid we had this Yorkshire Terrier called Harry who would rarely eat a treat if given it. Instead he would bury it in someone's bed and then guard it ferociously. In terms of my "safe" foods, I was rather like Harry. I would stockpile them as if I were expecting World War Three or a zombie apocalypse, and if anyone dare touch them I would feel furious.

"My poor husband had his head bitten off so many times for eating "my" foods it took years for him to relax in the kitchen." - T, adult in recovery from anorexia.

---

[171] Anorexia nervosa: Some connections with the religious attitude Huline-Dickens 2000

[172] Religious belief and anorexia nervosa Joughin

I could have a cupboard full of my special foods and still feel tetchy if someone else even looked at them. It makes sense that if your brain thinks that food is scarce you will feel the urge to hoard it, even if you can't eat it.

I've had enough clients upset by their own food hoarding to realise that I was not the only one who did this. If you notice that you are possessive around "your" foods, or that you stockpile them for safety, you will likely find that this form of OCD-ED mitigates itself as you come out of energy deficit as your brain will stop assuming scarcity. In the meantime, work on eating a wider range of foods to give your brain data to support the idea that you are not in a time of scarce resources.

Other Common OCD-ED

When I asked people in recovery from anorexia to tell me their OCD-ED I got pages of responses. I am going to list the most common occurring here:

- Having to be the last person to finish eating if with other people.
- Weighing yourself daily.
- Writing out calorie lists for every meal before eating.
- Eating in a specific order (usually leaving more enjoyable items for last).
- Eating a specific number of fruit and vegetables a day.
- Having a pre-eating ritual or "settling in" before a meal (most people mentioned a bathroom ritual before eating and cleaning/chores).
- Laying out the day's food in advance.
- Cleaning, handwashing, and other "contamination" practices before eating.
- Drinking specific amounts of water and other fluids.
- Counting bites taken or number of times food is chewed.
- Not trusting food made by other people.
- Choosing to be cold — not having heating on.
- Only buying discounted food and other items.
- Not being able to eat other than at designated times in the day.
- Only eating certain foods on certain days of the week.
- Only opening new packets of food on certain days of the week.

- Arranging food in cupboards.
- Having Best Before End rules such as not eating something within a month before the BBE on the packet.
- Saying prayers even when holding no religious beliefs.
- Saving and reusing plastic bags and other "disposable" items in an obsessive manner.
- Counting items such as nuts or crackers or chips.
- Excessively stirring foods or counting number of stir cycles.
- Always wanting hot food and drinks to be scorching hot.
- Always wanting food to look a certain way, or be arranged in an orderly manner on the plate. I.e. not dealing well with messy looking food.
- For any event that occurs on a daily basis, having to do it in a ritualised manner. This can be anything from putting makeup on to filling the dishwasher to making the bed.
- Having to savour every bite of food.
- Always leaving something on the plate.

OCD-ED stretches far past the obvious restriction-oriented behaviours. Those of us with a strong OCD element to our illness tend to find that there is some degree of ritual in everything we do. I will also stress again that for some people with anorexia, OCD-ED is not a large factor in the illness. Work with what you have, and if you have aspects of OCD-ED, then pay attention to overcoming them. Those neural pathways may weaken somewhat with nutritional restoration, but there will be an element that persists unless mental discipline and neural rewiring interventions are sought.

Rewiring OCD-ED

Just about every item listed in the Toolkit section is relevant for neural rewiring of OCD-ED. Overcoming OCD-ED is down to teaching the brain that it is safe to operate in a non-ritualized manner. The perfect way for you to do that is whatever way works for you.

While I believe that you have to have the goal of stopping the behaviour, I think that any way that you can get there is fair game. I have noticed that the same rule can be overcome in totally opposing ways for different people.

Here's an example. For one client, calorie counting was overcome by a very strict DRR (Detect, Reject, Redirect) approach where she would notice herself counting calories, reject the urge to continue or finish, and distract herself mentally by counting from 500 backwards until her brain was so confused with numbers that she had lost track of the calorie counting.

For another client, DRR simply didn't work for her with calorie counting. What did, was actually embracing the calorie counting as part of a pro-recovery tool. If she noticed herself counting calories, she took it as evidence that her brain was still hyper-focused on food and, therefore, in malnutrition. So every time she noticed she was counting calories she ate more food.. She found that, her desire to count calories became much less intense and naturally subsided. Here's a note from her:

"If I can't stop counting calories I might as well use it to my advantage."

You see, our brains keep doing things if those things are working to influence our behaviour. When you stop allowing calorie counting to lead to restriction, it stops working, and your brain will lose interest in doing it.

Then I had another client for whom the best approach to stop calorie counting was to make a "recovery rule" that if she started counting, she had to eat a cookie or chocolate, right then and there. This soon put a stop to her totting up.

What I hope to have illustrated, is that the same problem can be approached a multitude of different ways. There is no right or wrong: if it works it works. You will be able to work out what is effective for you so long as you are committed and determined. A good working communication with your support people will be the key as you can brainstorm and get your problem-solving heads in gear.

"My hope is that one day, I will be completely free of urge to do something I hate, that I will be strong enough to ignore the compulsion of the ED. That, to me, is true strength. " - E, adult in recovery from anorexia.

Section Four:

Anorexia Recovery Project Management

In this section of the book we will get right into how to project manage your recovery. Any project can be successful with enough organisation and good judgement, including your recovery.

For any project you will need to:
- ❏ Identify key players, team members and decision makers.
- ❏ Identify project goals, and objectives.
- ❏ Outcome tracking: define success criteria.
- ❏ Brainstorm potential pitfalls.
- ❏ Set project budget in terms of time and resources.
- ❏ Decide on a review process.
- ❏ Determine series of meetings among key players.

Then, as you get going, you will continually assess progress:
- ❏ Regularly access key player performance and switch out team members if needed.
- ❏ Identify problems and make changes accordingly.
- ❏ Identify successes and how to capitalize on these.
- ❏ Recalculate/reallocate budget as needed.
- ❏ Assess goal markers and targets.

Let's get on with this, shall we?

Chapter 14: Starting point realities

In this chapter, we will look at what you have right now in terms of resources and your starting point situation.

Resources

Identify key players, team members and decision makers
In a perfect world, everyone in anorexia recovery would be living with someone who was the perfect "recovery manager" — someone knowledgeable about anorexia who could help refeed and rehabilitate them.

In practice, we have to work with what we've got. In reality, even people who say that they treat eating disorders can give you bad advice or be trained in an outdated model of eating disorder treatment. It doesn't matter whom you work with so long as they know you, know what you are trying to achieve, and have the ability to learn about how they can best help you. I do think that for your own safety you should have someone on your team who is able to understand refeeding syndrome and blood work etc. So a medical doctor well versed in malnutrition or an RDN.

Support and *your* vital resources

The more support you have the better — so long as that is effective support. Effective support doesn't always have to be expensive support. Some of the most effective support is free: peer support. If you have been in treatment for years and not made the progress that you wanted, then that is not effective support. Effective support helps you make the changes that you need to make in order to reach full recovery. In this section I will describe some of what I consider to be the key support roles in this recovery project.

Your vital resources are specific to you. There should be no judgement involved over your choice to work with a therapist or not, or whether you use a dietitian, or anything else. This is all about you and what you need and find helpful.

"You need to work with an eating disorder expert. That expert might be a therapist, a dietician, a recovery coach, a parent … I don't care if your eating disorder expert is your local veterinarian. The title doesn't matter, the expertise matters!" - Therese Waterhaus, RD

The resources that you have available to you will differ for everyone. Some people are much more limited in a geographical sense to available help, other people do not have the financial means to afford the support they might like. I am going to list ideas of resources here, but keep in mind that you'll have to make the best of what your individual situation allows for. Even if your support is minimal, you can still eat food (once past the risk of refeeding syndrome). Not having adequate support currently in place, professional or otherwise, is not an excuse not to start recovery today. If you are working on your recovery project alone everything here still applies.

Things are changing. If your geographical location means that local help isn't possible, don't write off online resources as they are often incredibly supportive and effective. Be resourceful and look for support in non-traditional avenues. This is your recovery and how it looks is up to you.

Recovery Project Manager

I think it is a great idea to have someone who oversees your recovery and gets both the bigger picture, and the day-to-day details. Having someone else as an observer and feedback source is important as they can act as another pair of eyes to see what you don't see about yourself.

Your Recovery Project Manager should be someone who knows you well and either knows a lot about anorexia or is willing to learn. This is the person whom you will work most closely with, and be boldly honest with. As a recovery coach, this is usually my role, but you don't have to work with a professional recovery coach — anyone organised and invested in you getting better can fill this role. Often the most helpful aspect of working with another person is being able to bounce ideas off of them — anyone who can listen, learn, and give you feedback will do so long as you trust them and can communicate well with them.

If you have a partner, they might seem to be the obvious choice, but don't always assume that to be the case. I have worked with many couples and often the emotional drain is too much for a partner to be too deeply involved for a prolonged period of time. Also, while you may love your partner to bits, you might realise that they are not best suited for the job. One of the most common complaints that I hear when people are working with a partner as RPM, is that diligence is lacking. One woman said that her husband would come home from work too tired to ask her if she had eaten all her lunch, and this resulted in her skipping meals.

"If he doesn't ask, I feel like I don't have to do it."

Of course, the primary problem in the quote above is that the person in recovery has become dependent on her partner to always be asking her to eat. And that is not sustainable in the long term anyway. Your recovery depends on you, but if you do need that sort of accountability support it is vital you are a) able to ask for it and, b) given it.

Your RPM needs to be someone who is not afraid of or deterred by any anorexia-induced tantrums that you might (and are very likely to) encounter along the way. Incidentally, this may be another reason why not to have your partner as your RPM — most of us find we are more inclined to argue with people whom we are very close to. It is important to be honest with your RPM so you can both look at slip ups and failures and learn and move forward from them without making either of you feel blamed or despondent. If you can find an RPM who understands the doctor's lingo, even better — but with the internet these days just about anyone willing to learn can pick those things up pretty fast. I've known plenty of parent caregivers who are more clued up on anorexia medical complications than most doctors are.

I have known Registered Dietitians (RD) who have been fabulous RPMs. Dietitians can understand the medical lingo, and are often good for communicating with other support people, both professional and nonprofessional. So you can use a paid professional in this role if you prefer.

Your RPM should be willing to work with anyone else on your team including any family and friends. I frequently talk to my clients' family members, dietitians, therapists, and friends to help smooth communication.

Ideal skills:
- ★ Good planning skills — from goal setting to daily management.
- ★ Understanding of anorexia — and a willingness to educate themselves.
- ★ Time management skills — helping you keep on top of eating schedules etc.
- ★ Analytical skills — solving problems and helping you make decisions.
- ★ Objectivity — not allowing emotion to override.
- ★ Project focus — not allowing life's tangents to derail the recovery focus.
- ★ Compassion — recovery is hard!

- ★ Communication skills — needed if working with other therapists and family members, but most importantly communicating with you.
- ★ Availability — recovery doesn't take time off, while nobody can help you 24/7, availability is important.

The entire rest of this book, the exercises, planning, everything, should be done with your RPM and anyone else who is going to be a key player in this process — if you have them. While having other people to help is desirable, if you are working on your recovery project alone then don't think this means you can't achieve full recovery. You can. I recovered from anorexia without a therapist, without a dietitian, without any professional support whatsoever, and that was before the internet was as useful as it is too — so whilst that is not ideal, I know it is possible. If you can eat, you can reach full recovery. Other people to help will ease the process, but the only required ingredients are you, and food.

Your partner

If you have a supportive partner, it will behove you to bring them in on this whole process. If you have a good relationship with your partner include them in everything from doctor's appointments to therapy to mealtime support.

I have worked with many of my client's partners to bring them up to speed with understanding anorexia and helping them know what to do and say. I have generally found people to be wonderfully open to doing just about anything in order to see their loved one get well.

I have also known a couple of people whose partners were not interested in helping or were unable to be involved. We can work around this if that is the case. If you don't think that your partner will be helpful in your recovery, then don't rely on them for too much. Finding the balance between using other people for support but also being independent and not reliant on others is important.

Your family

Not everyone who enters recovery has family members available to act as a support, but if you do, use them. Family members can be your biggest on-the-ground, day-to-day anchors in recovery.

Be wary of the therapist who tries to convince you that your family members are to blame for your eating disorder. Energy deficit and genetics are to blame. Sure, if a family member stresses you out and this leads you to not want to eat as much, then this can worsen energy deficit — but that's a complication, not a cause. Therapists are picking at really easy targets when they blame parents for eating disorders. Blame won't get anyone recovered.

"Basically, I needed to go home and allow my parents to refeed me because I tried it on my own for too long. My fiance had become a sort of caretaker, and that wasn't the partnership we wanted. I wanted the fighting and stress to stop. I was either depressed or an anxious high

strung mess. I wanted a life. I wished so hard to turn back the clocks, so moving back home for three months was my time travel. No magic pill or wave of a wand or step in the DeLorean- just back to basics, honesty, transparency, and meal support to learn to live again." - Simon's Cat, adult in recovery from anorexia.

How you allow your family to help you is up to you. Sometimes financial support is needed if you cannot work due to your illness. Sometimes you'll use family for meal support, or helping you face certain challenges. Many of us are very wary of talking about anorexia with our families due to arguments we may have had in the past, but you will often find that people are more compassionate and willing to help when they understand what is going on. Consider that while talking to family about your illness can be stressful, it can also be a tremendous blessing. Anorexia can drive a wedge between you and those you love. Recovery not only mends your body and mind, but can work wonders on your relationships too.

As a recovery coach, I see my clients' parents, partners and other family members (regardless of the client's age) as valuable sources of information to myself, and support for the person whom I am working with. Generally the people who love you really do want to try and help — they may just be confused as to how the best way to do that is. With understanding and guidance, most families are supportive.

"My mom has been very helpful to me along this process. I would not be where I am now without her" - Ruthy, adult in recovery from anorexia

Peer support

"I realised there were many adults who were experiencing my difficulties, thinking my thoughts and finding their way through the same troubles. I realised I had people there to listen, take time to support and offer practical, compassionate and achievable suggestions that's making such a difference in my recovery." - Slack forum member

I am a fan of peer support for anorexia recovery. Here are a few of the reasons why:

1. People who have been through what you are going through can provide you with effective recovery tips, ideas, and resources.
2. Communicating with people who have felt similarly to the way you do now can help you feel less isolated.
3. Peer support is available online, and thus 24/7 accessible and convenient for times when you need it most.
4. Peer support is anything from totally free to affordably priced. This means you can use it more often.
5. Due to the more casual nature of peer support, anonymity, and lack of fear of judgement, many of us open up more which can result in us exposing and addressing problems that we were too ashamed to admit to in a clinical or familial setting.
6. Due to smartphones, we can receive messages from peer support friends anywhere at any time. This real time feedback and motivation helps us to shorten the feedback loop for pro-recovery action.

7. Online pro-recovery groups can allow us to feel a sense of belonging and togetherness without the physical comparisons that in-person groups can cause.
8. Speaking to individuals who have reached full recovery is priceless in terms of recovery motivation.

From a member of the online Slack group I created, for adults in active eating disorder recovery:

"There are scores of "recovery" groups online, but this is a very special one that is private, and free of charge. In different chat channels, we discuss, hold accountable, research, and reflect, while challenging each other to real change and life action. It is not a site for tourists, as it is honest and can be heavy. The beauty is that users are mature adults, and agree on the principle that eating is the only way forward."

There are downfalls, but these usually fall around what I would call "unstructured" peer support. That is, peer support where the person doing the support may not be fully recovered. In open peer support groups, such as those offered on social media, one has to be careful about taking advice from people who are in the woods themselves. For this reason I like support groups that are moderated and have guidelines.

For example, in the online private support group that I run, we have guidelines that all conversations have to be public. You are not allowed to post fattist comments about yourself or other people. You can't post anything indicating restriction, and nobody can indicate that they are exercising or participating in compensatory behaviours.

Basically, nothing that could be triggering or used the wrong way. To be accepted into the group, people have to be in active recovery — that means doing their best to eat unrestricted amounts of food, and resting.

"This is why this forum is priceless - immediate access to people who can show by example that the process can work" - Slack forum member

Another thing to consider with peer support is whether or not you are someone who gets overly fixated on comparing yourself to other people in recovery in a way that is not beneficial to you. This can still even happen with online groups as comparisons are not always about the physical aspects of the disorder. If you are somebody who does tend to compare too much, have a think about how you can overcome this.

Types of peer support

Online Groups

Online peer support groups are best in terms of accessibility and convenience. Online groups also have the benefit of no physical presence, and that means no physical comparison. However, they are the most subject to poor moderation as they are usually run by volunteers. When you look for an online peer support group, have a look for ones that are private, moderated, have guidelines, and are specific to your age. The challenges that adults face in recovery differ greatly from those of children and teens.

"Things I see and read here have so much more weight with me than if a professional said the same thing. Lived experience, insight, and encouragement is invaluable. I worked with a dietitian for years and never got anywhere, yet this Slack community had propelled me forward". - Slack forum member

Parents and partners of people with eating disorders can benefit from online support groups too.

In-person support groups

These are best once you are in a more stable place in recovery. Some people find that a nonspecific anxiety support group is just as helpful as an eating disorder specific group if they are worried that they will compare themselves physically to others in eating disorder recovery.

I am not a fan of in-person peer support groups for people who are still in nutritional rehabilitation. The comparison aspect is too much when people are underweight. This should be seen as a later-stage support possibility rather than early-stage. Personally, I think in-person support groups are riskier than online support groups in terms of triggers, and that there are few benefits of physically meeting over virtually meeting.

I do think that in-person support groups can be a big help to parents and partners of people with eating disorders.

Mentoring

If you find a long-term fully recovered mentor, this can really be beneficial. Someone who has been through recovery and is willing to lend an ear and some advice. I've heard stories of people experiencing mentors who they suspect are not in full recovery themselves, and this can be problematic. Mentors should not be underweight. Mentors should be able to eat without restrictions and have no food limitations. Mentors should not be compulsive exercisers. If a person is underweight and eats with restriction they cannot be a mentor to someone who is trying to eat unrestricted and recover. Mentors should not be giving medical advice.

Recovery coach

Eating disorder recovery coaching is when people who have recovered from eating disorders themselves offer help to others as a professional service.

A recovery coach needs to be educated in the most recent practices for treating eating disorders. There is currently no "standard" for a recovery coach, however, the best way to assess someone is their reputation. You want someone who is experienced and has a stellar reputation as an advocate for unrestricted eating, full nutritional restoration, and is an eating disorder specialist. No, a general life coach will not fit the bill. Remember, you need an eating disorder specialist on your team, not a generalist, and not someone who just took an online course in coaching.

Just like mentors, recovery coaches cannot be on any sort of restrictive diet, nor can they be people who exercise a lot. You need a recovery role model and someone who demonstrates what true freedom looks like — not someone who is a slave to the gym and restricts food. Recovery coaches should not be giving medical advice.

Unlike mentors, recovery coaches are professionals and help people in recovery for a living. This should be someone willing to offer support for you between sessions via text, email, phone etc.

Online meal support

One of the services that I set up with AEDRA is peer-led online meal support for adults who struggle to eat meals alone. Having a meal support session booked holds you accountable for eating, and will give you someone compassionate to talk to while you eat.

As mealtimes are often a very anxiety-provoking aspect of anorexia recovery, it makes sense that if a person in recovery needs mealtime support they should have it. It is not always possible for a family member to be there, and using a therapist would be too expensive due to the frequency. These are the reasons that I developed an online video-call solution using recovered and trained peers as meal support coaches.

"AEDRA is working wonders! I am afraid I would have relapsed by now had it not been for my coach supporting me through meal times and talking me through the process of transitioning to eating at home on my own!" - J, adult in recovery reflecting on AEDRA meal support.

Doctor

Having an Internal Medicine Physician who understands eating disorders well is a godsend. Unfortunately, the reality is that these sorts of doctors are few and far between. The vast majority of us have to advocate for ourselves in the doctor's office. If this is the case then it is well worth doing. I've had many lengthy discussions with client's doctors where I have pointed them in the direction of resources on things like refeeding syndrome and malnutrition complications. I have to say most of them have been very willing to research and learn.

You need a doctor for monitoring blood work, overseeing medical complications stemming from malnutrition, as well as to monitor physical symptoms and your vital signs.

Terrifyingly, many people (myself included here) have had very bad and even triggering experiences in doctor's offices. However I do believe that this is changing for the better, and it is so much safer to be working with a doctor than going it alone.

Inpatient Treatment

If you are at a very low weight, or physically unstable, you should go into Inpatient (IP) treatment to kick start your recovery process. If there is any doubt about your medical stability you have to avoid risks and seek a hospital setting initially. IP will not get you fully recovered, but it will get you started and get you to a physically more stable place from which you can continue. In a hospital setting you are in the safest place for medical emergencies that could come up in the initial refeeding stages.

In the USA there is a big market for residential treatment. I've not met many people who have made a full recovery due to help from a residential centre alone, but I do know people who say it jump started nutritional rehabilitation for them. It can expensive, and most adults find that when they leave and return to their home environment they slip back into eating disorder behaviours. Make sure that you have support in place when you transition back to your home environment.

Dietitian

Working with a dietitian is also optional. People have been recovering from malnutrition for a very long time — long before dietitians existed. Your mental (and sometimes physical) hunger is telling you how much and what to eat, so honestly if you can be accountable and respond to that, your own mental hunger is the best guide as to what your intake should be. However, a *good* dietitian does a lot more than just tell you what to eat and write meal plans.

You might be too fearful of your mental hunger to jump right in and respond to it. You might also be unable to give yourself "permission" to eat enough. In that case, having a dietitian to help you eat more may be an asset.

Here is a note from a good friend of mine, Therese Waterhaus, who also happens to be an RDN:

"If you do decide to use a dietitian, be sure to find an RDN who has had advanced training in eating disorder work. They might be credentialed by IAEDP or be a member of IFEDD (Int Federation of Eating Disorder Dietitians). Be sure to ask them what their training and experience is. If you are going the meal plan route, an RDN can create a meal plan or meal plan template, and at the same time they ought to be able to help you overcome any ideas that eating in normal fashion needs to be "perfect" and balanced all the time. A good RDN will help you work through and overcome food myths and misconceptions, simplify facts about foods, and help you build confidence in your ability to eat flexibly.

Additionally, a dietitian should be able to look at your recent food intake to determine if you are at risk of re-feeding syndrome and help you understand the mechanics of re-feeding and how this stage plays out in your body. They can coordinate with your doctor to analyze blood work, and help identify and correct any nutritional deficiencies. RDNs also have training in pharmacology and how various medications interact with nutrients and metabolism and sometimes this is helpful."

My biggest concern with people seeing a dietitian is that many dietitians spend their days trying to help people suppress their body weight and restrict food. The field in general is fat-phobic, and restricted eating is normal in our culture. So, finding the right dietitian — someone who understands anorexia, has a HAES approach, and encourages unrestricted eating — is vital.

Therapy

Some people with anorexia find therapy helpful. I think that is especially true for people who have other things going on, such as comorbid disorders. You can expect your anxiety to rise initially as you push yourself to eat more, and so these other things tend to also get worse before they get better. Having someone to help you process anxiety and other things can be a wonderful asset. I've met some people who say that their therapist was the key to their recovery. I have also met plenty of people who say their therapist was the key to their stagnancy. There is no right or wrong answer here as you are unique — and each therapist is a unique person too. I think my main issue is that it is so often assumed that seeing a therapist is essential to recovery, and for a good proportion of us, it really is not.

I never had therapy and made a very robust recovery. I believe not having therapy contributed to my ability to use common sense to refeed myself, as I saw my illness from a very physiological point of view. That is what worked for me, but that doesn't necessarily mean it is right for you. **You'll have to do what works for you**.

If you feel that therapy is an asset to your recovery, remember you are the customer and that your therapist is providing you with a service.

Not all therapists and therapies are created equal. You have to be discerning here too. If your therapist is not providing the services that you need, then look elsewhere.

"Official therapy did more harm than good, for sure. I'm sure I've banged on about it before, but basically they made me 'stay the same', telling me to keep doing exactly what I was doing (restricting and over-exercising) until they had a place for me on their 'outpatient pathway'. Disastrous, I had a really rapid decline. Since then I have been at best 'underwhelmed' and at worst 'devastated' by their treatment - they follow such ridiculously strict guidelines on how to treat people, assuming that everyone is the same." - R, adult in recovery from anorexia.

Some people find that therapies that focus on effective behavioural change without using psycho-analytical methods are helpful. A therapist specialising in Cognitive Behavioural Therapy (CBT), Acceptance and Commitment Therapy (ACT), or Dialectical Behavioral Therapy (DBT) who has an extensive understanding of eating disorders can provide effective tools in helping you overcome negative thought patterns and actions.

"I paid for a private ACT session once and it was great - it was via e-mail so I could write not speak (prefer that!) and do it in my own time" - R, adult in recovery from anorexia

The main thing that I want you to take away from this chapter on therapy is that therapy is subjective. Some types work for some people and not others. And whether you have any therapy at all should be entirely dependent on if it effectively helps you meet your recovery goals.

Cognitive Behavioral Therapy (CBT, CBT-BN and CBT-E)

The underlying notion here is that overvaluation of shape and weight and controlling shape and weight is at the core of all restrictive eating disorders. Thus, CBT works to counter this — at least traditionally. I am sure that you can see that this could be helpful, as can I. However, some CBT therapists (as well as other types of therapists) subscribe to the idea of discouraging patients from eating anything other than their prescribed meals and snacks, and this I generally disagree with for a person with a restrictive eating disorder as I believe it reinforces restriction.

While working with a CBT therapist may certainly help you with behavioural change, I think that many of the things that therapists label as therapy are common sense techniques that many people have already been using for decades in order to help them change their behaviours. The toolkit section of this book is probably an example of that. I never went to therapy, but with the help of a meditation practice and self-awareness, I was able to take the meditation techniques I was taught and develop my own ED-specific versions of them that helped my change my behaviour. The Toolkit section of this book are processes that helped me, you can and likely will develop your own processes that will help you. Maybe a therapist can help you do this faster. But set out to help yourself too.

"My CBT therapist is a godsend and I always come away from sessions more motivated to take recovery action." - EJ, adult in recovery from anorexia.

"CBT in england seems to be the gold standard but I never found it beneficial. It was almost just writing down what I already knew/ was common sense" - Es, adult in recovery from anorexia

Having spoken to a number of adults with anorexia who have tried CBT in the past, one thing that has been said to me a lot is that while CBT didn't help everyone with nutritional rehabilitation, it did provide them tools for life in terms of coping with anxiety and challenging negative thoughts. This is valuable.

Dialectical Behavioral Therapy (DBT)

DBT works on helping people accept change. It uses both cognitive and behavioral therapies to help people adopt healthy coping mechanisms. The core components are mindfulness based. It can help you learn how to relax, and chose alternative ways of dealing with stress. Incidentally, these are mindfulness skills that humans have been adopting and practicing to help manage stress for hundreds of years, just recently the therapy world repackaged it and started charging a lot of money for teaching you how to do it. 🙂

Cynicism aside, I do think that DBT can be helpful for many people. I also think that mindfulness in general can be helpful for many people.

In a similar vein as my comment above I believe that the majority of the stress that people with anorexia experience is due to ... having anorexia. Thus, long-term recovery works wonders. It is hard to be zen when one's body is starving.

Acceptance and Commitment Therapy (ACT)

This combines acceptance and mindfulness therapies alongside commitment to change. I've heard quite good things about ACT, as people say that it helps them find positive thoughts about themselves and therefore makes them more motivated to help themselves recover. Rather like connecting with one's purpose in life.

This is one sort of talk therapy that I think can only really do good. Helping someone find a reason to recover can't ever be a bad thing. But ... so long as that warm and fuzzy is followed up with eating food.

I like this comment from a person in recovery as I think it succinctly sums up ACT:

"ACT helped me because it made me identify what was important to me and I couldn't have what was important to me or what I valued unless I gained weight and kept it on." - Anon adult in recovery from anorexia

Psychoanalysis/Psychodynamic therapy

It is no secret that I am opposed to psychotherapy/psychodynamic therapy for anorexia treatment. I do not believe that we need to dig deep into our souls and search for an "underlying reason" as to why we are starving ourselves. But that's because I have always believed that there was a genetic element to this illness, and that the "big underlying reason" is genes. I do, however, understand that some people will have had trauma or other upset that caused them to go into energy deficit in the first place, but as outlined previously, when the brain is in malnutrition there is little effect that talking about the past will have on the future. Nutritional rehabilitation is needed first.

I believe that psychodynamic therapy, much more than any other type of therapy, confuses symptoms with causes; is based on theory rather than data, research, evidence, or common sense; often wrongly blames a patient's family for the illness; places meaning where there is none; and worst of all causes damage by prolonging the time between diagnosis and nutritional rehabilitation.

"I initially attended psychodynamic therapy due to the high anxiety levels I was experiencing. The therapist was so concerned that she referred me to a Consultant Psychiatrist who diagnosed me with anorexia. The psychiatrist informed me that unfortunately I did not meet the criteria for referral to the eating disorders unit. So I continued with the psychodynamic therapy for around a year by which time I had lost so much weight that when the therapist referred me back to the psychiatrist she was very concerned and immediately referred me to the eating disorders unit" - LC, adult in recovery from anorexia.

Much of my resistance to psychodynamic therapy probably comes from knowing adults with long-term eating disorders. I have known a number of people in their 30s, 40s and 50s who were diagnosed with anorexia in their early teens. They were treated with psychotherapy at that time, and thirty years later they are sicker than ever. They were stuck in an office with a therapist who did nothing but ask them about their relationships with their parents, or boyfriends. Their parents were excluded from the process and even blamed for the illness. Had they been treated with nutritional rehabilitation and given effective support for overcoming restrictive thoughts and behaviors I believe that they would have made it to full recovery half a lifetime ago.

Adult adaptations of Family-Based Treatment

Family Based Treatment is one of the approaches with the clearest evidence base for children and teens. It blew my mind when I watched the documentary "*Going Sane,*" to learn that therapists, once qualified, do not have to use evidence-based treatments when treating patients if they don't feel like it.[173] They have free reign to do what they like, and sometimes what a therapist likes and what works for the patient are not the same thing.

FBT is evidence based treatment for children and adolescents, because there is evidence to show that it works.[174] In a nutshell, FBT is a process by which parents take control of their child's health by feeding the child back to nutritional rehabilitation. It is taking control away from the illness, and therefore allowing the individual with the eating disorder to reach full health — at which point control is gradually handed back to them.

The concepts of FBT can be adapted to any situation because in a sense, FBT is peer support. It is on the ground support. It is in the home support. At its core, FBT is eating food support.

---

[173] http://goingsane.org/

[174] Evaluation of family treatments in adolescent anorexia nervosa: A pilot study. Le Grange, Eisler Dare, Russell. International Journal of Eating Disorders. 1992

Trauma therapy

I do not believe that trauma causes anorexia — but it can certainly contribute to the desire to restrict food, and complicate recovery. Trauma, and in fact stress, can of course cause lack of appetite which could ultimately lead to energy deficit. There are theories that the calming sensations that restriction gives a person with anorexia can lead to them using restriction as a means to self-soothe. I have observed and heard that nutritional rehabilitation can also cause trauma to resurface, which is a nasty side effect to say the least. You absolutely should not try and battle though that sort of thing alone.

If you have a history of trauma that is likely to compromise your ability to nutritionally rehabilitate, then you should seek professional help to deal with the trauma.

Finding a therapist

If you decide that therapy is for you, I think that the best advice about therapists can be found on online peer support groups. At the very least you will have people to help you figure out what are good questions to ask when interviewing a therapist. Via online groups you'll get a lot more opinions and can then weigh those all up more objectively. A couple of pointers from me would be to make sure any therapist you consider follows a HAES approach, and is not going to psychoanalyze your eating disorder or tell you that your family are to blame. They also have to understand the physical emergency state that malnutrition is.

Psychiatrist

A psychiatrist can help you with medication if you feel that you would benefit from it. I have known people who have really benefited from anxiety-reducing medication. I have also known people who have used it and not really benefitted. No judgement either way. I always say that anything that lowers anxiety in the recovery period is an asset so long as it is not a disordered behaviour. Antidepressants can also be helpful for some people.

If you do see a psychiatrist it is very important that they are an eating disorder specialist or willing to listen and gain understanding from someone who is. They need to know not to prescribe you anything that will artificially reduce your appetite. They also have to understand that some of your symptoms will be due to your state of malnutrition and that nutritional rehabilitation is the primary goal. Of course, you may be seeing a psychiatrist for comorbid disorders.

Teamwork, and honestly

Any project management book will tell you that good team communication is vital. That's true regardless of industry. From construction to software development, bad communication will wreak a project. You have to work as a team.

The first player here is you — the person in recovery. You may feel reluctant to talk about your illness due to shame or stigma. Most of us utterly hate talking about our anorexia behaviours because we are ashamed of them. Hopefully this book and the examples in it will help you see that everyone with anorexia does weird crazy shit. It's not just you at all. Take me, stealing loo rolls as an example of that! Anorexia makes us do ridiculous things, but rather than feel ashamed, feel proud of yourself for trying to change something that wasn't your fault in the first place. You didn't willfully create the behaviours, the anorexia response did, but you are going to fix them.

The people who are trying to help you recover are not there to judge you. They cannot help you unless you are transparent with them about what you are thinking and feeling, your behaviours, and the fears that are trapping you and stopping you moving forward.

The other players are the people on your team. They have to be able to talk to one another too. If you are working with anyone who is unwilling to be transparent and communicate well with you and others they are going to stall the progress you make.

The problems I see most here are: a) people in recovery being too ashamed of behaviours to talk about them, and, b) therapists not communicating with other team members (parents, spouses, etc).

It's all very well having a plan, but if you don't tell the people doing the work on the ground what that plan is, it won't work out well.

Team communication is critical. As is organisation, and that is what the next section is about.

Action: List your resources and start to brainstorm people whom you will ask to help

Section Five:

Project

Execution

This section we are going to finally get into the nitty gritty of planning your recovery.

Your understanding that you can do this is the most important piece in any of this. You can do anything if you are determined. You can do anything if you set your mind to it. In understanding your illness better, you will work out what you need to do in order to reach full recovery.

Chapter 15: Recovery Project Kick Off

Time to get started. You don't need to plan out your whole recovery in detail in order to start eating more food. You should have started doing that already. However, if you are working with support from other people it can be beneficial for you to get together and plan some things. This is where you lay out everything on the table and work out as a team the steps you will take to get to where you want to be. If you are working on this solo, you will still find the following structure useful in your own planning.

Goals

1. Establish recovery process structure in terms of key people involved and roles.
2. Establish short term, medium, and long term goals and objectives.
3. Define success.
4. Establish progress assessment.
5. Establish a sustainable recovery plan in terms of food, restriction and OCD-ED.

Establish Key People And Roles

Action: Questions this chapter should help you answer:

- Do you have a Recovery Project Manager or someone to closely help you?
- Are you going to be working with a therapist, dietitian, or any other professionals?
- Who will be helping with meal planning?
- Who will be helping in regards to checking in on restriction and OCD-ED?
- Will you be seeing a doctor for bloodwork and other checkups regularly?
- Will you be weighed, if so by who and how often?
- Are there going to be other family members involved for support?
- Do you have or will you look for a peer support network?
- Do you need meal support? If yes, who will do this?
- What are you going to use as a fun/stress outlet other than exercise?
- Who/what are you going to use as distraction from negative emotions before, during, or after eating?
- Do you have childcare duties that may be temporarily affected by the recovery process? If so who will be helping out there?

Resources can be anything from a therapist to an art class to a cat — and I don't value any resource higher or lower than any other. For me, my cat was much more of a recovery aid than any of my doctors were. For you, the opposite might be true. No judgement. You use what you need.

This includes things that make you happy. Recovery is hard, so you have to consider things that give you a mental outlet and make life worth living as a resource. You don't have to stick with the usual suggestions. If music makes you happy you might want to think about spending money on piano lessons — but with a caveat, you have to give double importance to things that directly result in you eating more food. (And if you have an exercise compulsion, you can't use movement until you are past that movement compulsion, even if it makes you happy.)

A pragmatic approach would be to sit down and first of all work out a realistic budget for recovery expenditure. Then, do a cost-benefit analysis for all your possible resources and see what is feasible, and what gives you the best return on your investment. For each resource, see if you can work out the return on investment by weighing the cost to the effectiveness.

Assessing Your Resources

Adopting an agile and responsive attitude

Being agile and responsive means adapting to the environment. If you have a spouse or partner present, then you can work out how they can help you. If you have a good friend or housemate who is able to help, then maybe they can help. If you are living alone, then you can use resources such as online peer support at mealtimes. If you have a combination of situations that differ from day to day, then you can work out how to be fluid and use what you have available to you at any one time.

"My dad has kept me going. And for so long my therapist told me it was inappropriate for him to be helping me so closely in recovery." ~ Mike, adult in recovery from anorexia.

Make the very best out of any given circumstances. Situations change, and you may need to change the way that you are doing things accordingly. Additionally, during the recovery process, you will change. When you change, tactics may have to change too.

I can tell you that my malnourished brain had a hard time with "agile and responsive." I was very fearful of change, and had trouble making decisions about when to make changes. Most of us struggle with inflexibility and insight when we are malnourished.[175][176] This is why you will probably do better if you are able to work with someone else to help you see the rigidity and challenge it.

---

[175] Impaired executive functioning influences verbal memory in anorexia nervosa J. Oltra-Cucarellaa, .et al.

[176] Neuropsychological investigation of decision-making in anorexia nervosa, Cavedini, et al

Are your resources relevant?

Go over current and potential resources available to you and assess for relevance. You will also continue to assess all resources that you are using on a weekly basis. After every therapy/dietitian/professional session give the helpfulness of the session a rating out of ten. If sessions are regularly less than 7/10 helpful then reconsider the relevance of that resource.

I hear far too many stories about underweight individuals who have been trying to recover and seeing the same therapist for two years and haven't gained any weight. Rather than keep spending time and money on a tactic that is not yielding a return on your investment, try switching it up and refreshing your approach.

When things work, stick with them. But, when they stop working, don't be slow to change and try something else. Be creative. Problem solve.

"I really love my therapist, but I have been seeing her for four years now … and it's rather the elephant in the room as to why nothing much has really changed in that time."- Anon, adult in recovery from anorexia

Whilst it can be argued that "things take time to take effect" and that it may be foolhardy to not give any one process long enough, I would counter that by pointing out that nutritional restoration is dependent on eating more food. When we stop psychoanalysing food restriction and start focusing instead on increasing intake as the primary goal, then anything that doesn't have the effect of increasing intake is a waste of time in that period. When nutritional rehabilitation has been achieved and is no longer the primary goal, then a change in goal for that period may mean that slower more therapeutic methods are employed.

For a resource to be effective, it has to:
1) Help you nutritionally rehabilitate.
2) Help you stop restriction and OCD-ED behaviours.
3) Bring you happiness and comfort that indirectly helps you with effectiveness categories 1 and 2.

The most important points to remember when evaluating resources:
- Everyone is an individual and responds differently to different resources.
- You don't have to use a resource that is not working for you.
- Effectiveness needs to mean that the resource is helping you gain weight, stop restriction and OCD-ED, or indirectly contribute to doing this by reducing stress.
- Resource importance should be weighted towards resources that help you gain weight and stop restriction and OCD-ED as these are the most important goals.
- Good communication is crucial.

Dealing with limited financial resources

I'm not going to pretend money isn't often a barrier to getting the support you need. If the "free" resources that you are being provided by your national healthcare or health insurance are not effective, then you may consider finding better help privately.

If you don't have the means to pay for private services, your options here are to a) put up and shut up and hope for the best, b) borrow money or apply for some sort of financial support to help you get the help you need, or c) try to recreate or simulate the resources that you think that you need but cannot afford.

For example, if you have had DBT therapy in the past and know that it is helpful to you but cannot afford it now, there are books and online resources that you can try out. Is this as good as a great DBT therapist? No. Is it better than nothing at all? Yes. Is it something that you can do right now while you try and find a good affordable therapist? Yes.

Likewise, with just about any other type of resource other than the strictly medical aspects. Can't afford art therapy? Look for a meetup group or local art collective to join. Can't make it to the local Eating Disorder Recovery support group because you have to look after the kids? Find an online group, or better still prioritise your recovery project and ask someone to watch the children for you.

When you cannot afford something that you think that you need, or for whatever other reason it seems out of reach: get creative. One of the pluses of having anorexia genetics is that you are a smart person. You can work this out.

Action: List the resources that you cannot currently afford but would like, and brainstorm alternatives.

Location and resources

Planning and choosing your resources in terms of professional and other support is all very well in areas where that support is available. I am only too aware that for many of you, good professional support is not available. That's unfortunate, but it doesn't mean that you cannot be successful. If you do not have local professional resources have a think about what you need. See if you can come up with a next-best alternative. More and more, online resources are turning out to be accessible and effective.

Another problem that some people are still faced with is lack of local support due to stigma and misunderstanding about eating disorders in general. I have worked with people in countries in Europe, China, India and other parts of the world where eating disorders are really poorly understood. Again, do your best to work out what you need and where you can get that. Sometimes we don't just have to think outside the box in order to get what we need in recovery, we have to build our own door out of the box!

Action: List resources that you would like to use, but don't have geographical access to, and brainstorm alternatives.

Identify Project Goals And Objectives

You cannot work out how to get where you want to go until you know where you are. Let's assess your current situation. You should assess from a relatively detached standpoint so that your emotion about your situation doesn't derail you. Put yourself in a third person seat and assess your current situation as if this were a project at work.

Assessment benefits from external eyes. Due to anosognosia (that's the medical term for when you don't know that you are as unwell as you really are) it is unrealistic to think that you would be able to impartially assess the truth of your situation — but that is not to say that your opinion is completely invalid on all things. There are a couple of areas that are notoriously difficult for us to self-assess and are therefore good to talk with other people and get feedback on. Mainly:

1. How much weight we have to gain in order to be healthy. Remember your brain typically magnifies what is on your body, and you do not always perceive the truth.
2. Our current state of physical health. High pain threshold and anosognosia can make us believe we are fine when we are not.
3. The adequacy of our own intake — people with anorexia are really prone to thinking that they are eating enough when they are not.
4. Our output: exercise, movement etc. We aren't that great at perceiving that we are doing a lot when we are.
5. The amount of help that we need from others. I'm a fabulous example of someone with a disastrous mental block around asking for help.

Things only you will be really able to assess (and therefore need to be brutally honest about):

1. Current state of mental health (i.e volume of restrictive thoughts, mental hunger, emotion around food etc).
2. OCD-ED behaviours.
3. Restriction: the non-obvious sort.
4. How much you really want to eat. Your mental hunger guides you here.

Your recovery planning should be a joint effort with whomever is helping you, but there will be some areas where I advise you to listen to what the people helping you think and going along with their suggestions much more than you allow your own judgement to influence things. If anyone tells you that you are not eating enough, you have to accept that and eat more. If anyone tells you that you need to gain more weight; don't argue. Of course you won't agree all the time, if eating more and gaining weight felt okay then you would not be in the mess you are now. You will likely have to place trust with other people for certain things.

Nutritional Rehabilitation Goals

Next, let's look at your nutritional rehabilitation goals. If you are underweight — i.e. you have been using restriction, exercise, or other compensatory behaviours to suppress your natural bodyweight — then nutritional rehabilitation via unrestricted eating should lead to the restoration of your natural, unsuppressed bodyweight.

This chapter should help you answer the following questions:

1. Can you respond to mental and physical hunger at all times?
2. Can you eat unrestricted. Do you understand what that means?
3. Do you need help from a dietitian to kick start the goal of eating unrestricted?
4. What other support do you need to move towards unrestricted eating?

Recovery Goal One: Unrestricted eating

(Remember, the information here is general concept. You are an individual and your recovery will reflect that.)

When you are underweight and suppressing your bodyweight via restriction, exercise, or compensatory behaviours, your body will be giving your brain feedback that you need to eat more food. This leads to mental hunger; something that is not present in a person who is not restricting.

Therefore, unrestricted eating and responding to mental hunger should see you to full weight restoration. Your mental hunger will likely remain high until you are nutritionally rehabilitated. Remember, you have been eating abnormally low amounts of foods, so in order to get back to a balanced state of health, you will likely have to eat abnormally high amounts of foods.

As you become nutritionally rehabilitated, your mental hunger levels should naturally decrease. This means that unrestricted eating will look different as you move into a more energetically balanced state. You will no longer desire to eat the whole house. Rather, in the same way one doesn't continue to gasp for breath after one has enough air, you will desire to eat enough to maintain your weight restored body. As your body moves into energy balance its need/desire for massive amounts of food decreases, and your mental hunger will decrease until one day you are left with normal, physical, hunger cues.

The mental hunger is there for a reason. When you are in energy balance, nutritionally rehabilitated, and eating regularly and well, it dissipates.

Quit the food judgement

Anorexia loves to judge everything about food. *When* you eat. *Why* you eat. *How much* you eat. And of course, *what* you eat.

Unrestricted eating means that you respond to hunger — be it physical hunger cues or mental hunger cues — at all times. It also means that you do not judge the type of food that you want to eat, and do not negotiate by eating "safe" foods when what you really want is a big slice of cake.

Mental hunger as your intake guide

I used my mental hunger as my guide as to the quantity of food I ate in the nutritional rehabilitation stage of recovery. It clicked that the constant thinking about food was my body communicating to me what it needed. In order to recover this way, you have to be brutally honest and accountable with yourself. If you genuinely are not in touch with your mental hunger, or are able to block it out as a minority of people with anorexia do seem able to do, then work with an RDN to establish an intake that will help you nutritionally rehabilitate. Even if you are taking the meal plan route, you can still challenge restriction and rewire by treating the meal plan like a minimum and making brave decisions to eat scary foods. Remember, this is your recovery, do what works for you in the present moment.

The catch ...

The catch is that you have to be honest. And accountable.

I know that personally I had two opposing forces present when it came to responding to hunger. I was thinking about food, but somehow that part of my brain terrified of food could convince me that I was not. Deep down I knew that I was ... but admitting that, even to myself, was scary. Thankfully I finally managed to find that brutal and unapologetic honesty. I was hungry!

Does this mean I perfectly ate to mental hunger all the time? Of course not. I made mistakes. But I learned. I also got to a point in recovery, where if I didn't eat enough at one meal, my body would take over and I would feast eat at the next meal, and so I learned that restriction had stopped "working" for me anyway. That kind of forced me into not even bothering to try and restrict. At the beginning there was certainly an impatience to my hunger. But then as I nutritionally rehabilitated, I moved on to times — sporadic at first, but gradually becoming more persistent — where there was less urgency to eating, and it felt less frantic. More "normal." I was getting windows of having an increasingly "ordinary" relationship with food. The overall result was that as my body came into a place of nutrition, my eating leveled itself out accordingly.

So, the big question here is: do you have the power and the control to be honest about your mental hunger, and accountable to yourself for responding to it?

Here's a clue: If you are underweight, you have to be eating enough to restore your bodyweight. Do not allow yourself to believe that you can eat unrestricted and also stay underweight.

It is absolutely your responsibility to gain weight and get out of malnutrition and you can't allow anything to detract from the simplicity of this. That is your anorexia getting the better of you. Eating unrestricted will mean you eat enough to gain the weight you need to gain. If that is not happening be suspicious of your ability to really respond to mental hunger and increase what you are eating.

If the concept of unrestricted eating feels cloudy, or if you are in any doubt that you can jump in to unrestricted eating and be accountable for really *really* responding to mental and physical hunger, then you need to work out what you need in order to get you there. Think outside of the box. There are more on ideas of how to jump start yourself later in this chapter.

Respond to mental hunger

1. If you are thinking about food, you have to eat food.
2. Eat what you desire without compromise or judgement.

It feels radically over simplified, doesn't it?

For years you have probably been told that refeeding yourself is this complicated exact science. That you have to micromanage your diet. Yet, here I am telling you: just eat what you really want to eat in the quantity that you *really* want to eat it. Surely that can't be it?

I think that people likely recovered from anorexia before we even knew what a calorie was. And I believe that humans certainly would have worked out how to recover from famine and malnutrition using common sense and animal instincts. All the information I needed about how much to eat, was right there in my mental hunger.

It will be messy!

Don't expect yourself to straight out know what you want to eat all the time. Don't expect decisions to always feel easy. Don't expect your mental hunger to always be crystal clear. Some days you may eat so much it hurts. Other days hunger may feel missing or disconnected, and you'll get to the end of the day and realise you didn't eat enough. One of the biggest issues that people in recovery from anorexia have is second guessing every decision they make and overthinking it all. That, and catastrophizing everything.

If a decision feels murky, just do your best — and remember that when you are underweight, eating is never the "wrong" thing to do. If you don't know what you want to eat, just eat something, and don't fret if it didn't feel like the "right" thing. If you eat so much that you feel over-full, don't freak out about it. Your body will manage, and it needs the fuel. If you think that you may have accidentally restricted, don't beat yourself up; rather, learn, and change things. Just do your best and don't expect things to feel tidy. Do not allow this to be overly complicated. Channel your inner mammal and drop the human tendency to overthink.

Other paths to unrestricted eating

There is never just one way of doing something. I advocate for responding to mental hunger and unrestricted eating because I think this is the fastest path to true freedom. When you push back against the "safe" rules you neurally rewire at the same time as nutritionally rehabilitating. However, it took me years of trying to recover before I got here. Recovery is messy. While unrestricted eating is your primary goal, you may need some alternative routes to it.

It's not like I just woke up one day, realised I was emaciated, and decided to eat unrestricted. Nope. I was actually already theoretically "weight restored" when I clicked that my constant thinking about food was actually hunger and that I should respond to it. I had already gained a significant amount of weight in a very restrictive, binge/purge (exercise) manner over the years leading up to that. And it was through doing so, and still being as mentally messed up around food and exercise as before, that led me to understand that there was more to full recovery than eating enough to get my weight to a point where it was in the green so far as a BMI chart was concerned. My own path to unrestricted eating was very messy, and I made over ten years' worth of mistakes to get to where I am now. So don't ever write yourself off. Rather, problem solve: What do you need in order to get to where you want to be? And what have you learned by getting to where you are now?

If you cannot be accountable to responding to mental hunger at this time, then there are other options such as working with a set intake and building on this, or working with a dietitian to help you figure out how to eat more. If you are working on a set intake, then try eating over and above your meal plan each day. If you can go over and above your meal plan with every meal and snack then even better — that is you taking control!

Some people do really well with having a set plan, and a goal of eating more at every meal in a semi-structured way. So sitting down at the start of each day and loosely planning the minimum that they will go *over* the "plan." Or even planning to have an "unplanned" extra, such as going into a cafe and allowing your partner/friend to choose what you eat alongside your usual afternoon snack. So that way, you can challenge your need for having to plan every bite you take, whilst also having enough structure that you feel safer as you gain confidence.

Other people do better with a set plan, but having the mission of eating over and above that at every meal, without pre-planning how. Accountability is key here, so that you don't allow yourself to wimp out at the last moment. I think that you can find a balance that suits you between structured meal plans and also trying your best to be accountable to responding to mental hunger on top of this. As you grow in confidence, you will find you become more able to respond to eating what you want when you want, and not being fearful of eating more.

Whatever route you choose, be wary of feeling too safe and comfortable about what you are eating, as this likely means you are not pushing yourself hard enough. When you challenge your anorexia neural pathways you will probably feel unsure, and unsafe — unfortunately, these uneasy feelings are proof that you are changing. It is important to be challenging yourself enough, and to not fall into complacency.

Answer the question: "what is unrestricted eating, and what do I need to do in order to get there?"

Weight gain

If you are underweight, nutritional rehabilitation means weight gain. You may need support to help you deal with that truth, and if that is the case work out what you need and seek out that support. You are going to gain weight. *You need* to gain weight. I think the sooner you can own this idea, the better. Personally, I would repeat the worlds *"I need to gain weight,"* to myself over and over in my head (don't say it out loud or people will look at you funny). I needed to brainwash myself with that truth when I was underweight, because otherwise my anorexia brain would convince me to be scared of eating enough.

"Strong, authentic people do not suppress their natural body weight." This was another thought that I played over and over in my head to help me deal with the reality of weight gain. I suggest you find a mantra that works for you, and brainwash yourself with it.

Being underweight is a medical danger that should not be underestimated regardless of how fine you feel. You have to have regular medical check ups.

The real bulk of the concepts behind the suggestions in this chapter were outlined in Section Two of this book. You may want to reflect back on that chapter.

Bodyweight goals

Personally, I do not believe that it is helpful, realistic, or necessary to set a target weight. You have to get yourself above the lowest "healthy" weight for your height and then keep going until your physical symptoms of malnutrition disappear, and your mental state shows signs of shifting. (More on that later)

That's my opinion, as an adult who put herself through recovery. I understand that target weight may be more helpful for parents who are refeeding children and young adults. What I tend to observe, is that a person's true healthy weight cannot be defined by any resource other than that person's body. And that trying to define a person's healthy weight by a chart or a graph can lead to weight suppression more often than not.

Health At Every Size (HAES)

Health At Every Size is a movement towards celebrating body diversity. Erroneously, it is often thought that people in larger bodies suffer poorer health *because* they are in larger bodies. HAES states that this is not the case, and that a person in a larger body cannot be determined less healthy than a person in a smaller body simply on the grounds of weight.

What remains incredibly concerning to me is that many healthcare professionals not only discriminate negatively against people in larger bodies, but they assume that people who are in smaller bodies are healthy and therefore ignore signs of ill health. Doctors are too fast to tell overweight people to lose weight, and too slow to tell underweight people to gain weight.

Women in energy deficit may lose their periods and their doctors don't consider that they need to gain weight or that they are in a state of malnutrition. People can present to their doctors displaying physical and mental signs of malnutrition and their doctors cannot see that being underweight is harming their bodies. In many cases people who are underweight are congratulated for being so, and encouraged to remain in a state of malnutrition. People who are in larger bodies are encouraged to eat in a restrictive and disordered manner, and to exercise excessively. Ironically, medical professionals are often the worst offenders for encouraging malnutrition and disordered eating behaviours. Even worse, many eating disorder professionals discriminate against larger bodies by telling their clients to eat less when they pass a BMI of 19 or 20. This is weight discrimination and is not demonstrating an understanding that people come in all shapes and sizes.

It drives me mad that many professionals consider that all people reach nutritional rehabilitation and weight restoration at a BMI of 19. This is ludicrous! Most people in the general public have a natural weight that is higher than a BMI 19, so how can it be assumed that all people are healthy at this low weight? If a person's natural, genetically predisposed weight is BMI 24, then they are underweight and will display the symptoms of energy deficit until they are at a BMI of 24. This is why many people who are discharged from treatment because they reached a BMI of 19 never reach full recovery — they never actually got to *their* unrestricted, energy balanced, bodyweight.

It gets worse: people in recovery from anorexia are told that they now need to reduce their meal plan (restrict what they are eating) when they reach a BMI of 19. It seems impossible to be true that a person in the primary stages of recovery from anorexia would be told to eat less by a medical professional only after putting on a marginal amount of weight, but it happens all the time.

If a person in a larger body goes to the doctor, they are often told that their health problems will be remedied if they lose weight. This is size discrimination. Just being in a larger body doesn't make you unhealthy, and it is often the case that losing weight will not solve other health complications. In fact, if a person is genetically supposed to be in a larger body, losing weight would be unhealthy for them.

A Health At Every Size approach is vital for people in recovery from eating disorders. Ask your physician about this. If you are working with someone who either doesn't support HAES, or doesn't know what it really is, move on. It will be worth your while to find somebody better educated.

Dealing with fat phobia

Unfortunately, we live in a society where many people, including most healthcare professionals, do not accept body diversity. Most doctors have been taught that having fat on one's body is a threat to health, and do not support a HAES approach.

I have often had to educate my clients' doctors, therapists, family and friends as to how they demonstrate implicit weight biases. Doctors, and other people who have professional status, tend to be able to do the most damage because as a client you will find you give their opinions more consideration due to the perceived authority they have over you.

Do not be afraid to tell your doctor or any other professional that you disagree with their opinion. Sometimes you have to be really brave. A common example of this is when your doctor or therapist tells you that you are recovered because you are now at a "healthy" BMI, but deep down you know that you are still restricting, and that you likely need to eat more and gain more weight in order to reach full nutritional rehabilitation (and mental freedom). I know it is much harder when you have active anorexia to advocate for your right to gain more weight — but you have to do it.

This is your body, and your life. Do not allow other people's weight discrimination issues stop you achieving the full physical health and mental freedom that you deserve.

Action: Talk to your support individuals about HAES, and make sure everyone understands the importance of this approach.

What is my healthy weight minimum?

I hate the idea of setting a target weight. It always gets treated in the anorexia brain as a maximum. Nobody has a weight that they stay at. We naturally fluctuate in terms of what we weigh. At any one time you have a weight range rather than a weight.

I never set a "target" weight for myself. Rather, I looked for an upward trajectory of weight gain. If you eat unrestricted amounts of food you should gain weight, but when your body reaches it's happy, unsuppressed, natural weight your mental hunger will decrease accordingly and your hunger and intake should settle at whatever it is your body needs to sustain itself. We don't need to set you a target weight because your body will sort all that out and get to where it needs to be if you provide it with with unrestricted fuel.

So what is the equation for calculating your healthy weight minimum?
Eat unrestricted amounts of food. Gain weight. If you are not gaining weight, eat more. Keep going until your physical state and mental states shift out of malnutrition.

Don't treat your body like a machine — and don't allow anyone else to either.

Mental state rather than target weight

Once you start to get into the healthy weight range and the physical signs of malnutrition begin to amend themselves, the clues that indicate healing is happening become evident in your mental state.

If you are still having a high volume of restrictive thoughts and mental hunger, then this indicates that anorexia is still active and that you have not been eating enough food for long enough to convince your brain that the famine is over. Or, and this takes honestly, are you still restricting and trying to suppress your weight gain? So long as you continue challenging restrictive thoughts and eat without restriction you will get there.

For me, an indicator that I had achieved a weight at which I was out of energy deficit and switching out of the scarcity mindset was that I was not as scared at the thought of gaining weight anymore. When I was underweight the idea of gaining 10lbs terrified me. At my recovered weight I have zero emotional reaction to the thought of gaining 10lbs. Ziltch.

Aim high. Start seeing weight gain as a trophy.

I know this sounds vague. I know that you hate how vague that is. I know that you want me to be able to give you a formula that tells you exactly where your weight should be. That wanting to know is generated by the anorexia system that hates ambiguity because weight gain is perceived as a threat. Think of accepting the unknownness of your final weight as part of the mental work that you have to do. Stop questioning. Stop "what-iffing."

Adopt the "Fuck It! Attitude" to your recovery weight. Eat food and quit worrying about it. Your weight has to go up and no matter what it is anorexia won't like that. Where did listening to your anorexia mind ever get you anyway?

Indicators of mental state shift

★ Dissipation of mental hunger.
★ Reduced fear of gaining weight.

- ★ Being able to eat without guilt, anxiety, shame, restrictive thoughts, or any other negative emotions.
- ★ Restriction ceases to feel rewarding.
- ★ Feeling less drive to participate in OCD-ED and other compulsive behaviours.
- ★ Reduction in hyper-awareness of food and other people eating.
- ★ Being able to eat any new or unplanned food without spikes in anxiety.
- ★ Movement compulsions dissipate.
- ★ Reduction in general anxiety.

These are just some of the indicators of your brain coming out of energy deficit and the scarcity mindset. The overall effect most of us feel is a return of the pre-eating disorder versions of ourselves (if you were old enough at onset to know what that was). The most notable and wonderful marker for me was the dissipation of my mental hunger. Although it makes perfect sense that when you are nutritionally rehabilitated the mental hunger goes as it no longer has a purpose, it was still a welcome surprise to me when I realised I was not thinking about food every moment of the day. So many years of having mental hunger had led me to see it as a normal state of being for me. That, thankfully, wasn't true. My mental hunger was there trying to tell me to eat more, and when it no longer needed to do that, it left. My brain became free to think of other, much more interesting things.

If your brain moves out of energy deficit for long enough, it will begin to turn off the famine response. With that, your fear of "overfeeding" is no longer required, nor is the compulsion to move. Whilst there may still be neural pathways in place supporting these behaviours, many of us find that the driver behind them is weaker. It becomes easier and easier to go against the behaviours when you are moving out of the scarcity mindset. Behaviours and rituals that used to feel like a solid brick wall start to feel like a rickety old fence that will fall over if you push against it. The thought of eating spontaneously stops pulling up a solid *"Hell No!"* fear response and you notice that you feel curious, and more open to that offer of a slice of cake as you walk past Starbucks. Disobeying your entrenched behaviours gets easier and easier. If you can take the seat of the observer and watch this process within yourself, it is fascinating to live through.

As energy deficit is a chronic state that takes months of being in daily energy surplus to amend, you cannot rely on weight gain alone as a marker of amending energy deficit. This is why I prefer to use the term "nutritional rehabilitation." While weight gain is a necessary step, weight gain alone is not the end of the story. Your body and brain have to heal from the effects of malnutrition and therefore may require a higher than average food intake for a while post weight gain. Hence, pay attention to your mental state rather than your weight in order to determine if you are in energy balance or not.

Rate of weight gain

I do not think it is helpful or advisable to try and control the rate at which you put on weight. Don't judge it either! If you suppress your rate of weight gain by not responding fully to physical and mental hunger, you are restricting. Restriction feeds anorexia. Restriction tells your brain that there is not enough food in the environment. Therefore, the anorexia response remains active.

It has been shown that people put on weight in different ways.[177] Rather like we all grow at different rates when we are kids. Some people increase rapidly at the start and then level out; some increase steadily throughout; some increase slowly at the start and then speed up. Either way, you end up where you need to be — no micromanaging required. Gaining fast versus gaining slow doesn't mean that your final weight is any different. However, your body does it, you don't get to control it, and it will all work out in the end. Don't fret about it. Don't judge it. Roll with it. And remember, trying to control your rate of weight gain is an act of restriction.

If you eat in accordance to mental hunger you will gain weight and end up settling at your healthy, unsuppressed, body weight. If you aren't able to jump in and eat unrestricted, or if you are working with a meal plan, then make sure you are fast to increase what you are eating if you are not gaining weight. Nutritional rehabilitation is the primary focus, don't lose sight of that. Don't be scared if you gain weight fast to start with (as some of us do) and don't decrease what you are eating if your mental hunger is asking you to eat more. Your body will increase metabolism when it is ready to do so.

Your nutritional rehabilitation goals needn't be complicated. If you eat without restriction and in accordance to your mental hunger you should eat enough to gain weight. If you can't do that, then use a Safety Net intake approach to force yourself to eat enough to gain

---

[177] Int J Eat Disord. 2017 Weight gain trajectories in hospital-based treatment of anorexia nervosa.Makhzoumi et al.

weight. If you are underweight and not gaining weight, the simple truth is you are not eating enough and need to eat more, so change something.

Note: while physical signs of healing such as return of menstrual cycle in women could be considered a nutritional rehabilitation progress marker, they are not anything more than that and are certainly not indicative that a healthy weight has been reached. Some people get their periods back at low weights and others don't lose their periods at all. We cannot determine anything too conclusive from it.

Should you know your own weight?

Totally up to you. You are an adult, so the decision will be yours to make.

You do not have to know your weight if you don't want to. I have successfully worked with clients who have gained weight, and neither of us have actually known the number. We've gone by dress size and clothing fit to indicate that change is happening; family members giving me feedback that they are noticing change; and doctors assessing the medical side of things. If you are eating unrestricted, weight gain is a given. We don't need to interfere with it. I tend to prefer to focus on enabling and supporting unrestricted eating and taking the focus away from a dumb number on a scale that means nothing anyway.

Alternatively, I have worked with clients where they have known their weight. That's fine too — so long as the focus is on unrestrictive eating rather than the number.

And then I've had clients who didn't want to know their weight, but wanted me to know it so they blind weighed and got a family member or their doctor to send me the result. There are many ways of dealing with the scale, from not at all, to using it sparingly.

When it comes to the question of you knowing your own weight be honest about what works for you. Some people are fine about knowing their weight or want to challenge their reactions to it and they weigh themselves. Some people prefer to do this with another support person there with them. Some prefer to do it alone. And some don't do it at all. There is no right or wrong answer here. You do what works for you. If weighing yourself is its own compulsion, however, you probably want to challenge that and abstain from doing so. Be honest and tell people what you need. If you don't know what you need, err on the side of caution and don't look at the scale.

Action: Have a think about and discuss with your support people whether or not you should know your weight.

If you do weigh yourself, don't weigh any more than once a week and my suggestion is that you don't weigh on the same day every week as this can create a boogie day in our heads.

Weight gain anxiety

You have anorexia. The illness is defined by fear of eating which results in fear of weight gain. You are going to have anxiety about gaining weight regardless of how "on board" you are with recovery. My own fear of weight gain always fascinated and confused me. I didn't even like being thin, yet I was still scared of gaining weight. Bonkers!

For some of you, being thin will be something that you perceive as desirable. You may have triggered anorexia initially by going on a diet in the first place because you were unaccepting of your unsuppressed body weight. You still have to eat unrestricted, and you still have to gain weight. You will have to work on accepting your beautiful body the way it was designed to be. Your weight gain anxiety will likely be greater than that of those of us who don't enjoy being thin. But you can and you will grow to accept and respect your unsuppressed body if you stick with it and give your brain time to begin to see it as home. Put the support and resources in place that you need to help you deal with your weight gain anxiety, because full recovery is not possible in a weight suppressed body.

Regardless of how you perceive thin — desirable or undesirable — the fears generated by anorexia are not necessarily entirely your fears. I could logically know I needed to gain weight and want to gain weight, but still be scared of doing it. It was never my fear. It was anorexia-generated. Hence, an indicator of full recovery is loss of a good proportion of that fear. I do believe, that we have the ability to neurally rewire this fear of weight gain fully regardless of what the original source was — just for some people this means more and ongoing work to do so.

Action: Talk to your support people and come up with a proactive plan to help you deal with weight gain anxiety. Have a look through the toolkit and see what items are relevant to you. I recommend PNSP to visualise yourself in a larger body and work on remaining calm whilst doing so.

As a feminist, I was able to use my anger at the oppression of women to help fuel me into taking action to gain weight. One can't very well be a feminist and suppress one's own weight to suit a thin ideal. I was not suppressing my weight to suit a thin ideal, but everyone assumed I was. I hated to think of people looking at me and thinking I was starving myself in order to fit into a cultural ideal that I strongly disagreed with. When my weight-gain anxiety started to bite at me I would bring those thoughts of wanting to present a strong, confident, full bodied woman to the world into the forefront of my mind.

That image of a non-conformist, fearless woman helped *me*. What will help you?

Action: See if you can answer the following questions (and of course, use other people to help you with these to get external viewpoints).

1. For now, should I know my weight or not?
2. What are the mental state markers that I should be using to determine my state of nutritional rehabilitation. How can I use these markers to counter anorexia thoughts that tell me I no longer need to gain weight?
3. What do I need in terms of support for dealing with weight-gain anxiety?

Recovery Goal Two: Rewire Restriction

Anorexia is a very judgemental disorder. A lot of the restriction we experience comes down to judgement. Judgement of "too much." Judgement of "bad quality" or "unhealthy."

The rewiring process is about proving to your brain that the judgements that you have around food are not required. You do that by doing the opposite of what the judgemental thoughts tell you.

Action: Have a think about the following:
1. What are some of the obvious and less obvious ways that I restrict?
2. What are redirects I can use when I detect these urges to restrict?
3. What foods do I avoid eating that I have to focus on eating?
4. Who can I contact/talk to/call/text to help me with restrictive thoughts in the moment?
5. What environmental cues or situations make it easier for me to restrict, and how can I avoid or overcome them?

Eating in an unrestricted manner is very important in terms of rewiring the brain. In order to tackle something as intangible as restrictive thoughts and behaviours, you have to be deeply honest and open to seeing the restriction in your behaviours.

Restriction is like an onion. There is the obvious outer layer — not eating. Once you pull that away and start eating, you will notice all levels of restriction are present. All sorts of rules about what you can eat and when and how much. They all have to go. Every last one. As you move through the recovery process, you will notice new restrictive thoughts and behaviours crop up. It can feel discouraging, but once you really get into the groove of running into the fear and challenging restriction head on, that will change.

Restriction list

Action: Start by making a list of the most obvious, to the least obvious ways that you restrict.

Examples of obvious restriction:

> ➤ Not eating all the food on my plate.
> ➤ Not allowing myself to eat when hungry if it's not a mealtime.
> ➤ Not allowing myself to eat more than X calories a day.
> ➤ Delaying eating breakfast until 9am.

Examples of non-obvious restriction:

> ➤ Not responding to mental hunger.
> ➤ Not admitting to liking certain foods .
> ➤ Eating lower calorie food rather than higher calorie versions.
> ➤ Claiming an allergy to certain foods when no allergy really exists.

Yes, you'll have to be honest, especially with the latter part of the list. For years I swore that I didn't like pizza. Turns out that not liking pizza was an anorexia truth, not a Tabitha truth. Being able to tell the difference was a took a lot of work. Many of us feel ashamed of this more covert restriction, but don't allow those feelings to hold you back. You are doing the right thing when you call out the restrictive thoughts and actions. This is what allows you to overcome them.

Restriction redirects

Next step is for every restrictive thought or behaviour, make a goal that will help you change it. This is a redirect. (DRR)

These goals are not quite as straightforward as nutritional rehabilitation goals.

Examples of restriction	Examples of goals
Delaying eating	Never delay eating
Saving food until later	Eating throughout the day
Compensating after eating more than usual at one meal by eating less at another	See meals and snacks as independent events
Ignoring mental hunger	If thinking about food, eat food!
Restricting caloric intake	Never count calories and eat freely
Buying only discounted food	Buying the food you want

These are some of the more common ways that we restrict food. You will have plenty of ways that are unique to you. You will have situation dependant restriction that crops up in different places. You will have timing restriction that is relevant to your lifestyle. You will have restriction that depends on the level of exercise or movement that you did. It all has to stop. Break all the rules all the time. No half measures. When you are making restriction recovery goals get it all out there and start working on it all at the same time. Restriction is like a leaky bucket. If you only plug one hole the water will just come out stronger in other areas. Plug all the holes at once.

Recovery Goal Three: Rewire OCD-ED

OCD-ED is covered in detail in Section Four, you may want to reflect on that section to help you plan here. If you don't have any OCD-ED, (compulsive exercise. movement, or ritualised behaviours) then of course you can skip this section.

Action: Answer the following questions:
1. What are your most prevalent OCD-ED behaviors?
2. What are your redirects (list)?
3. What environmental cues or situations provoke OCD-ED and how can you overcome or avoid them?
4. What can you use as a distraction to stop you from carrying out OCD-ED routines?
5. What can you use to make you sit down and rest more overall?
6. Who can you contact for support when you are struggling with the urge to act on an OCD-ED thought?

OCD-ED thoughts and behaviours, like restriction, have to be tackled in mass. It can take some time to fully disentangle all your OCD-ED from your life. In my case it turned out that almost everything I did and every move I made was OCD-ED. From my morning pre-breakfast ritual to the way I stirred my yoghurt at lunch. From the mid-afternoon walk to the shops to taking the bins out.

This is another goal area that you will have to be deeply honest with yourself about. If you are in any doubt about why you do any of the things that you do: assume OCD-ED and plan to resist the urge to do that thing.

In the same way you did for restriction planning, make a list of OCD-ED behaviours and goals.

Examples of OCD-ED	Examples of goals
Eating with same cutlery of utensils	Be able to eat with any cutlery
Having to clean the kitchen before and/or after eating	Relax and stop the cleaning
Compulsive exercise	No exercise
Eating in a certain order	No food rituals
Counting calories	Never count calories
Measuring food	No measuring, no food limits

Those little things that add up to an uncomfortable existence

Relevant to this planning section are the little things that you make yourself do, (or don't allow yourself to do) that add up to an uncomfortable existence. For example, me not allowing myself to take the car to the grocery store that was only a five-minute walk away. This in itself was not a huge act of self-harm, but it combined with so many other little discomforts that accumulated to make me dread getting out of bed in the morning.

Action: Answer the following questions:

1. What are the tiny, almost insignificant ways I make daily living harder than it should be?

2. How can I make life easier for myself?

Tactical planning

Now we will make a list of tactics that you can implement to help you overcome each behaviour, be it restriction or OCD-ED. Ironically, many of the traits that you use to enable these behaviours — determination, stubbornness, grit etc — are the very same traits that will help you ace overcoming them. Dr Laura Hill,[178] one of the leading figures in the neuroscience behind eating disorders, talks about using your character traits to your advantage in recovery. I thoroughly agree with her there!

Action: For each major goal you have, answer the following questions:

1. What are your character traits that will benefit your ability to change this behaviour?
E.g. Determination, stubbornness, self-compassion, bloody-mindedness, courage. What is relevant to this goal?

2. What are your circumstances/thought patterns that will be problematic to your ability to change this behaviour and how can you sidestep or work around these problematic elements?
Take, for instance, the common OCD-ED behaviour of measuring food. Many of us justify this behaviour, claiming it at least helps us to eat a minimum. The counter thought, or redirect, to this would be that because there is no maximum amount of food that you can eat, then if you are in any doubt that you poured enough cereal without measuring it, you simply pour and eat some more.

---

[178]http://tabithafarrar.com/podcast/tabitha-talks-dr-laura-hill-neurobiology-behind-eating-disorders/

I know that this is a scary idea — and that is exactly why we need to do it. Run into the fear.

Another example would be the delaying eating food. Many of us do this as we fear having eaten our allotted amount and then being hungry and having to wait a long time to eat again, so we delay eating. Your redirect thought for this would be to tell yourself that you can eat as much as you want and the more the better — therefore you can eat again later too if you are hungry. What often comes up as a problematic element here, is being afraid of not being hungry in time for your next meal if you increase your snacks in between meals. The redirect for that would be to realistic — most of us are hungry all the time in recovery. You'll be able to eat okay!

What I hope to have generated with those examples is the way that your anorexia brain can try and weasel out of your good intentions and generate other thoughts that seem to make restriction make sense. Try and identify these, and bring it all back to your primary focus of rejecting restrictive and/or OCD behaviours in order to achieve freedom from them.

Action: For some of your goals you will be able to draw on past experience. List things that might have worked for you in the past and see if they are relevant here.

For others you will have to try some new tactics. How you redirect a behaviour or thought has to be down to what works for you. Don't be afraid to try new things if a redirect stops working.

Brainstorm where your resistance comes up and have pre-planned responses to that restriction. Below I have illustrated this. While it may seem like overkill on the organisational front to spell it all out like this for every behaviour and every goal you have, don't be fooled. When you get hit by that moment of anxiety you will need reassurance not to have to follow through with whatever behaviour it is that you are trying to redirect. It is worth taking the time to do this properly.

Behaviour	Goal	Obstacle	Redirect/ Tool
Measuring food	Stop	Will I get enough? Fear of going "over"	Eat more There is no such thing as too much food
Pacing	Stop	Pure anxiety/ movement compulsion	Breathing/ mindfulness/ text someone for help
Delaying breakfast	Eat earlier	Fear of hunger later	You can eat more later too!
Cleaning kitchen before eating	Stop	Anxiety/ OCD-ED	5 min meditation before eating rather than cleaning
Only allowing one bread item a day	Eat bread unrestricted	Anxiety/fear	Eat a bread item as soon as you get restrictive thoughts a

Goals Summary

By now, you should have a list of nutritional rehabilitation goals, restriction elimination goals, and OCD-ED cessation goals. In addition to this, you should have a detailed list of restrictive and OCD-ED thoughts and behaviours written out with a plan on how to overcome and redirect. And of course add any goals that you have that are specific to you that don't fit into any of those categories.

Remember, these are your starting point tactics. You can and should change any tactics should they cease to be effective.

Define success

You've got your goals, now's the time to figure out what success looks like. Before I even get into this chapter I want to make one thing clear: success is not black and white. There is some success in every failure, and there is some failure in every success. The point of defining success is not so that you can get all down on yourself for realising all the things you are not yet doing. It is about having a reference for understanding what is working, and what is not.

You want to get an idea of:
1.   What unrestricted eating success looks like.
2.   What OCD-ED cessation success looks like.

Weight gain success

If you are underweight, you should be noticing weight gain as a natural, optimal and intentional result of unrestricted eating. If your weight gain isn't happening, reflect and change something.

The hard part here, is that at the start of recovery, when you still get a reward feeling for energy deficit, you will likely be scared when you know you are gaining weight. The same concept applies throughout recovery — run into that fear.

Weight gain is your trophy. If you don't feel good about gaining weight, fake it. Tell yourself that you do. Repeat it over and over in your head and brainwash those weight-loss oriented neural pathways out. Weight gain has to happen. You cannot recover and remain underweight, so work out what you need to do in order to not freak out about it. Determine the support you need too, and be proactive.

When I surrendered to unrestricted eating — yes, totally eating as my mental hunger wanted me to — I ate a hell of a lot of food. And yes, I gained weight. But here's the important message in all this: nothing bad happened. I ate. I ate a ludicrous amount of food. My body gained weight up to where it needed to be, then my hunger subsided and my eating naturally reduced to what it is now. My body sorted it all out.

The even more important point I need to make here, is that it was scarier for me to eat a restrictive amount of food and gain 2lbs a week than it was for me to eat an unrestricted amount of food and gain more.

I'll elaborate. When I ate only a couple thousand calories a day and my malnourished body began to gain weight on that, it scared me. I would step on the scale at the end of the week, see it rise, and reflect on the fact that I had been starving hungry all week and I still gained weight. I could have eaten so much more. That felt out of control. Conversely, when I went gung-ho and ate as much as my mental hunger really wanted, I stepped on the scale and saw the weight gain — but I felt in control. Of course I had gained weight! I had eaten with that intent!

It is soul destroying to be eating a little more but still restricting heavily and gain weight. It is devastating to see the scale rise and reflect on the past week and realise that you had been hungry the whole time. I decided I was going to take control of my own weight gain by eating enough to really gain weight. As I have said numerous times, there is no one-size fits all recovery method. But I want you to be brave. And I want you to remove any arbitrary limits that have been put on your ability to eat and gain weight. I want you to take control and gain weight your way — but that has to mean taking action and making it happen.

We all gain weight at different rates. Any weight gain is a success, but don't settle for "almost" recovered.

Restriction and OCD-ED elimination success

In the early stages of recovery, success will look like actually getting better at detecting restriction and OCD-ED. Once you start to "see" it more (which is the main benefit of making that list and writing it all down), it will begin to drive you nuts, so your motivation to stop these thoughts and behaviours usually follows naturally.

If you have identified a behaviour, and determined a redirect, your success evaluation will look at the effectiveness of the redirect. Also, if the redirect is successful, you want to double check that it did not result in a compensatory behaviour later on. For example, if the restriction rule that you are trying to eliminate is only allowing yourself to eat one bread item a day, and your redirect was to eat as much bread as desired, then a compensatory behaviour would have been restricting other foods, or going on a walk motivated by desire to burn calories. We often try to negate the increase in eating by increasing movement, or vice versa. Be very careful to assess for this, and be very honest with yourself and your support peeps about it. If you don't expose what is going on, you cannot plan to overcome it. Do not allow stopping one compensatory behaviour to result in others developing to replace it. Trust me, whilst it feels like a relief at the time, you only end up with an even more tangled web of behaviours and thought patterns to try and unravel.

Ultimately, success in terms of restriction and OCD-ED thoughts and behaviours looks like the elimination of compulsive behaviours but also the absence of the stress and anxiety that is usually associated with not doing them. The latter will lag; so when you first stop the behaviours you can expect anxiety to rise. Of course it will, your brain has been trained to believe that these behaviours are important and that stopping them is dangerous. Your brain is going want to pitch a bit of a fit.

Stopping compulsive behaviours is not dangerous, and we have to retrain your wonderful brain by giving it data to the contrary. Every time you don't act on an urge to restrict or OCD-ED you are giving your brain data that it is safe not to, so long as you stay calm. This is where those breathing techniques and tools come in. I was often surprised at how quickly my brain stopped invoking an anxiety response when I didn't conform to restriction or OCD-ED urges — but some behaviours took longer than others to overcome. You just have to keep going until the behaviours and thoughts are gone and the anxiety is gone.

The reduction in anxiety will happen slowly. It will become evident in moments like someone asking if you want to take the dog for a walk on a sunny day and you replying that you would rather relax and watch the rest of the Netflix show you just started. Because that was what you wanted to do with your life in that moment on that day. And you'll surprise even yourself with that response, and beam inwardly as you realise that you feel absolutely fine about staying on the sofa as they leash up the dog and head out the door. It was these tiny freedoms that people without anorexia take for granted that would fill me with bliss and gratitude for my recovery.

Tracking Success:

Action: Here are some things that I want you to keep in mind during the process of goal setting and progress assessment:

1. What are the markers that you will use to determine success?
2. How will you evaluate your progress and decide when it is time to change tactics?
3. How can you check in on a daily basis to make sure that your recovery tactics are still working?
4. For every goal that you have, make sure that you have a Plan A and a Plan B to pull in so that you can move to Plan B quickly if you need to.

Learning And Adapting As You Go

The gift of failure

Eating disorders are not stationary targets. They move as your recovery progresses. Therefore, something that was working initially can stop working after a while. Likewise, some tactics that make sense on paper don't work when we put them into action. That's okay! It's fantastic actually because with every slip up, blip and tumble you learn something about your eating disorder that you can ultimately use against it!

Failure is a gift — but only if you learn from it.

In order to learn from failure, you have to be able to detach yourself from the emotional reaction that we all have to it. That emotional reaction to failure, like all other emotions, evolved with a functional purpose. We feel bad when we don't achieve what we wanted to achieve, and this is what keeps humans ambitious. To some extent, this would have originally kept us alive too. If Mrs Cavemen didn't feel crappy about not getting the buffalo that she needed in order to feed her family, then she wouldn't have built a better spear, would she?

I'm a pro at failing. Failing is my scientific specialty. I failed at recovery for years. I failed in just about every way possible; l learned. I paid attention to where and how I failed and I used every nugget of failure information I could gather in order to finally put it all together and eat my way into full recovery.

In a sense, this whole book is based on lessons from failures. Every success has a plethora of failures behind it. Failure is where the clues to success lie. Do not waste your time getting all down in the dumps when something doesn't go right. Get excited; use the information and adapt.

Learning from blips

You will have "blips" in recovery. Therefore, now that you know that, you can remove the personal blame and feeling like a failure, and know that these learning experiences make you stronger. You are growing your ability to make decisions, and exercising more and more freedom. There are consequences for all decisions, and you can use these in your favor. Part of recovery is recognizing those consequences. Let's look at it from a project management perspective:

1. What happened and what can I learn to prevent it from happening again?
2. What were the events leading up to the blip?
3. What were the warning signs and how can I be more observant of them? How was I ignoring those signs, and what did it feel like?
4. How did I react after it happened?
5. What might have been a better way to react?
6. Who/what resources should I use if this happens again?

Learning is in every experience, good and bad. Say you did not eat a big enough breakfast because on Thursday your kid had to be in school half an hour earlier, and you got up late. Maybe this tension increased your desire to restrict, and you panicked. So, keeping plenty of snacks handy, and in the car, is a way to counter this and promote action that is right for you. This is an organization issue; not a character issue. No big deal.

If you have had previous "failed" recovery attempts don't despair! This just means you have a plethora of experience and knowledge about your eating disorder. There is so much information in the past that you can use to inform this current project.

Action:
1. Have a think back over some times that stand out to you as blips or failures in recovery. What can you learn from these past experiences?
2. Think back to past treatment experiences if you have them, what would you change about those in hindsight? What have you learnt from those experiences.

Common indications that you need to change or rethink tactics

- Stagnancy. If you get stuck in terms of making success with responding to physical and mental hunger via unrestricted eating, or even with your ability to overcome OCD-ED behaviours for more than a couple of days, you should talk to your support friends and come up with a plan to get things moving again.
- Not reaching goals. For example: Not gaining weight if underweight. This isn't always a signal that what you are doing is wrong. Sometimes it can mean that you are on the right

track, you just need to push yourself harder to eat more. However, if you are missing this goal by a long way, or continually, this indicates that you need to change your strategy. Maybe you need more support to help you with unrestricted eating.

Chapter 16: Being Realistic. Being An Adult

Plans are all very well. Life doesn't always conform.

Lifestyle hurdles

In an ideal world you would be a millionaire, have a supportive partner and family, have a cheerful housemaid and live on a beach in Hawaii. The reality, for me at least, was that I was single, lived in a dingy flat somewhere in rainy England, had a crappy job, and my closest friend was a cat called Sprout.

I didn't have kids, but I will talk about them in this section as I have worked with a number of parents. This chapter is about common lifestyle hurdles that you may need to be prepared for in active recovery.

Work/Money considerations

You may not have the money that you need in order to employ certain recovery resources. Work comes into this, as many people find themselves unable to work due to the illness, or at least the anxiety generated by the illness or some other medical problem.

I always say that if you can possibly stop working during the initial stages of recovery at least then this is the best option. If you can take a year off, even better! That time can be used to totally reset all habitual behaviour and get back to the blank slate. Another reason for this is that many of us realise that our preferred occupation is actually anorexia-geared, and that recovery brings a desire to change track.

I worked as a nutritionist and personal trainer, and also a chef when I was sick with anorexia because my world revolved around thinking about food and working out. I actually got fired from one gym for spending an entire shift on the stairclimber despite multiple warnings that employees were not supposed to exercise whilst on duty. Anyway, you get the picture: all day every day was spent in a gym. Then my evenings were spent cooking food in a pub kitchen. Once I had switched out of the anorexia mindset, the thought of returning to either of these jobs filled me with dread. The thought of being a personal trainer actually appalled me. I am sure that you can imagine why for me at least, my old career was not an option.

In the later stages of recovery I think it can be healthy to start experimenting with what you might want to do as a career, but without committing or getting overly invested. I changed more still in the years following my nutritional rehabilitation.

If you have to work to pay the rent and there are no other options, then consider shifting to a low-stress, low-activity job. It is no coincidence that many people with anorexia work on-your-feet jobs such as bartending, waiting, or manual work. Have an honest think about these things or talk it through with someone. Ultimately you want to do what is right for greatest recovery success with the options that you have. If you cannot afford not to work, switch waiting tables for sitting at a supermarket checkout or doing some low-key admin for a local business. Please consider how incredibly critical it is to rest your exhausted, undernourished body. Remember, your career is a moot point if you don't reach full recovery anyway. There is no point in having a great job if you are miserable inside. Recovery is more important than any short-term fears you have about switching jobs for a while. Jobs that involve walking, lifting, standing or any other type of physical activity can be an opportunity for the eating disorder to engage.

Schoolwork has to be talked about too. Going away to university was almost the nail in the coffin for me personally. Not so much the workload as I cannot really claim I went to lectures, but more the free rein for my anorexia to make all the decisions and call all the shots. Had I stayed close to family and friends I would have received more of the pro-recovery support I desperately needed. Some of my clients have not been able to focus on schoolwork due to the malnutrition brain fog (note: not everyone gets the brain fog, some of us remain very mentally able to focus despite our malnutrition) so have had to take time out for that reason. Others have been able to focus fine on schoolwork, but found recovery gets pushed aside when they are studying. Conversely, some people find that a desire to do well in school provides extra motivation to get better and helps them eat more. There is no right or wrong here, there is only what works for you that needs to be considered.

Here is a note from MK, a client, who writes:

"I let go of work, even as it was an at-home editing position. It was entirely too stressful, and I couldn't eat the way I needed. I didn't like the job, anyways, though I fought hard to keep it going. I realized that it was

deficit nature that kept me attached to things like this, even though I hated it. It felt like something, and I was afraid to see what was on the other side I quit going to my graduate classes, too. I stayed at home, ate, talked with Tabitha, ate, napped, and ate, and ended up with the best grades of all my classmates. More importantly, I had to let go of driving my car. No one with low weight and mental illness can be trusted to manage a speeding loaded weapon. So, I got help with transportation, and set weight goals for driving. Then, when I was driving, I set a restoration rule: I had to meet the minimum intake the day before, in order to put the keys in the ignition. Even then, it was only to go to the market and back. When you are operating on death fumes for so long, you lose judgement, and I had to be honest with these things."

Action: Questions to help you figure out your work plan:

1. If you are working or at school, can you afford to take some time off to concentrate on recovery? On the flip side, can you physically and mentally afford to remain in your work or school situation?
2. How long can you take off in terms of savings and financial resources?
3. If you are at school and do have a heavy workload, is this going to impact your recovery in a good or bad manner?
4. How long can you take off in terms of long-term career impact? Is it true that, perhaps, a better career lies ahead, when you take the time off that you need?
5. If you are to continue working/studying, would it behove you to talk to your boss/colleagues/teachers about your recovery process and explain the allowances that you may need to have in order to eat, and to attend medical appointments.

If you will continue to work, identify situations at work that may cause the eating disorder an opportunity, and plan ahead on how to tackle them. For example:

➔ Standing desks should be set to sitting at all times.

➔ Take the elevator rather than the stairs.

➔ Do not engage with colleagues who may discuss diets.

➔ No compulsive exercising or walking at lunchtime.

➔ Actually eating a large lunch at lunchtime, and having numerous food breaks throughout the day, even if your colleagues are not eating.

Family Dynamics

Every person has different family dynamics, family commitments, and levels of family support. There are so many variables at play here that the best approach is to talk about family aspects broadly with your recovery support people and your family. Good family relations are always a benefit to recovery. Unfavourable family relations cannot be allowed to get in the way. The vast majority of the time, family members are an asset.

"Snappy Turtle Syndrome!"

Sometimes the support that we receive from well-meaning and concerned family members can feel smothering. I used to become incredibly irritable and downright aggressive with my mother or my partner should either one of them express concern over my weight, my eating, or my levels of exercise. Let's have a look at that for a moment:

As explained in Section One, a malnourished body is not a particularly happy one. Couple that with an innate fear of eating more. When we are underweight and under stress, we tend to be aggressive and defensive — especially when it comes to things that our brains perceive as threats. As also explained in Section One, the scarcity mindset alters our perception and we assess more food to be a threat. Therefore, when people lovingly inquire if we have eaten enough, we bite their heads of — or at least feel like we want to.

I was so irritable and inclined to snap people's heads off when I was underweight that my nickname, given to me by one of my best friends at the time, was "Snappy Turtle." Hence, I call the recovery irritability "Snappy Turtle Syndrome."

Do not take Snappy Turtle Syndrome personally. It means nothing about you as a person. It indicates nothing about the type of person you will be once you are fully recovered. It doesn't mean that you don't love the people close to you. All it means is that your brain and body are in a state of stress, and that food, eating, and overcoming anorexia thought patterns is needed.

Even when we have declared to the world (or close family) that we are in recovery and that the plan is weight gain, we can still feel that prickly annoyance when people ask us about it sometimes. Or when they remind us that we are supposed to be having second helpings of dessert after dinner.

I have, in the past, specifically asked my husband to remind me to eat more than usual, then bitten his head off when he does. From a partner's or parent's point of view, this can be hurtful and confusing. Therefore, it is important that nobody takes these incidents to heart.

How to deal with Snappy Turtle Syndrome
Toolkit suggestions: DRR, Urge Surf, Breathing

It is understandable as to why you feel irritable and want to bite people's heads off. It is still not okay. It is not okay because you have the control and ability not to be a Snappy Turtle just the same way you have the control and ability not to restrict or follow through with any other OCD-ED thoughts or behaviours. Surf the urge to snap. Smile —

even if you have to force it. Breathe, and say "thank you very much dear ... I will have another slice of cake after all."

Laugh. Find humour in the absurdity of the situation. Laughter shifts the brain from fight or flight aggression into logical and reasoned thinking.

Because, after all, the fact that you want to murder someone just for offering you a slice of cake is indicative that you really, really, should be eating more cake.

Family commitments

Action: Some family-oriented questions to think about:

1. What family commitments could interfere with recovery?
2. Can you forgo these for the process of recovery? If not, how can you make sure they don't have any negative impact on progress?
3. Do you need to involve or talk to family members to explain what is happening?
4. Who/what do you have available to help you with children/animals while you recover?

If you have children, adjustments may have to be made for the recovery period. For example, a lady whom I was working with as a recovery coach had to allow her partner to take over the morning school run with the kids so that she could get meal support at breakfast time. The biggest obstacle for her partner and I was actually convincing her to allow this temporary measure while she got more accustomed to eating breakfast. This is the case more often than not; family members are happy to jump in and help, but we feel guilty for allowing people to help. This is something that we have to get over in recovery. You need what you need. Let others help.

Another woman I worked with was a single parent with no partner support. She had always walked her children to school, but she did admit it was compulsive as on the weekend when there was not school she felt she had to make up an excuse to walk that same distance every morning and again in the afternoon. I suggested for the recovery period that she stop this school walk, but that wasn't straightforward as she genuinely didn't feel that allowing the children to do it alone was safe. She also didn't have a car. This is exactly the sort of situation where it would be so much easier to "let it go" and brush off the behaviour, but I think it is important to think out of the box and make changes that allow these behavioural neural pathways to shift. In the end we were able to work out a school run shift sharing between other family members and her good friend who lived close by. After a month or so of that arrangement it was summer holidays, and by the time the autumn term started up she was in a strong enough place in her recovery to not allow that short walk to become a compulsion. But don't worry, we had that school run shift sharing solution all ready to go had it started to feel compulsive again.

Kids are one thing, but you may have elderly parents or other people who are dependent on you. You will have to talk about how these things may affect your recovery and what you need to do to overcome them. Don't forget to include care of animals in your family commitments planning. Animals are family too. Dog walking is something that can fast become compulsive when you have anorexia, so you may have to find a dog walker for a while.

Chapter 17: Mealtimes

Food is vital. Mealtimes can be difficult. Planning helps. Support, in whatever form you prefer it, is crucial.

Where you are at vs. where you want to be:

Current eating status: Restricted, fear-based eating.
Eating goal: Unrestricted eating.

So often, anorexia reduces food to calories and/or macronutrients. Ironically, eating disorder treatment specialists also often reduce food to calories and macronutrients. I have to be honest, the "exchanges" meal plans where you get to choose two proteins and two carbs or whatever at breakfast makes me cringe. When you reduce food to a collection of macronutrients, you turn it into a math equation. When you do this, you are giving the eating disorder power by overcomplicating something humans have been doing since the beginning of mankind.

Adults with anorexia do not have to be taught how to eat.

Humans have been cooking and celebrating the taste of food for thousands of years before anyone even knew what a calorie or a nutrient was. If you are human, you know how to eat.

Adults with anorexia have to be *empowered* to eat without restriction.

Find your basic mealtime structure

We've covered unrestricted eating. Now for putting that into action. You need to eat at regular intervals throughout the day, and you also need to eat as frequently as your mental hunger desires. I suggest having 3 meals and 3 snacks as the standard breakfast, snack, lunch, snack, dinner, snack intervals throughout the day — and then seeing how much you can respond to hunger above and beyond this. So snacks in-between snacks etc. Be brutally accountable to your physical and mental hunger and your state of health. If you are underweight you need to eat for weight gain regardless of hunger.

If that basic structure doesn't work for you, find something that does. I have worked with people in all parts of the world and this educated me to the fact that different cultures have differently normalised eating structures. Of course, go with the culture that you are in to establish your basic structure of meals, Regardless, if you are fully responding to mental hunger you will likely be eating all the time initially anyway, so that basic mealtime structure will be totally swamped. As you move into nutritional rehabilitation and your mental hunger dissipates, your eating cadence will change, and most of us find mealtimes become more defined.

Mealtimes are even more important if you are unable to respond to mental hunger and are following a meal plan. If you are experiencing a lot of mealtime fear and using meal support, then you will likely only be able to have that support available at pre-planned times. This doesn't mean you are not doing recovery right if you cannot respond to mental hunger and eat without restriction immediately. You will get there in the end. Focus on doing your utmost best and keep trying and you will surprise yourself.

For example, one of my clients had incredible mealtime fear and was thankful for the support of her parents at mealtimes. She had been in treatment eleven years and never been encouraged to eat over and above her designated meal plan, so when I suggested it she looked at me as if I was asking her to fly to the moon. She was adamant she could not. *"I can barely eat my planned meals,"* she told me, *"let alone extra!"*

I told her so long as she was eating her meals and doing her best we were making progress, but over the next couple of weeks kept on putting it out there that is was, indeed, entirely possible for her to go into the kitchen and get herself whatever she wanted, unplanned, in between meals and snacks. Just over two weeks from that initial suggestion that she could help herself to food, alone, and I got a text saying, *"I'm shaking. I did it. Three Oreo cookies!"*

Those three little cookies were the first bites in over eleven years that this woman had given *herself* permission to eat. They were the first thing she had eaten that had not been written on a meal plan. This was her first successful attempt to respond to desire and hunger, and eat more than her meal plan. Over the next couple of months she grew enormously in confidence and moved towards unrestricted eating.

There is no one way to success. As long as you are doing your very best, you will get there in the end.

Making Food

If you struggle to make your own food without undercutting on ingredients and allowing your anorexia to interfere, you would ideally have someone else prepare all your meals and snacks and deliver to you in the first stages of recovery. Realistically this isn't possible for most adults out of an inpatient or residential situation (which you absolutely can consider as an option). There are other options. You can buy pre-made food. If you cannot make a sandwich without freaking out over spreading butter on the bread, or choosing the lowest calorie bread on offer in the supermarket, I suggest you buy them pre-made initially. The long-term goal is to have you being able to make your own food without following through with any urges to undercut.

Buying food

Not buying food and having it readily available in your house is a form of restriction. You have got to get out there and buy those foods that scare you.

When buying food, run into the fear by always choosing the scarier option. Imagine that it is only scarier because your brain sees high-calorie or nutrient dense foods as a greater threat because it associated them with hunting — which is risky in a famine environment. Use this theory for where the fear comes from to tell yourself you don't really have anything to fear. If you can see the calorie difference on two packets of sandwiches then pick the higher one just to prove that you can regardless of taste preferences. You are in control. Not the fear.

After years of anorexia, choosing the lower calorie options can also become habit. A habit that keeps you in that scarcity mindset. So either way, make it a new rule that you choose the scarier, higher calorie foods when you know the caloric value. Even better is not looking or not knowing, but that is hard because these days the calorie amount is usually plastered on everything.

When deciding what foods to buy, remember that if you are trying to choose between a couple of options that buying and eating both is not outside of the realm of possibility. Of course your scarcity mindset will hate that idea as not only will it lead to you eating more, but you will spend more money too. If anorexia hates an idea that is all the more reason to do it. If a choice has to be made, choose what you are scared of.

Meal frequency

The more often that you can eat the better. I like the 3 meals, 3 snack structure as a minimum — mostly because that fits in with the culture I live in and it provides no more than a couple hours between eating. Of course, the more that you can eat in between meals and snacks the better. The reason that I like this frequency is I notice that the longer a person with anorexia goes without eating, the stronger the scarcity mindset becomes, and the harder eating becomes. If you go without food for too long you'll often notice that you feel more threatened by the thought of eating and that you dither over food decisions more. For this reason, breakfast is a common "difficult" meal, and a very important one.

Too long without food increases the urge to restrict

Some people get hangry when they are hungry. I've noticed that people with anorexia get their own version of hangry that involves an increase in eating disorder urges.

When you are in a state of malnutrition and have anorexia, going more than a couple of hours without eating reinforces the brain's assumption that food is scarce. Hence the desire to feed little and move more gets stronger. I discovered that while I was in energy deficit, even the shortest time without eating made my urges to restrict and exercise increase in strength.

Conversely, if I ate a big breakfast, and snacked all morning, then I felt less stressed about a big lunch. This dynamic is also affected by exercise or exertion and is another one of the reasons why rest is so important. Many of us find that rather than increasing our desire to eat, exercising makes the urge to migrate more intense.

Here is a quote from a member on our recovery Slack forum:
"It is seriously amazing to me how food changes my mental state. And not even big picture, I mean meal to meal. I really find if I even wait too long for a meal, the ED thoughts come back. This morning, I had this thought that I should be a raw vegan. I mean obviously this is something I'd never do (even at my worst point in ED), it's just these compulsions. Then I ate breakfast, a big one. And suddenly, I am thinking--yeah, raw veganism is not for me" - Ranger, adult in recovery from anorexia

Eat big and eat often.

Action: Some questions to consider:

1. Are you going to make your own food or is someone else making it for you?
2. Who is going to help you buy food?
3. How are you going to push yourself to try new and different foods?
4. How do you currently find yourself vulnerable to social diet/ nutrition culture?
5. Is looking for new foods/recipes going to mean that you are exposed to more online dieting/calorie counting influences? How can you make sure you don't allow these to have a negative effect on you?

Mealtime fear

Mealtime fear is there in some way shape or form for the majority of us. It is not a fear that we can afford to gloss over because you have to eat and you have to eat a lot.

Being scared of eating is an irrational fear, but as your perception shapes your reality that doesn't matter. It is fear. Fear feels horrible. Fear makes us want to flee or punch someone in the face. When we cannot do either of these things, fear morphs into frustration: tears, shaking, feelings of depression.

Mealtime fear has to be talked about with your support people. Don't be ashamed to admit that you are a grown-arsed person who is afraid to eat. I've been there. I have been reduced to tears by a piece of buttered toast. That is what anorexia does. Accept mealtime fear and anxiety for what it is and devise a plan to help you overcome it.

Action: See if you can answer the following questions:
1. What has helped in the past in terms of mealtime success?
2. What has hindered in the past and made mealtimes harder?
3. What thoughts or actions help you redirect/overcome mealtime fear?
4. Does distraction help?
5. Are there certain times of day/meals that are harder than others?

Meal support

Meal support is useful in terms of both accountability — having someone with you so that you are not tempted to skip out on the meal or eat less — and distraction. Someone there to talk to about something other than the food you are eating. Having a conversation can be useful in drawing attention away from the thoughts in your head. What this does, is it helps you stay in your parasympathetic nervous system as you eat — you are calmer. When you are calm you are giving your brain data to confirm that eating is not something it needs to freak out about. The more data like this that you give your brain, the less primed those neural pathways that associate eating and threat become. Food also tastes better when you are not in a wild panic.

Types of meal support

Meal support can take a number of forms. I encourage you to think unconventionally about this if you need to. I actually used people as meal support without them even knowing it on a couple of occasions. I didn't feel I needed meal support all the time, but on the big fear foods I really did. I was lucky in recovery to have one good friend, and I used to invite him over for pizza or whatever it was I knew I needed to tackle. He didn't know I had an eating disorder (he likely guessed, but we never spoke about it due to my stupid pride and the stigma around anorexia at that time) but he would never hesitate to tell me to "fucking eat more."

Thankfully a lot more people now understand that anorexia is not a choice, and therefore I hope you feel you can talk to people about it and ask for help. You can have meal support in-person with a friend, partner, or family member. There are also professional services where dietitians offer meal support but realistically this is going to be expensive to do every mealtime. Online peer support is also an option here and is much less expensive than other professional services.

The right meal support solution for you is up to you. Some people do better with family, others find that too intense and therefore feel calmer and more comfortable with a meal support coach. There is no right or wrong answer here. What works, works.

Don't be shy about asking for mealtime support. This is not something to be ashamed about, it is just your reality and it is where you are right now. We all need different things in order to overcome the misplaced fear that anorexia generates surrounding eating. Deal with it by getting whatever help you need.

Action: Think about the following:

1. Do you require meal support?
2. What form will this meal support take, and when do you most need it?
3. Do you do better with in-person support, or would you prefer online support?
4. How often and for what meals do you need to arrange external meal support?

Pre- and post-mealtime anxiety

Some of us are very anxious and stressed before meals. Most of us get those feelings of guilt, shame, disgust after eating too. While, honestly, most of this doesn't really go away fully until you are out of energy deficit, there are things you can do to keep yourself calmer in the meantime.

Pre-eating meditation:

1. Close your eyes, focus on your breathing. If you have certain music that you like put it on to help you calm.
2. Count the seconds to inhale and seconds to exhale for at least three breath cycles. Try and make your inhales and exhales as long as possible.
3. Think of the things that you want in life that recovery is going to make possible. Remind yourself that in order to have the happy, healthy life that you want you need to eat this meal.

4. Think of an image that is going to remind you of your goals. The face of a loved one, a goal, or something that you can associate with recovery (for me it was being recovered and able to get back into horse riding). Write the name of this image down on a piece of paper and have it with you at the table or in your pocket.

Staying calm while eating

1. If you start to feel stressed whilst eating, close your eyes, focus on your breathing.
2. Count the seconds to inhale and seconds to exhale for at least three breath cycles. Try and make your inhales and exhales as long as possible.
3. After 3 breaths, visualise yourself calmly eating. Focus on the feelings of success that you will feel once you have eaten.
4. Open your eyes and start eating.
5. If you feel your rate of breathing or rate of heartbeat increase at any point during the meal, stop, and repeat steps 1-3. Remind yourself of your recovery goals by taking out the piece of paper with the name of the image on it that you wrote before.

After eating: DRR

1. Be prepared for the feelings of guilt, shame. disgust and regret. Don't be surprised that they show up.

2. As soon as you detect any of these negative feelings, reject them. They are only the anorexia mindset trying to disincentive feeding. You do not need to pay attention.
3. Redirect. Distract yourself and refuse to give those negative emotions space.

Setting up for mealtime success

Action: Answer the following questions:
1. Are you going to pre-plan your main meals?
2. Who is in charge of stocking the kitchen?
3. What are you doing in terms of scheduling eating times and accountability for eating?
4. Who are you going to contact for support if you are alone and having thoughts about restricting or skipping a meal?
5. What are the techniques that you will use pre and post eating in order to help you stay calm if anxiety arises?
6. Who is going to be responsible for grocery shopping?
7. If you are grocery shopping, what is the plan for helping you make pro-recovery choices and not getting stuck with indecision.

Find a meal planning strategy that suits you

You do not have to pre-plan meals if you don't want to. Honestly so long as you eat enough and frequently I don't care how you do it.

Some people do well on really thorough meal planning at the start for their main meals because this stops them from eating only safe foods. Other people find that planning like this doesn't work for them, and instead they hand the reins over to someone else to feed them. Other people have a vague plan in place that acts as a default, but they know that it is actually a greater challenge for them to "go with the flow" when it comes to meals, so they try not to overly plan ahead. I didn't really plan anything, but rather doubled dared myself to go eat the scariest foods that popped into my head. There is no right or wrong here, there is simply seeing what suits you best. Whatever strategy works for you (and remember "what works" is subject to change as you move through recovery) the focus always has to be responding to hunger and eating over and above whatever you have planned if that is what your mental and/or physical hunger is asking for.

Additionally, make a list of all the items that you need to purchase and do so as soon as possible. Managing recovery well means being organised in terms of your food supply.

Do not delay eating

Delaying eating is a pretty common urge that we get with anorexia. For me, I used to do it because I was afraid of getting hungry later and not allowing myself to eat because I had already eaten my daily quota. Also, I would get a rush of positive emotions if I delayed eating, which made it all the more tempting.

I had to learn that my daily "quota" had no upper limit on it. This allowed me to eat early and know that if I wanted to eat again later that I could.

Start every day as you mean to go on. Eat breakfast as soon as you wake. Eat early, and if you are hungry later you eat more.

Make meals substantial

You have to eat a lot of food. Much more than a "normal" person who is not in malnutrition would eat.

I found that in the early stages of recovery when I tried to make my own food, the restriction drive was so strong that it would make me undercut on what I was making. For this reason, making your own food — such as a simple chicken sandwich for example — can be really hard. The urge to restrict may tempt you to choose the lowest calorie bread, or skip spreading butter on the bread. This is why getting someone else to make food for you can be beneficial.

Much of the problem was that I had been eating such silly small meals for so long I found it hard to put more food on my plate. One day I realized that trying to gain weight on small portions of food was ridiculous. I decided that I would not allow my plates of food to look anything less than would be served in the local pub. Sandwiches had to be doorsteps. Breakfasts had to resemble something that would feed a warrior before a day in battle. Dinners had to be enough to satisfy the hungry farmers that came in for a pint and a pie at the end of the day.

I started eating substantial meals in recovery, and I haven't ever stopped. 😊

Rest after eating

Many of us experience a sudden urge to move after eating. I would get such intense urges to move that I would jump out my seat and start cleaning or pacing. This was not a good habit for me to create, and I had to work hard at making myself urge surf and stay sat down.

I started by setting myself a 30 minute sitting down time after eating. While initially I was very twitchy about this, after a couple of days I relaxed and learned to enjoy this time. Of course, should I be able to sit for longer than 30 mins that was even better, but setting myself that time slot was helpful in overriding the initial urge to move after eating.

Food Shopping

Fight, flight or freeze can happen in places other than at the dinner table. Shopping used to be a huge challenge for me due to the conflicting thoughts and motivations. On the one hand I would want to challenge my OCD-ED and restriction by buying new and delicious foods, on the other I would feel stuck not only in the habitual behaviour cage, but also in my inability to spend money.

I cannot count the number of times I marched into Tesco's brimming with ideas of all the exciting and scary foods I was going to buy — roquefort, blueberry cheesecake, sticky toffee pudding, sausages, brioche buns — only to check out with an apple and a couple of lifted Black Jacks from the Pic 'n' Mix (those usually wound up in the bin on the high street).

Due to a ridiculously strong freeze response to buying new foods, I had to employ a number of different techniques in order to keep shopping trips to less than three hours. Here are some of them:

- Write a detailed shopping list of challenging foods and stick to it. While I would love to say I could walk into a store and be spontaneous about what I was going to buy, the reality is that only became possible for me towards the end of my recovery. Until then, when I wanted to challenge myself into buying new and different and more caloric foods I had to be very organised otherwise I would go into freeze mode in the store.
- Have a minimum spend amount for every time that you go to the store. I found this helpful as I had so much resistance to spending money that I had to force myself to do it. I would go

into freeze-mode on seeing price labels on food, so I had to be committed to spending the money.

- Listen to music or a podcast while shopping. This would help me distract a little and stay calm.
- Repeat a mantra that works for you. Mine was "Now or never!"
- Have someone ready and able to provide support for you via text in case you get an anxiety freeze in the store. As a recovery coach I sometimes do this with clients and that little bit of support gets people to the checkout with what they intended to buy in half the time and with much less stress.
- Urge surf when you feel the compulsion to compare the nutritional value of foods. I also had a rule that really helped me that was if I did compare the caloric value of foods I had to choose and buy the higher calorie one.
- Take a friend. Take one of your support people. I would say that any friend will do, but be careful not to go shopping with someone who eats diet foods!
- If the anxiety is stalling you, ask someone else to shop for you. This was hard for me to mentally give another person control, but when I did it worked wonders in terms of timesaving. If I froze when trying to purchase a new food, I would ask someone else to get it for me. Once I had eaten it at home I was much more able to buy it without freezing or feeling like I was going to have a nervous breakdown in the store.

Have fun! One of my clients, Christina, plays a reality television game at the grocery store to distract herself from her anxiety. She pretends that she has a show for brave eating disorder recovery, and talks to the audience, as she makes awesome choices, and avoids silly nutrition obsessing. She distracts herself, brings a sense of humor, and lessens the tension. "If I were on national television," she says, "I would behave in a proper manner, and not have a meltdown in aisle 4." And, true to her belief, if you can dream it, you can do it. This has been a huge help for her, and she tries new things, every day. She shops, every day, as well. Her priority is an abundance of food, coming out of total life restriction. At the market, she meets people, stocks on food, and wears something to make it an outing. You can do this, no matter your body size.

"I find that having a time limit to shop can be helpful - if I don't have time to spend hours looking and comparing i have to grab and leave and often ends up more successful" - Anon, adult in recovery from anorexia

Recovery Project Kickoff Outcomes

By now, you should have a plan for at least the following:

1. Recovery resources: the who, what, when, and where of any resources such as therapists, other professionals, peer support, social support, and family support.

2. Nutritional rehabilitation plan: You don't need to have a specific target weight (unless you want one), but you do need to determine how you will evaluate if you are making progress in terms of weight gain and unrestricted eating.

3. Mealtime plan: who, where, when of the daily mealtimes.

4. Restriction plan: a list of your restrictive behaviours and thoughts and kickoff strategies (see toolkit) to employ to help you work on living and eating in an unrestricted manner.

5. OCD-ED plan: a list of all your OCD-ED behaviours and thoughts and kickoff strategies (see toolkit) to employ to help you work on redirecting and rejecting these compulsions.

6. An idea of what success looks like and continuing assessment and evaluation intentions.

What do you do now?

You start. Immediately. Don't wait until the beginning of the week. Don't wait for anything. You can start eating more and working on restriction/OCD-ED right now.

Chapter 18: Project Execution — Day-to-Day Recovery

Recovery, as the process of rewiring the neural pathways in the brain — changing thought processes and behaviours — calls for unrelenting focus in the primary stages. Doing the opposite of what anorexia wants you to do leads to an initial spike in anxiety for most of us. These are all reasons why you have to make sure that your recovery stays at the forefront.

Recovery Project Meetings: Cadence

I suggest you have at least two weekly meetings with your RPM. My general cadence with a client is two short meetings a week and daily email or text contact in the first couple of months or so into recovery at least.

This is where you get right into assessing and troubleshooting what may have come up that week. I would keep this meeting cadence up for the duration of the nutritional rehabilitation phase of recovery and as long after as is needed for you and your support team to feel that both your weight and your mental state are in a stable place. Additionally, have a daily check in at the very least. I work via text and email with my clients on days when I do not speak to them to help them stay on track and troubleshoot any resistance that may arise on a daily, sometimes hourly, basis. I believe that this regular check in makes a vital difference to my clients' ability to keep recovery top of mind. I also encourage clients to look back at each day and retrospectively tell me where they could have improved.

"In hindsight, I think I could have had extra for breakfast. I could have had a bigger snack mid morning, a dessert for lunch and fitted something else in somewhere too ... " - Anon, adult in recovery from anorexia.

Any other recovery focused meetings that you have — say with a therapist, meal support coach, or dietitian etc. — should be additional to these two recovery project meetings. Think of these meetings as strategy evaluation rather than therapy or treatment.

If you are working alone, I recommend you still set aside meeting time like this where you focus on your recovery efforts and plan. This is not ideal as being able to bounce ideas off someone else can help you overcome obstacles easier, but I know that some of you realistically won't be able to find that sort of support. You can do this anyway. Your presence is the only required presence for you to recover fully. If you don't have the ideal situation, do your best with what you do have.

Ongoing Recovery Meeting Agenda

Here is an example of a working agenda for these meetings. As you will see the aim is to have a functional and effective meeting where you can talk about the things that are concerning you and plan for the days ahead. Of course, what you determine is important in your recovery meeting agenda may be different from what I have here, so just use this as an example. Over time you will understand more about what is important for you. The key areas are your goals and staying focused on structuring your day so that recovery is helped as much as possible. However, I always like to check in on feelings around weight gain as that sensitive topic tends to fast become the elephant in the room unless spoken about frequently.

1. Status: Do a quick take on how you are feeling and how your recovery has been going overall.
2. Retrospective: A more detailed look back at the last couple of days:
    a. Make a note of the successes and talk about how you can learn from success and use that information going forward.
    b. Make a note of the problems that were encountered, how they were dealt with, and if there are learning points to be taken from these experiences.
    c. Look back at the goals that you set and talk about how the last couple of days has been in regards to overall goal success.

    d.   Talk about any other recovery-orientated meetings or events that have taken place (therapy sessions, support groups etc) and continue to assess these.

3.   Food and eating:

    a.   Has unrestricted eating (or meal plan following if you are doing that) been successful?

    b.   Were there any times when you felt that you struggled to eat, and can you identify why this might have been? What can you learn from this?

    c.   How has your current mealtime plan been working and do you need to make any adjustments?

    d.   How has your overall level of anxiety been at mealtimes?

        i.   How successful have you been about rejecting/ignoring the negative emotions (shame, guilt, regret, fear etc) after eating more or differently than usual? What do you need to do to make yourself better at not getting sucked in to these emotions?

    e.   How have levels of hunger been? Were you able to respond to hunger when/if hunger came? Were you able to eat even if not hungry?

    f.   Identify any times when you felt that you allowed OCD-ED food rules or restriction rules get the better of you. What can you learn from this and what measures can you put in place to help you overcome?

4.   Exercise and OCD-ED:

    a.   Were you successful in overriding any urges to exercise? If not, what do you need in order to be able to do so?

    b.   Go through your OCD-ED list and talk about every item on there that you are working on. Evaluate and restructure your approach if needed.

5.   Communication and using resources:

    a.   Have you asked for help when you needed it?

    b.   What is it that stops you or deters you from asking for help?

    c.   How have other resources and recovery meetings been?

6.   Body changes and weight gain:

    a.   How are you feeling regarding your body and the weight gain goal?

    b.   What do you need in order to help you deal with any anxiety the reality of weight gain invokes?

7.   Miscellaneous: Leave a space to talk about anything else not covered in the agenda.

8.   Planning: Make a plan that includes any tactical changes or alterations that may have come about as a result of your discussion.

You'll be surprised at how much you have to talk about each session. Recovery is a fascinating process if you can take the seat of the observer. Some days you will be able to feel your mental shifts as you become better at detecting the anorexia neural pathways at work and rejecting the thoughts and behaviors that it promotes.

I suggest that you sustain twice weekly recovery meetings until everyone involved agrees that they are no longer needed. Don't cut these short too soon as you will be surprised how quickly the recovery mindset is lost if you are not meeting to specifically discuss recovery.

When you believe it is the right time to reduce the frequency of your meetings, do so slowly. I usually take people down to one meeting a week, then every two weeks, and finally once a month. The most important thing to remember is that weight gain does not equal full recovery, and just because you start to gain weight doesn't mean you should reduce support. Your mental state shifts are the clues to look for. Weight gain alone should never be considered a reason to reduce support.

Section Six:

Recovery

to

Recovered

Recovery is the process that we go through to get fully recovered. Fully recovered is when unrestricted eating means that you naturally eat enough to sustain an unsuppressed body weight, but it is also a mental state of freedom from any desires to restrict, compulsive exercise, and all other OCD-ED and anxieties. For me, full recovery was the re-establishment of my pre-anorexia self. I am excited for you. A world in which your brain does not perceive food to be a threat is a wonderful place to be.

Full recovery is a life without restrictive thoughts and OCD-ED. Because you achieve energy balance, the mental hunger leaves you alone. It is body and mind at ease. It is bliss! The process of getting there, however, was by far and away the most difficult process I have ever been through — and messy as hell. And not only due to the physical changes, there was a lot more tied up in my anorexia identity than I had thought.

In order to recover from anorexia, I had to lose the anorexia identity that defined me for over a decade. I had to let go of thin, fitness fanatic, martyr, vegan. For me, letting go of my identity was not as difficult as letting go of being good at something was.

Letting go of being good at anorexia

I was really good at not eating. I was an A* student at restriction. Whilst I have no desire to be good at restriction now, that is because I am not in the anorexia mindset anymore and I don't get a feeling of reward for eating less and moving more.

When my brain was in the anorexia mindset, even if everything else in my life was in shreds, there was a sense of contentment and peace to be found in the fact that I was really good at eating less than anyone else. That is a horrid truth to admit, but a truth all the same.

When I started to eat a lot of food; stop restricting; stop the OCD-ED; and gain weight in recovery, I mostly felt scared. But I also felt powerful. I knew I was doing it. I was doing recovery. But there was at times, a sense of loss. I didn't know what I was good at now that restriction and exercise were not an option.

It is a bit like taking a chessboard away from a world class chess player. The game I had been winning at meant nothing in the real world. The only thing that I was really great at held no value. I struggled a lot with missing being good at something. It was important for me to do something that made me feel successful in the recovery time. I started volunteering (running the social media for a local nonprofit) and started writing. That filled a gap.

"I had always felt a failure my whole life and anorexia was the only thing I was good at and it offered me a feeling of success that nothing else ever has. I live in hope that one day recovery from anorexia will offer me

488

that same feeling of being successful" - LC, adult in recovery from anorexia.

The recovery process is an incredible time — that is, if you can step outside of yourself enough to be brave and curious about it. Due to the number of "is this normal?" texts and emails that I get every day from my clients, I feel that a section on what to expect is needed. This is not extensive (because we are all different) but an idea of some of the most common recovery happenings.

Chapter 19: What To Expect

Malnutrition is a big deal for your body. Coming out of a state of malnutrition can also be a big deal. Here are some things that you may experience.

Water retention/edema

In the initial period of eating more, many of us notice this very uncomfortable gaining of water weight. This is your body trying to achieve rehydration. It can happen really suddenly too!

Many people go into recovery knowing that water retention could be a factor, yet most are still shocked to discover just how extreme it can be. It can be painful too, I mean physically painful. If you experience edema it is worth getting checked out by a doctor.

If you gain a lot of weight initially as you start to eat more, it is usually just water. The endocrine system adjustments required to slow our metabolism lead to the increased retention of fluid as we start to eat more.[179][180] As a reaction to dehydration the kidneys sometimes retain more water and salt and the permeability of the your capillaries increases. Hence, a tendency for water retention. Apparently, one is especially susceptible to this edema or water retention if suffering from the symptoms of hypothyroidism such as bradycardia, low blood

---

[179] Low serum triiodothyronine (T3) and hypothyroidism in anorexia nervosa. Croxson MS. Ibbertson HK J Clin Endocrinol Metab. 1977 Jan; 44(1):167-74.

[180] Effect of caloric restriction and dietary composition of serum T3 and reverse T3 in man. J Clin Endocrinol Metab. 1976

pressure, cold hands and feet and slow reflexes. This is because those symptoms indicate that the thyroid is under stress — it is these that lower the metabolism, and so as you begin to eat more foods metabolic changes will be large as your body gears back up to normal functioning. Purging behavior also increases propensity to become dehydrated.

It is suggested that eating diets higher in fat can help — and I fully support that, as many of us are mentally resistant to eating fat so adopting a high fat diet in recovery is doubly effective in healing the body and rewiring the brain.[181]

The body can hold onto water in a way that it cannot hold onto food. It can retain water immediately, so your weight on the scale can be altered from one day to another in the way that it cannot with true weight increases. Of course, your disordered thoughts will tell you that you are broken and that you have suddenly overnight gained a ton of weight. You haven't. It would be impossible for you to gain several pounds of bodyweight in a day. Believe me, I have tried.

(I always recommend getting any persistent edema checked out by an eating disorder specialist medical professional)

[181] O'Connor G, & Goldin J (2011). The refeeding syndrome and glucose load. The International Journal of Eating Disorders, 44 (2), 182-5 PMID: 20127933

Digestion problems

More often than not, anorexia recovery is characterised by tummy trouble of one or many distinctions. If you think about it, that makes total sense, because your system has not had to work properly for a while. Common physical effects include: gas, bloating, diarrhea, constipation, acid reflux, frequent bowel movements, and indigestion. I had every one of these, and sometimes all of them on the same day.

In a conversation that I had with Dr Jennifer Gaudiani[182] — one of the only internists who truly specialises in the medical complications of eating disorders in the US at this time (2018) — about GI issues in eating disorder recovery, one of the most prominent things she said to me:

"All that is required for the processes that we have been talking about to resolve back to normal, lovely, GI function is full weight restoration and great daily nutritional intake."

Let's look into that in a little more detail:
- Your stomach and intestines have not been given any maintenance or repair work due to lack of funding (food). Before this system is going to work well again, repairs will have to be undertaken.
- Inadequate intake leads to the slowing down of the emptying of the stomach, so, initially, eating more can lead to nausea, cramps, constipation etc. as the system recalibrates.

---

[182] http://tabithafarrar.com/2017/09/dr-g-tummy-troubles-in-eating-disorder-recovery/

- A low volume of food over time leads to reduced elasticity of the stomach.[183] During this process, some people suffer from functional dyspepsia — when the stomach lining is less able to stretch in order to accommodate the increase in food that leads to early satiety, stomach distension, bloating, and upper abdominal discomfort. When you start to eat again, you may be uncomfortably full until this rights itself and your stomach expands.[184]

- Not eating enough and limited variety leads to a reduction in gut bacteria and a culling of many other than the die-hard bacteria who can survive on practically nothing. Just another area in which your gut has to gear up a notch and recover optimal processes.

- For most of us with anorexia, eating more food creates anxiety initially. Anxiety places you in your sympathetic nervous system which is the fight or flight one. We were not designed to digest food well while in the sympathetic nervous system. Over time you will start to feel less anxiety about eating, and your digestion can improve because you start eating from your parasympathetic nervous system instead.

IBS/Temporary food intolerance

You may get IBS symptoms when you start eating more food. Unless you get a valid diagnosis of a true allergy or intolerance — and you

[183] Am J Clin Nutr. 1996 Feb;63(2):170-3. Reduced stomach capacity in obese subjects after dieting. Geliebter et al

[184] World J Gastroenterol. 2012 Prevalence of functional dyspepsia and its subgroups in patients with eating disorders. Santonicola et al

should consult with a medical professional on that, not some quack — don't stop eating these foods! Think of it as a case of needing to keep practicing in order to get your digestive system up to scratch.

Bloating, constipation, indigestion, cramping, nausea, gas, diarrhea, and general discomfort were all with me as I started to eat more. I have yet to meet a person in recovery from anorexia who has got there without any periods of stomach discomfort. There is a lot going on in there, and your system is working it all out. Chaos may reign. Generally, time is all your digestion needs. If you want to get checked out to make sure, why not?

Tummy troubles summary:

- Continue to eat at regular intervals regardless of how awkward it feels. We have to train this system up!
- Reduce intake of any fruits or vegetables. These are low nutrient density, and high fibre is probably the last thing your poor stomach needs. Give your tummy foods that are easy for it to process and highly nutrient dense.
- Drink adequate amounts of water and fluids, but not so much to fill your stomach. Drinks with calories in are good!
- If you are eating a low-fat diet: stop. Fat is your friend.
- Use breathing practices before and after eating to help you reduce anxiety and stay in the parasympathetic nervous system.

I should also mention that most of us seem to cycle through periods of constipation to diarrhea as our digestive systems get used to processing food properly.

As with absolutely everything, if you are really worried you should seek the help of an eating disorder specialist medical doctor. Be wary of seeing any doctor who doesn't follow a HAES approach or is eating disorder savvy, because they may tell you to restrict — and that is the last thing you need to do!

Hunger

As you start to eat more, you can feel full to the point of bursting one minute, and empty and hungry the other. I think this happens as your system tries to re-calibrate itself to your new increased intake. I believe all this is mostly due to delayed gastric emptying. Your stomach is full, full, full! And then it all suddenly moves through and it feels empty, empty, empty!

While your system tunes up, you will spend a lot of time having to eat when you are not hungry, or when you feel full. This all feels just ... wrong. It will feel "wrong" for a while. In a way, it has to feel wrong in order for your system to change. Regardless of how wrong it feels, eating is always right.

There is no normal here. Some of us go into periods of extreme hunger. Some of us continue to feel full throughout the entire refeeding process. I was really very gassy and some days my tummy felt like an orchestra trying to tune up! There is no norm here, it can all happen. The body is an organism. The only blanket statement is that if you are underweight you have to eat regardless of your lack of physical hunger and regardless of how full you might feel before a mealtime.

Hunger isn't always convenient

My own physical hunger used to have a very annoying habit of being nowhere to be found until about five minutes after I had eaten a meal. Then it would ask me for more food — something that I found mentally hard to accept but learned I had to.

Another common mental hurdle is eating when not hungry. As hunger cues are often not present when we are in energy deficit, recovery for most of us requires eating when not hungry. Your Safety Net plan should account for this. Absence of hunger should never lead to you eating less, but presence of hunger should always lead to you eating more.

Your attitude to hunger changes as you recover

I found that as I moved through recovery, my attitude to being hungry changed drastically. Hunger went from a trophy feeling, to something I could not tolerate. Hunger no longer felt rewarding or superior, it began to feel like an irritant.

"I feel I've moved on another step in recovery; eating more, finally enjoying food, actually wanting good recovery type food (bread and butter, cheese with everything etc. not just making myself override ed's

cravings for veg or safe fats etc), feeling hunger, adding extras on top extras with more ease etc. alongside massive positive cognitive shifts. However, where as previously any slight inadvertent energy deficit caused a 'high' and encouraged activity I don't get this, I instead feel headachy, nauseous, dizzy, extremely tired etc. I'm finding this really encouraging. It's like my body is ruling my mind more, rather than ed. I get nearly teary as soon as my body is anywhere near needing food but for the right reasons (because I want to eat, not as I'm scared of food)" - RR, adult in recovery from anorexia.

I appreciate what RB is saying in the quote above, as this is how I came to feel in recovery too. I simply could not be hungry. I would feel physically compromised, and mentally furious should I not eat enough. It was rather as if my body had taken over my recovery, and now there was no question of me eating when I needed to. The option to go hungry was gone. I remember feeling some security when this happened, as if I had no choice but to keep going forward because hungry didn't work for me anymore, nor did it feel like an option.

"Even though living in a malnourished state is basically a life of chronic hangriness, I've found that now that my emotions, hormones and general spirit have been flipped back on with recovery, when I accidentally get into deficit, I reach such desperate levels of hangry I sometimes frighten myself, haha. Like the other night dinner was delayed by just a bit and I'd had a snack to hold me over, but I felt a little bit like the Hulk inside. Like I could've flipped a table over. Reassuring because I feel like my body is no longer checked out due to being ignored. It's kicking a** and taking names." - J, adult in recovery from anorexia.

Increased anxiety/irritability

"My anxiety has hit the roof this week. Apparently donuts to my ED are like a red flag to a bull."- JC, adult in recovery from anorexia.

When you start to eat more and you disrespect all your food rules, do not be surprised if your anxiety increases. You are literally going against everything that you know. And remember, anorexia uses the emotions of shame, regret, fear, and guilt to try and disincentivise you from eating more. These will flare up as you start to eat more. You will feel untethered, there will be a lot of doubting thoughts. Recovery is a process of sitting on the very edge of your comfort zone all day every day for months and months. In a sense, if you feel comfortable, you are likely not pushing hard enough.

Anorexia makes you feel that energy deficit, exercise, and restriction are all good things. It rewards you when you do these things. In the same vein, it doesn't reward you for going against this. It makes you feel all sorts of anxiety. This is a good sign. It may not feel like it, but this mental discomfort indicates you are on the right path.

The trouble is, we often turn into nightmare people to be with. As a recovery coach I always opt for damage reduction tactics here by making sure that family members know that this is likely to happen especially at the start of the recovery process and not to take anything too personally.

One of the reasons that I am quite forthright in telling you to try your best not to be snappy and irritable with the people who love you as you navigate these high anxiety stages in recovery is because I thoroughly regret many of my own actions and words in this time. The people involved may have forgiven and forgotten, but I would still have preferred it not to have happened. I've forgiven myself too, but I wish I had known then what I know now. I think had I been able to see that my increase in irritability was due to the recovery process and not due to the person in front of me, I would have been better able to dismiss those emotions.

Nothing seemed to irk me more when I was in recovery than people offering me food. Doing so was bound to get your head bitten off. To me, offering me food was a threatening behaviour — never mind the fact that I was hungry and was also trying to eat more. Just because I was in recovery didn't mean my brain suddenly stopped processing food as a threat. It takes a lot of data for this to happen. Data, like eating a lot of food to prove to your brain it is not a threat. Data, like eating new foods. Data, like eating foods prepared by someone else. This data takes time to accumulate. In the meantime, your brain will likely still react to food as a threat. Hence the stress.

General fatigue, aches and pains

I mentioned earlier that anorexia tends to bring with it a higher than normal pain threshold. I think that additional to this, we tend not to feel a lot of pain simply because our bodies are not doing repair work.

When I started resting and eating more, I experienced general aches and pains. It felt a lot like the growing pains I used to get as a kid and in a sense I guess that would be accurate as there must have been a lot of regrowth occurring too.

The general fatigue that recovery often brings too can be disconcerting. You'll have doubts, and you will wonder why you are feeling more tired than ever when you rest. You were always tired, you just couldn't feel it. You have probably been tired for a very long time. Only in recovery, you feel it. It's okay. When the time is right your energy will return.

"When I eat more, I get more tired. This makes me feel like eating is bad for me." - R, adult in recovery from anorexia.

Feeling tired can throw a spanner in the works for many of us because we sometimes interpret that as a sign we are doing something wrong. I asked Shan Guisinger about this, and she explained to me that it is another facet of recovering from the migration response. Apparently the same happens in the laboratory "anorexic" rats — they start to cut back on exercise and seem tired in refeeding. When your body thinks it needs to migrate it will direct all energy to movement. When an increase in incoming food signals to your body that you are out of the famine, it will stop directing all energy to your limbs, and start directing it to repairing.

For a couple of months, I was feeling in the wars and pretty bloody sorry for myself. I was ridiculously hungry, irritable, dog tired, achy, bloated, and quite cross. But over time I did begin to feel my natural energy levels return.

Most commonly reported are general achiness, and specific muscular and joint aches. I remember for a couple of days my wrists really hurt, then another time I had a week where my back ached. Added to the fatigue, stomach discomfort and low-level depression that many of us have, this can be a pretty testing time. It is still very worth it!

Increase in volume of restrictive compulsions

If you have a OCD-ED element to your illness this often gets worse before it gets better too. Especially for the food rules. It makes sense really, as you are eating more so anorexia has more food to make rules about than it had when you weren't eating as much.

For example, if you aren't eating bread at all, you don't need restrictive bread rules in order to limit your bread intake. If you start eating bread again, anorexia has a field day making up lots of bread restriction rules such as only being allowed bread once a day, or not being allowed to eat bread at consecutive meals etc. In a sense that makes it feel like the rules are getting worse, but that is only because you are eating more. If you have exercise or movement OCD-ED the compulsions sometimes initially get stronger as you start to eat more too.

As well as the increase in the OCD-ED rules around food, I found that I got serious "ants in my pants" some days in recovery. I had gone cold turkey on all exercise and superfluous movement, so exercise wasn't an option, but I would get these very strong pangs of wanting to move. Things like I would be sitting down and suddenly have to jump up and go and do something as if I had been bitten on the bum. I used to call them energy shots, as that is what it felt like. Ultimately, I worked out that if I stayed still, and urge surfed, the energy shot would dissipate. This initial stage it is very important that you rest as much as possible, because even if you are eating more, your body isn't into building muscle mass yet. Right now, your body is directing all the nutrients and energy at your vital organs first.

The recovery tummy

Weight initially gathers around the vital organs. This is all very well — your body is invested in protecting the organs that are more needed for survival — but it means that you will have fat on your stomach. Bam goes reality! This is what needs to happen. This is what your body is designed to do as you start to gain weight again after a period of starvation. This is what you have to know is likely to happen so that it doesn't surprise you when it does.

In a way, this is like the recovery acid test. In order to reach full recovery, you will have to sit with fat around your stomach for a number of months, and in my case well over a year. It will redistribute, but it will take it's time.[185] Nothing you can do will change this. If you react by restricting your body will likely assume that food is scarce again and it needs to resume starvation mode and store even more fat. If you react with increasing exercise, the same will likely happen. You can scream and cry and wail, but your body will still store fat around your stomach until it is good and ready. You might as well

---

[185] Adipose tissue distribution after weight restoration and weight maintenance in women with anorexia nervosa Mayer et al

accept that now and get on with it.

I know one person who made friends with her recovery tummy by giving it a name (Roy!). I know others who have told it daily that they are thankful it is there as they know it is part of their recovery. A bit like a recovery trophy. I made myself place my hands on my recovery tummy every day and think nice things about it. With the right mindset, you will find what works for you to cultivate peace, not war, with your tummy.

So why? Other than to totally traumatise a person who is scared of weight gain even further, why would this happen? It may be that this abdominal fat is due to hormonal imbalances, which are commonly observed in anorexia nervosa patients.[186] It has also been suggested that decreases in gonadal steroids, which is common in anorexia, may also be a reason that their body prefers to distribute fat in this way, as sex hormones have a large say in how and where we accumulate fat.[187] It is generally concluded in the literature that people in recovery from anorexia seem to gain more fat around the abdomen than someone gaining weight without anorexia would do.

Whatever the reason, stomach fat should redistribute to other parts of your body naturally over time.[188][189] There are a number of studies that show this to be true, and the one year mark is the general length of

[186] Corticotropin-Releasing Hormone System in Human Adipose Tissue JANETTE SERES et al

[187] Body fat distribution before and after weight gain In anorexia nervosa Zamboni et al.International Journal of Obesity February 1997

[188] Endocr Pract. 2008 THE ENDOCRINOPATHIES OF anorexia NERVOSA Lisa S. Usdan

[189] 2005 American Society for Clinical Nutrition Body fat redistribution after weight gain in women with anorexia nervosa Mayer et al.

time this redistribution takes. To note, I do know people for whom it has taken longer than this, and some that it has taken less. Ironically, it was around the time that I really accepted my recovery tummy, and became ambivalent to it that it finally left and redistributed to other parts of my body. My recovery tummy turned into bigger boobs, broader shoulders, curvy calves, and thighs. Finally I became a woman with curves. And I love them.

Tips for dealing with the "recovery tummy:"
1. Understand that this is a healthy sign of recovery and that your body is healing.
2. Be patient. Recovery is a long process due to the many physiological systems involved.
3. Find someone you can talk to about it in a structured and effective manner.
4. Work to discipline your thought patterns. When you find yourself obsessing over your body in an ineffective and detrimental manner: shut those thoughts down.
5. Keep eating.
6. Wear loose, comfortable clothes.
7. Don't start exercising or doing tummy crunches. This will not help. In fact, Dr. Gaudiani explained to me in a podcast conversation that this can actually make things worse.[190]
8. Don't let yourself freak out about it. It really is not a catastrophe that you have a tummy (even though your anorexia will try to convince you it is). This is a perfect opportunity to practice shutting down negative thoughts and not allowing your brain to obsess over things.

[190] http://tabithafarrar.com/2017/09/dr-g-tummy-troubles-in-eating-disorder-recovery/

Depression

Depression happens enough in the recovery process that it is certainly worth mentioning here. Most of us feel a large amount of fatigue in recovery, and for some people, there are bouts of depression too. I certainly had some down-in-the-dumps days, but luckily other than that, depression didn't bother me too much. I know that for some people it can be pretty awful.

I have noticed that people at some point in the refeeding phase quite suddenly move from hyperactivity to a state of depression. There are hibernation theories that this is a storage phase, however if you look at the devastating effects that malnutrition has on the body, it is very understandable as to why the body goes into a state of temporary depression in order to continue the restoration process.

As ... undesirable ... as depression is, it is a functional state.[191] There is an animal equivalent to depression when a creature is ill or wounded, this illustrates the biological advantages in withdrawing when one is recuperating. It makes healing faster because all energy is directed to the process, and not towards being social.

"I developed depression very quickly after going cold turkey on exercise and stopping any restrictions with food. Although I had experienced depression for some time, this was different, I couldn't leave my bed, I slept a lot but still felt exhausted, I didn't want to speak to anyone, all I could do was to cry. I'm not going to pretend it

---

[191] The bright side of being blue: Depression as an adaptation for analyzing complex problems. Andrews et al, Psychological Review

wasn't awful because it was a terrible time, but it did serve a purpose and made me rest when my body needed it. So while I wouldn't wish this on anyone it did have a benefit to me. - LC, adult in recovery from anorexia.

It can be hard to think about depression as a functional response to anything, but in evolutionary terms it must be. So what could the functional benefits of a state of depression be?

Possible functional aspects of depression in anorexia recovery:

1.   Awareness

Depression can make you acutely aware that something is wrong. Restriction phases are commonly affected by anosognosia — inability to see how sick one is. Depressive phases act the other way, and make it very obvious to ourselves that we are unwell. Obvious to the point that we tend to dwell on and analyze our illness. In evolutionary purposes, this fixation on an egregious problem would have evolved to motivate us to fix it.

2. Problem solving

Depression makes us better at solving certain types of problems, and motivates inaction and stillness.[192][193] Deep, analytical thought is "expensive" and costly in terms of energy. Physical fatigue, and lack of interest in social situations also come into play here to make one focus

---

[192] Clinical Child and Family Psychology Review 2001 Family Processes in Adolescent Depression

[193] Joshua Wolf Shenk (2005). "Lincoln's Melancholy: How Depression Challenged a President and Fueled His Greatness". Houghton Mifflin.

on oneself. This want for stillness is beneficial in recovery from anorexia.

3. Stress reaction

Taken from the "Arrested Defenses" model of depression, where the body feels overwhelmed with stress. When coming out of energy deficit, the false sense of energy that many people with anorexia gain from restriction could subside and the underlying stress invokes feelings of depression.[194]

4. Inner conflict

Looking at anorexia recovery depression from the point of view of the "Behavioural Shutdown" model — where if an organism faces more perceived risk than reward for activities, the best solution is to withdraw from them — depression could occur due to having to eat food, and fighting that very strong and persistent urge to restrict.[195] So when everything within you is screaming at you not to eat, and your family and doctors and everyone outside of you are telling you that you have to eat. You feel torn and depressed.

5. S.O.S

Taken from "Honest Signalling" theory, depression is a way of truly demonstrating that you need help. This is an interesting theory, as it implies that depression is needed most of all when we don't feel we have the ability to "ask" for help — the depressive state makes it so obvious that we need help. I think that this can be interesting when we

---

[194] Evolution and depression: issues and implications PAUL G ILBERT Mental Health Research Unit, Kingsway Hospital, Derby, UK Psychological Medicine, 2006

[195] Toward a revised evolutionary adaptationist analysis of depression: the social navigation hypothesis Paul J Watson

consider the shame surrounding eating disorder, weight gain, and the social problems that recovery often encounters.

6. Self-preservation

The theory of depression that most interests me in respect to anorexia, is the "Prevention of Infection" hypothesis. This implies that depression is a protection against a hostile environment, disease, or any other danger in the outer environment. It promotes that depression forces us to rest physically, and keep ourselves holed up and safe until the coast is clear.[196] It makes sense from an evolutionary perspective, that when migration is complete, and food has been found, time has to be spend recuperating and resting. Resting and eating.

It should also be noted that illness of course can provoke depression — when the immune system is compromised. Most of us find that we don't get ill when we are at a very low weight, but in recovery, when our bodies have the resources to process infections and viruses, we are under the weather a lot! This really annoyed me because I always used the fact that I rarely caught colds as an argument that I was healthy when I was underweight. Then almost as soon as I started to gain weight I was a snivelling snotty mess for a while.

I have known people try depression medication in recovery, but overall, it seems that nutritional rehabilitation is the tonic, and that depressive bouts dissipate as you move into full recovery.

---

[196] An Evolutionary Hypothesis of Depression and Its Symptoms, Adaptive Value, and Risk Factors Kinney et al. Journal of Nervous & Mental Disease: August 2009

What to do if you are feeling depressed in recovery:

1. Keep eating. Don't allow depression to make you get complacent about this.
2. Stay quiet if you need to rest. If it is helpful, and helps you eat more, temporary withdrawal is okay. Don't immediately pressure yourself into going out etc. If you want to rest, rest.
3. Talk to people. Pick up the phone. Human connection helps and you don't always have to go out galavanting in order to communicate with people. You can do that from home.
4. Get a kitten. Okay, this might not work for everyone. I didn't have many friends left when I started recovery. I was very lonely. When I committed to not exercising and staying in and resting, I got a kitten from the local rescue to keep me company. Animals are wonderful companions.

Feelings of resignation

"I thought every bit of progress I made would feel good (and it sort of does), but it also just unveils how much more progress I need to make. It's like that game at the fun fair where you whack a gopher with a mallet then another one comes up, then another. Then the ones you'd already whacked come up again. I'm tired already but not as tired as I am of anorexia." - R, adult in recovery from anorexia.

I know how "R" feels. I loved her description of whacking gophers. Her recognition of herself feeling tired of the process also brought her to her own realisation on why pushing forward would be worth it. That's one of the reasons I love working with people with anorexia — they are so smart.

Recovery is hard work. No, it is fucking hard work! And it is a long process. Even if you get your intake up, you have to keep it up in order for your body to really start to make the repair work that it needs to. You don't get a day off from eating. Most of us go through a kaleidoscope of emotions as our system starts to re-calibrate itself. These are all indeed good signs that change is happening.

Feeling like it is just not working

Another phenomenon that I have witnessed in others and experienced in myself, is the feeling that rather than things getting better the more you eat, they feel like they are getting worse. I know I went through a patch of what felt like uncontrollable hunger that just got worse the more I ate. And, alongside this was incredible fatigue that seemed to increase rather than decrease. So I was eating more, yet feeling no relief — just more tired and more hungry.

"Is it normal that the more I eat the hungrier I am? I feel like I must be doing something wrong" - O, adult in recovery from anorexia.

It isn't that you are doing anything wrong, it is just that your body is responding to the increase in food with "It's about time! Now I'll let you know how hungry I really am!" And likewise, it is finally telling you how very exhausted it is. I think that this is because when you eat more food your brain has consistent data to tell it that you are no longer in a famine. The migration response begins to switch off, and with this that protectionary element of not feeling how tired and hungry you are begins to dissolve. You are incredibly tired and hungry and it can feel as if eating only makes it worse. Stick with it, and be compassionate.

Many of us, myself included, get impatient with the recovery process. And honestly, if you think about it, what right do we have to be impatient with our bodies? I got impatient, yes. Twelve years of starvation and exercise abuse in which my body bravely soldiered on, and I got impatient with it after three months of eating properly? WTF?

It doesn't work like that in recovery. You don't get to call the shots in terms of how your body heals. You don't get to dictate your rate of weight gain, or how long it takes, or which systems start to heal first. You don't get to decide how long it will be before your recovery tummy redistributes. You don't get to be frustrated because you feel fatigued and listless. You get to eat and rewire. That is your job. The rest is left to your body. The good news is that your body is best qualified to know what it is doing in the healing process, so you are in the best of hands. Leave your body to do its job while you concentrate on resting and eating.

What you get control are your actions and reactions. You choose to obey restrictive thoughts or not. Anorexia can generate thoughts, suggestions, but it can't make you do anything. You get to choose your reaction to them. A lot of recovery is about you taking back control and committing to eating without restriction and resting. It tickles me that so often I am told by psychoanalysts that "anorexia is about control." Anorexia isn't about control — but recovery is!

Don't think you are "done" too soon

One of the biggest recovery mistakes that I continued to make was being so in awe of my relative change in weight and mental state that I would be lulled into thinking that I was "done." Compared to what I was eating before, I was eating a lot more food. Compared to how much I was doing before, I was resting a lot more. Compared to how restrictive and OCD I was before, I was so much freer and happier now.

The seemingly enormous relative changes tricked me into thinking that I was all better. And yes, I was better than before. But, I still had work to do. It's a bit like I'd been skint for decades, and I had found a couple of pound coins on the pavement, but was so busy celebrating having found them that I hadn't yet looked up and realised there was a wad of hundred pound notes a couple yards farther down the road. There is a much bigger bounty ahead if you keep going.

Focusing on the relative changes would trip me into stagnancy. I found that the key was to constantly be suspicious about my state of recovery. Rather than comparing the current situation to my past situation, I did better if I compared the current situation with what I wanted the future situation to be. When I did that, I could see that I still had a way to go.

Hormones and periods (Teenage Brat Syndrome)

Malnutrition causes our bodies to lower metabolism and one of the major ways your body does this is by shutting down many aspects of the endocrine system. When this starts to crank back up again you may be in for a pretty topsy-turvy time. I went through a stage of being like a complete teenage brat!

Logically I knew that getting my period was a possible effect of nutritional rehabilitation. I still don't think that I ever really believed it would happen to me. I had never had a period in my life. I assumed I had broken my body to the point it would never recover a menstrual cycle. I was utterly flabbergasted when it arrived.

That time was like puberty for me. I was emotionally volatile and physically in discomfort. I felt rather alone, as most adult women of almost middle age have been dealing with periods for half their lives already. I was having to work out sanitary protection properly for the first time aged 30. I hadn't a clue what to buy, and was too embarrassed to ask anyone. Thank God for Google, eh?

Personal experience aside of what this incredible event feels like, the main point I need to make here is that getting your period doesn't signal anything other than things are on the right track. Getting your period doesn't mean that you are nutritionally rehabilitated. Getting your period doesn't mean you are not in energy deficit anymore.

I have known women who got their periods at very low weights. I have known woman who never lost their periods at all even at startlingly low weights. I have known, others, like myself, who didn't see their periods until a long time after they had reached a physical and mental state of real nutritional rehabilitation. We are all different. Your period is a good sign for sure, but it is not a definitive indication of anything other than an improvement in physical state.

Tips for when you restart your period

- Put emergency sanitary protection items in your bag, your car, every bathroom in the house, in your draw at work. Basically all places you frequent. I got caught out countless times in the first year of having my period because I was not in the habit of needing that sort of thing and therefore would often forget to have sanitary protection handy.
- Don't assume that your periods will be regular. In the first year my periods were all over the calendar. Don't be alarmed, it is your body working things out. They should settle down in time.
- Try and enjoy the "down time." When you get your period your body has a lot going on and often we feel low and tired. I'm not saying you have to turn into a damsel in distress, but I also don't buy the notion that you have to be "out and at it" like the girls in the old Bodyform commercials when you are on your period either. Look after yourself.
- Cramps are no excuse to eat less, neither is bloating. If you find yourself more tempted to restrict when you are on your period put a Safety Net plan in place.
- Congratulate yourself. Your body is healing.

Chapter 20: Mental And Physical State Shifts

In this chapter I am going to explain why full recovery is not as simple as weight gain alone, and outline those mental state shifts that signify nutritional rehabilitation and neural rewiring.

Initial weight gain

Many of us greatly fear gaining weight more the lower our actual weight is. Conversely, for some of us, as we gain weight, our fear of gaining weight diminishes. However, despite being very afraid of gaining weight, when we are very underweight it is easier for many of us to mentally justify gaining weight. Then, as our bodies become heavier it is harder to mentally justify eating more — for some at least, not all. Either way, the point is that your attitude to gaining weight will likely shift and change as you move through weight gain.

No matter how gung-ho you feel about recovery, and no matter how on board you are with gaining weight, you will still likely feel like you were kicked in the stomach by a horse the first time you feel your clothes tighten.

Remember to not allow these emotions to affect your actions. Your body knows what is doing. You do not get to freak out and eat less because you got scared that you were gaining weight too fast too early.

When you start eating more in recovery, you should see/feel your weight increasing — sometimes fast, sometimes slow, sometimes evenly. This is the goal, and all the while you are focusing on eating without restriction. It is nobody's job to interfere with your weight gain. And remember, regardless of how much you are eating, if you are not gaining weight it is not enough.

I am often saddened by witnessing therapists and dietitians start to panic if their clients experience rapid initial weight gain. I have often had to hand hold professionals through this process in order to stop their own implicit weight biases and fears from transferring to their clients. I have to explain to them not to judge their clients weight of rate gain, and that if they don't interfere their clients body will stabilize. It upsets me to think of how many people in recovery are being negatively affected because their professional support gets cold feet when they actually begin to gain weight.

Your body knows what it is doing. Let it get on with its job the way it sees fit and do not allow yourself or anyone else to judge the rate at which you gain weight. Keep responding to hunger and your body will wind up where it needs to be. You cannot interfere by suppressing your intake and restricting. If you do so, you are basically still in anorexia, just at a slightly higher weight.

"At each stage of weight gain, I think "OK, I'm all right here, but NO MORE! I can't take any more weight gain!" And then yet, I gain a little more weight and I'm OK again. Like, the world didn't end." - Anon, adult in recovery from anorexia.

Toolkit ideas for weight gain anxiety

So what does this negative reaction to weight gain redirect look like? For me, I used a meditation practice that put me ahead of it a couple of steps. I used the PNSP as described in the Toolkit. As I anticipated that the reality of weight gain would be difficult, I started "practicing" being in that larger body ahead of time. When we mentally rehearse anything, or even if we straight out imagine a scenario, we give our brains a data point to refer to. By imagining being in a larger body I was giving my brain data to support the notion that this larger body was not a threat after all. I would sit and visualise myself gaining weight, seeing the number on the scale rise, and feeling at peace with it. I did this meditation multiple times a day, just for moments at a time — longer if I had the time to.

You will gain weight. Gaining weight is a non-negotiable requirement to reach full recovery. You will likely have negative reactions to gaining weight. Don't judge yourself for these, but don't allow them to control you.

Energy Debt

Here is something that took me a long while to work out about recovery: weight gain doesn't mean you are out of energy deficit. One can be gaining weight and still in energy deficit due to the debt of energy that one created over the time that one was underweight.

Many of us notice that there is a lag between the physical nutritional rehabilitation and the mental restoration that takes us out of the scarcity mindset and improves our mental state. I believe that this "lag" is because a person is still in energy debt despite having gained some weight. Problems arise when you stop eating as much too early. Then, you never really get out of energy deficit. Remember, you can be in energy deficit in any size body.

You have to keep eating

If you start restricting as a response to weight gain you will never get to that point where you have amended energy deficit and come out of the scarcity mindset. Hard as it is to do so, you have to keep eating. Unrestricted. Pull together whatever support you need in order to do this. Too many people start sliding backwards at this point because, a) they think that recovery didn't work for them as they put on weight but still had just as much mental stress, and b) other people assume that because they put on weight they are recovered and support was reduced too early.

What you need to know about energy debt:
1. Short term weight gain doesn't equal full nutritional rehabilitation.
2. Until energy debt is negated, you will still be in the scarcity mindset and therefore weight gain will likely put you in a very painful place.
3. You need more support than ever as you ride out the debt in order to get to a place of energy balance.

4. You should not start exercising when you are still paying off that energy debt.
5. Did I mention that you are going to need a ton of support? And that you have to keep eating unrestricted amounts of food regardless of how scary that feels.

Recovery Weight

I wrote about recovery weight in Section Two, but I am coming back to it here because it is important that you understand how this works. Recovery weight is what your body does in order to save up to pay off your energy debt. Or I should say, what some people's bodies do. Not everyone.

In the Minnesota Starvation Study, it was found that most of the participants overshot their pre-starvation weight by around 10 percent in the recovery stages. Most of them returned to their pre-starvation weight (i.e their normal, pre-experiment, unrestricted, unsuppressed, healthy weight) around a year later. So the body gains a little more weight than is normal for it, and later that weight is lost without the person restricting food.

Recovery weight is you getting a new job but still having to spend a year or more saving money to pay off those credit card bills you racked up when you were unemployed. Your body is putting energy in the bank when it stores fat. It will do so until it knows that there has been adequate energy coming in for long enough for it to assume that you really landed in the Land of Milk and Honey. It needs to know that there is going to be a consistent supply of energy coming in before it will spend energy on making expensive repairs. This is a natural, intelligent, physiological response to a period of starvation. Admit it, if it didn't scare the hell out of you, you'd be hugely impressed about how smart your body is being when it does this.

Sadly, knowing this logically will not stop your anorexia brain freaking out about it. You will have to employ Direct, Reject, Redirect to a lot of thoughts, and you will have to Urge Surf many desires to restrict. Hang in there, and surround yourself with support.

Nutritional Rehabilitation

How do I know when I am nutritionally rehabilitated?

Being nutritionally rehabilitated is not a number. It is an increase in weight until the point the mental state markers of recovery start to emerge. Of course there are medical markers that indicate that you are nutritionally well, such as a normal hormonal state, protein status etc, and your dietician or doctor should be able to help you track such things.

Getting nutritionally rehabilitated is not a case of picking a number of a chart and heading for that. It is a mental state marker rather than a physical weight marker. For me, the biggest clue that I was out of energy deficit was that my mental hunger gradually went away and I no longer feared weight gain.

Recovery Mental State Markers

When you come out of energy deficit, the anorexia response turns off. Indications that this is happening include:

- **Food ceases to be so emotional**
    - Your brain no longer needs to use negative emotions to disincentivise eating (fear, regret, disgust, threat etc decrease) nor does it need to use positive emotions to motivate you to combat malnutrition (lust, desire, obsession over food decrease).
    - Restriction stops feeling rewarding.
    - You don't feel anxiety about not knowing the calories in food. You stop feeling the need to calorie count at all, or it begins to get easier to ignore.
    - You can eat something that didn't taste that great and not wallow in regret for hours afterwards.
    - You no longer treat food as a reward.
    - All-in-all, food stops being such a big deal.
- **Hyper-awareness around food lessens**
    - You find that you no longer remember every detail of every meal you ate recently.
    - You stop noticing what other people are eating and comparing.
    - You feel no anxiety about deciding what to eat and can make spontaneous food decisions.
- **Mental hunger diminishes and eventually dissipates.** Mental hunger is there for a reason when you are malnourished to motivate you to eat. When you are out of energy deficit it is no longer required. You will notice that you think about food less

and less. You can have chocolate cake in the fridge and it doesn't call at you like a magnet. One day you will realise you had a two-hour conversation with a friend and you were able to give them your full attention without getting distracted by thoughts of food. Then, there will be a day when you can't remember the last time you obsessed about eating. If you had any cookbook reading habits, or cooking show watching, you may begin to lose interest. It is an incredible freedom when the mental hunger subsides.

- **You find yourself predominately thinking about non-food aspects of life**. Work, sex, friends, family etc start to dominate your brain space as there is no longer any need for your brain to obsess about food. Now that your primary survival needs — food, water, oxygen — are all met, your brain will move onto higher level thoughts and aspirations.

- **Restriction, OCD-ED and exercise compulsions cease**. You began to feel a large reduction in the drive to move all the time. You can watch someone else go running and not feel angry or jealous. You are able to take a walk and not feel like you *have* to go the next day too. Your OCD-ED urges disappear, leaving you free to do with your day what you want. Restriction begins to feel pointless and unattractive.

- **The mental effects of malnutrition begin to subside**. You feel more social, less irritable, less angry, less anxious. Your ability to feel compassion for other people increases. You begin to feel more flexible, and less prone to stick to routines. You may notice you start to feel more extroverted and social. You may notice that you are developing interests that are different from those that you had when you were in malnutrition.

- **Brain fog lifts.** If you had the malnutrition brain-fog, you should begin to gradually notice that you are thinking clearer. You may also notice perception changes, and even things like more vibrant colours and smells.

Mental state, not target weight.

You cannot assume that just because you gained enough weight to get into a "healthy" BMI range that you have gained enough weight to be fully nutritionally rehabilitated. You absolutely have to be prepared to allow your body to guide you in the process of nutritional rehabilitation, and the way you do this is to gain weight until you in a healthy weight range or higher *and* you feel these mental state shifts.

You do not get to control your weight, neither does anybody else.

The New Body Problem

New Body Problem = the thoughts and feelings that arise when we move through physical change in anorexia recovery.

Even those of us who want to — in our rational brains at least — put on weight can get caught out by the reaction when it happens.

Due to my competitive nature, I wanted to win against anorexia, and winning meant putting on weight. My body became a trophy. But even then, catching my reflection in the mirror brought a momentary shock wave as I thought, "Who is that stranger in my house … oh wait, it's me!"

Or the "*what's that?*" jolt that came if my legs rubbed against one another and caught me off guard. The disappearance of the thigh gap was welcomed by my healthy brain, but that didn't stop it feeling weird and different. The same was true every time I flexed my arm and felt flesh touch flesh on the inside of my elbow. That feeling was new, alien to me. My whole body was alien to me. I had been underweight for over 10 years. The way my healthier, larger body moved was different. The spaces that I fit into (or didn't fit into) had changed. I had gone from driving a Fiat Cinquecento to a Bentley. Moving around the world was altered in every sense from the way that strangers greeted me to the fact that I could no longer sit in a child-size seat without getting stuck. All different. Changed.

"I feel so lost. Like I know I should like the fact I don't look emaciated … but I don't. Will that change?" - Ser, adult in recovery from anorexia

What "Ser" is describing there is something so many of us go through. My answer to her would be that given time, she will learn to like, then possibly even love her new body.

The first 6-12 months of nutritional rehabilitation

For some of us, the period between gaining weight and the mental shift out of the anorexia that makes us okay about gaining weight is awfully hard. Don't take it personally. Not liking your new body right now says nothing about you as a person, and it doesn't indicate much about the future either. It is a reaction that is very normal in eating disorder recovery, and is not indicative about your true feelings regarding your body.

The initial weight gain period of recovery is certainly difficult. But for many people it is the first 6-12 months post nutritional rehabilitation that are the hardest. This time here, when you are in a larger body, you don't really know how to operate it, you are exhausted, emotional, and terrified that it will never end. This is when you really need support to hang in there. It is important that those supporting you understand this too.

Other people wrongly assume that just because you gained some weight you are suddenly all better. That is not the case, and it can be painful that in the time you are feeling most vulnerable and confused you are often treated as if you are well.

Dealing with weight gain comments from other people

Comments from other people are always awkward. It is an odd situation really. In the west, it is considered pretty taboo to comment

on a person's weight gain, but there is a large weight bias present —
even when an emaciated person gains weight, some of us get
comments to imply that our life-saving nutritional rehabilitation was
unfortunate. People with anorexia in larger bodies have to deal with
lack of understanding not only from peers, but from professionals too.

I have worked with people from all over the world and some cultures
are kinder towards weight gain than others. A client I had in India lived
in a region where commenting on another person's weight was as
common as talking about the weather — just much more accusatory.
She had to deal with people telling her she would not find a man
willing to marry her should she continue to gain weight. (I am happy to
report that the woman in question is a role model for deciding not to
care what other people think, and she continued with a full nutritional
rehabilitation regardless.)

*My primary care doctor remarked to me once that I had gained over
40lbs in the time that she had been seeing me ... as if it were a bad thing!
- Jenni, adult in recovery from anorexia*

Almost every person whom I have worked with at some point has
brought up that they really fear comments from other people about
their weight. Sometimes this is fear that other people will judge them
as lazy or attach any of the usual stigma that people in larger bodies
have to deal with all the time. More often, however, people worry that
others will assume that they are all better if they appear better in
terms of physical appearance.

"I don't mind meeting new people. It's harder when I see old friends for the first time. I worry that they will be wondering what is going on with me and why I gained all this weight." - R, adult in recovery from anorexia.

First let's address the size discrimination element: Often, when clients talk to me about the comments that they get from others, we discover that they have projected their own weight bias onto other people. I used to do this too. I remember this old chap in our local pub remarking to me "Well girl, haven't you put on weight!" when I was early into nutritional rehabilitation. I assumed this comment to be a negative remark. My anorexia brain translated that innocent remark into "Well girl, you put on far far too much weight," which was not what he said at all. Anorexia isn't wildly concerned with being accurate about things like that — it'll pick whatever it can out of the information coming in to prove its own biases as true.

Looking back now, with non-anorexia perception, I can see he wasn't being negative at all. He meant it as a positive remark. He was congratulating me. He was relieved for me. When people see us looking as if we are on death's door, they are pleased for us when we start to look better. It was only my anorexia-lens that stopped me from seeing the true intent behind such a remark. Harks back to the whole perception concept I started with at the beginning of this book.

What I found, was, well meaning or otherwise, someone commenting on my weight gain sparked adrenaline in me. I would then become tongue tied. I would usually say nothing, or something silly and awkward. The next day, I would think of a brilliant comeback and kick myself for not having thought of it at the time. After a while I perfected a couple of explanations and one-liners to deliver if anyone commented. If people seemed sincere, and open to it, I would explain to them that my weight gain was a good thing as I was in recovery from anorexia. That took a lot of courage, but I was often rewarded by people who took the time to try and understand.

Now let's look at the fear that some people have around being congratulated on looking well, because they are worried that this will mean others assume they are all recovered, done and dusted.

Why would a person possibly be scared of other people assuming that they are okay?

Here are some direct quotes from people in recovery on that:

"People think that eating disorders are about weight and being skinny, so they think when you are not skinny anymore then your ED is all better. They see you eating, they see you gaining, life is great. Inside you are struggling harder than ever though."

"How can I possibly ask for support when I look "all better?" It feels fraudulent, selfish and just wrong."

"Afraid people will see it as just attention seeking (like many people think eating disorders are in the first place)."

"That there will be no support left once weight is restored, when support is needed more than ever, to deal with ED thoughts, to deal with being in a bigger body, to deal with anxieties and fears that still exist. But...I thought you were recovered?!?!"

We know that people judge our wellness based on our appearance. Most of us also know that the first couple of months in a larger body is when we need support the most. I suggest proactively talking to your support team about the support that you will need in the period of time between putting on weight and the mental state restoration that will allow you to accept and even enjoy being in a larger body. Let's not pretend that there isn't usually a time lag there. The body heals faster than the brain.

When I first started coaching almost every client voiced this fear of being perceived as being recovered when still not mentally there yet, and it confused me. I had not had this fear myself. I struggled to understand it. After a while I noticed that everyone who had this sort of fear had been through treatment and "relapsed" at least once — usually as soon as they had been dropped by their treatment provider who assumed them to be all better. Maybe the reason people were scared of being there was because they had been there before — in a larger body — and abandoned.

(I say "relapsed" using inverted commas, because it's not actually a relapse if you never got to full recovery, and weight gain alone is not full recovery.)

It is vital that support continues as long as needed, regardless of the physical appearance of the person in recovery.

Clothes

Whenever I start working with someone going into nutritional rehabilitation I tell them to throw out all the clothes that currently fit them, and to stick with baggy and elasticated. Many people are dubious and wait a while before doing this — everyone does it sooner or later. I cannot count how many "OMG", calls, texts, or emails I have had from distressed clients who have pulled on a pair of jeans only to get them halfway up their thighs. I've done this too. No matter how recovery motivated you are, this sort of physical confirmation of weight gain will throw you. It's like reality suddenly hits, and it punches hard.

Trust me, save yourself the unnecessary freak out and throw your clothes out. You will not need them where you are going. Only wear baggy and elasticated clothes for the recovery period.

Your perception of your body

Your body is going to change. If you are underweight you have to gain weight. And remember, underweight means under the weight that your body would naturally be without restricting your intake. You can be underweight at any size.

I found it helpful to realise that I was noticing change. And that was all. I was noticing differences in my body. I also found it helpful to understand that anorexia causes people to hallucinate more fat than is actually present. That is not to say I didn't gain fat — I did and so will you because all people need fat on their bodies to be well. But anorexia made it all seem bigger than it really was. I could not trust myself to judge my body. That was both an alarming and calming truth.

Sometimes I wasn't even sure if differences felt bad or not. Sometimes it was a rather impartial reaction, but I still noticed. It is only natural that you notice. Try not to assume that just because you notice change, that this change is bad. Take a couple of deep breaths to calm your mind, and then observe your emotional reaction to whatever it was that you just felt.

Fattist comments

You likely tell other people off about being fattist and for fat discrimination. What about yourself?

No double standards. Thinking mean thoughts about your body is not allowed. Discriminating against your own body is not allowed. You would not do it to someone else so do not do it to yourself. When you notice such thoughts aggressively send them to the spam folder. Do not tolerate weight discrimination from anyone, least of all yourself

Your body is the only living being that will be with you every day of your life. Your body is your best friend. It is important that you treat it with respect both in your actions and in your thoughts.

Internal perception of self and body image

The insula, is a part of your brain with relevance in your body representation, and your perception of self — that is, the way that you think of your body. It works with other brain areas such as the somatosensory cortex involved in perception of self. In doing this, the insula stores an integrative model of your own body. It is a bit like Google Maps in that sense. Google Maps might be the insula for Planet Earth. It is thought that for people with anorexia, a faulty representation is given that makes a person perceive their body as different — larger — than it really is, and this is the theory behind body dysmorphia.

What I am interested in, is why for those of us without severe body dysmorphia, it still takes a while before we are able to feel happy in our recovered bodies. Even those of us who want to gain weight often struggle when it actually happens. We feel alien. We forget we gained weight and feel shock when we see ourselves in the mirror. I remember a number of times being caught out by forgetting I was in a larger body. Seeing a reflection in a shop window and thinking it were someone else, only to get closer and see it was me — my internal image of myself was so much thinner than what I saw in the mirror.

I didn't have stereotypical body dysmorphia. I always knew that I was too thin, however, as I gained weight I still felt shocked by the changes — and for a long time after those changes had actually happened. As if I painted my house red and a year later Google Maps was still showing it as blue.

Let's look at these emails from a client of mine, I will call her Jane. Jane lives in the UK, is 38, and had anorexia since she was 15. These comments were in the time after Jane started to nutritionally rehabilitate.

April:
I don't feel real, somehow. I feel like I am in a fat suit. I know that this is the weight I am supposed to be at, and I know that I am a healthy weight now, but it just feels alien. Like, I touch my skin and it doesn't feel like my skin. Today I walked past a mirror and I swear it took seconds before I even knew it was me. Is this normal?

June:
I mean I know that something is better I guess. I don't feel like an alien quite as much and sometimes I am not as aware of my body as I was in a good way. Like it's just my body and not weird anymore. I still feel self conscious. Like yesterday when I saw our old milkman and I hadn't seen him since I was sick. I feel like everyone is judging me and I know that cannot be true. Sometimes I feel like I am a bit protective over my healthy body and don't want anyone to say anything about it. Make sense?

October:
OMG Tab, it dawned on me today that yesterday we went out to a party and I didn't even worry about wearing a strappy dress. I mean I didn't even think about it until now … I didn't have any thoughts about anything other than looking forward to seeing my Uncle who was going to be there and I haven't seen for yonks. Literally didn't feel abnormal or like a

hippo in a bathing suit. If anything I am feeling proud of myself. Maybe this is what being a regular person feels like!

I don't want to paint too rosy a picture here. For months Jane would email me daily and be in the same doubting, panicking place that most of us are in when we start to eat more. But even she was stunned when she started looking back over emails to notice the change in her own perception of herself over the months. October was a bit of a turning point for Jane in that her hyper-awareness of her change in body size lessened. Of course there were other things she was still working on at this time, but for the most part, she started to feel more "at home" in her own skin. Please don't pay too much attention to the timeline I have shown for Jane here. Don't compare your own recovery overly with that of others. It may take you more or less time to get to a point of acceptance.

How to deal with weight gain:

1. Throw away all your clothes. Don't try them on to check if they fit or not, just shove them in a bag and take them to a charity store. For the recovery process all you need are loose, elasticated clothes. Do not buy any new clothes until you are weight and state restored fully.
2. Remind yourself daily that your goal is to gain weight. Keep telling yourself this. Write it down. Use these words as your screensaver. You have to get this concept fully absorbed by your brain.
3. Have some canned responses to dole out to anyone who comments on your weight gain. They don't have to be sassy or

sarcastic (unless you want them to be) but be prepared with something.

4. Every day, place your hands on your recovery stomach and tell it that you love it.

5. If you find yourself body checking. Stop. Be very strict with yourself here.

6. Surround yourself with the support you need to help you.

Mid-Recovery Clusterfuck (Charlie Foxtrot)

When I went through what I refer to now as my "Mid-Recovery Clusterfuck" I didn't know what it was. I thought that — despite considering myself at the furthest end of the insanity scale already (just hiding it like a champ) — I was getting crazier. Turns out, years down the line and after having worked with other people in recovery from anorexia I see that Mid-Recovery Clusterfuck (MRC) is a "thing." It happens to most of us at some stage in recovery. In the midst of the nutritional rehabilitation process, most of us experience an onslaught of emotion somewhere along the way.

"I cry about the weirdest things. I started crying at work and had to go to the bathroom because I listened to this song that got me all emotional. I am not a guy who cries a lot. Wow!" - M, adult in recovery from anorexia.

What is Mid-Recovery Clusterfuck?

According to Urban Dictionary, "clusterfuck" is a military term for an operation in which multiple things have gone wrong. Related to "SNAFU" (Situation Normal, All Fucked Up") and "FUBAR" (Fucked Up Beyond All Repair). I think that any of these terms could be adequately used to describe the recovery process, so feel free to use them interchangeably.

In radio communication or polite conversation (i.e. with a very senior officer) the term "clusterfuck" will often be replaced by the NATO phonetic acronym "Charlie Foxtrot."

For those of you who don't like swearing, there are options. I happen to think that Clusterfuck hits the nail on the head, so I'll stick with that. Think of it as Charlie Foxtrot if you prefer.

MRC describes many of the realisations about my life that I went through between starting recovery and reaching full recovery. As my body and mind healed, I had a number of awakenings — not all were entirely pleasant.

Being underweight has a numbing effect. The body is too low on resources to bother with emotions and the brain wants to focus primarily on food. Emotional responses pertaining to non-food aspects of life are dampened. I started to gain weight, and a couple months into that a clusterfuck of emotion hit me like a Whitney Houston flash mob. Suddenly I felt everything. Ten years of emotion had consolidated and launched itself at me. I was happy about getting better. I was mourning my eating disorder. I was lonely. I was frustrated. I was angry. I was bored. I was overwhelmed. I was excited. I was regretful. I was aspirational. I was hopeful. I was sad. I wanted a career change. I wanted love.

Oh ... all those things I hadn't thought about for 10 years started to come up again. Here I was, 27, and I was crying about something a boy said to me when I was 16? What? I didn't even really like him. Maybe I was crying just because I was sad that this was the last time I'd ever been close to a boy at all so it was more of a pity cry? Maybe I was crying not about him at all but about the fact I'd now been alone for 10 years? Maybe it was more about regretting not slapping him in the face. ... Maybe I'm just really hungry.

And then: I'm very upset with myself for not going to my friends wedding three years ago because I couldn't handle the pressure of having to eat or looking so thin in the photographs so I made up some excuse about not being able to take time off work and now I feel like a bad friend. I messed that up. Who doesn't go to a wedding? What sort of person am I? Maybe I should call her and tell the truth? Maybe I can make it up to her? ... Maybe I'm just really hungry.

And then: I cannot believe I spoke to mum like that at Christmas dinner in 2002. Who yells at their mum on Christmas Day just because she offered some gravy? Who does that? What is wrong with me? I wonder if mum remembers. I wonder if it hurt her at the time. I wonder if it is too late to apologize. Maybe I should call her? I'm such a prat. Maybe I can make a special effort this Christmas? ... Maybe I'm just really hungry.

And then: I hate my career. I hate it. Who am I kidding, I don't have a career. I wasted 4 years at university. I have wasted by degree. It's too late. It's over. What am I going to do with my life?

And so on and so forth ... you get the picture. What you might not get is that rather than being isolated moments of emotion, these sorts of things — and so many more — seemed to hit me all at once. I'd not been totally void of all emotion at all times before. Sure, I had felt regret and loneliness and sadness and snippets of hope. But watered-down versions. And not all at the same time. Hence: clusterfuck.

In this time I also experienced intense feelings of grief and mourned my "anorexia identity." There was sadness about not being about to achieve that feeling of success that restriction had given me. There was also fear of the future and what the heck I was going to do with myself now I wasn't obsessed with food and exercise.

Another layer on top of this was a very intense feeling of impatience and frustration. I wanted it over. I was done. So much of my existence wasted to anorexia. I wanted a life and now! But I had no idea how to get to where I wanted to be. In some respects things had been easier before I had any ambition to have a life. Now I had the desire, but no roadmap.

(Note: If you have trauma experiences to deal with then it can be the case that these affect you more in this recovery time. Please seek support and help for dealing with these.)

Keep going

No, it wasn't easy. Yes, I doubted myself. But I ate. I ate out of anger. I ate out of fear. I ate out of bliss. I ate out of loneliness. I ate out of hate. I ate out of regret. I ate out of exhaustion.

Some would call that comfort eating. Some would call it emotional eating. I would say: *stop trying to psychoanalyse eating*. I am eating because I have been starving for years. I am eating. That is all. And anyway, even if it were "emotional eating" then I had ten years to make up for. So out of my way and make me a cheeseburger. Double.

Mid-Recovery Clusterfuck is disconcerting. It's both enjoyable and painful at times. For some people it seems to happen shortly after they begin recovery eating. Some people (like me) much further down the line. It marks a death and a birth.

Enjoy it if it happens. MRC is neither the start nor the end — but it is somewhere in between. That is worth celebrating!

Recovery

Moving towards full recovery

I believe that full recovery is possible for all. To me, "full recovery" means that your anorexia goes away. It gets easy and enjoyable to eat, and to sustain your natural, unsuppressed bodyweight. You can eat without the slew of negative emotions and anxiety. The fears dissipate. Full recovery is life without anorexia in your head. If it were anything less, what would be the point in all that hard work to get there?

If you have the genetic predisposition for anorexia, it is true that should you go into energy deficit, even years after recovery, you'll likely trigger the anorexia response again. But it's not like you have no control over it. You do. It's actually as "easy" as never allowing yourself to go into energy deficit again. If you stay on top of that, you'll never have anorexia again. Don't get complacent, ever ... and you will be okay.

Being human is risky. If you break your leg and it heals there is no guarantee that you won't break it again. But that doesn't mean you should spend your life acting as if your leg is still broken.

You can do your best to be careful, but health is not a guarantee. I still don't think this is any reason to say that full recovery from anorexia isn't possible. That's not to say I ever take my recovery for granted. But I think the risk of me developing anorexia again is probably around the same as the risk of me running for president. I've learned too much to allow energy deficit to happen, and I am not going to pretend it is out of my control. I have the ability to ensure I always eat and rest enough, and it is my responsibility to do so.

I also think that the term "relapse" is often problematic. Just because a person put on some weight doesn't mean that they reached full recovery. As full recovery is evident in a person's long-term mental state shifts — not just their body size. Often people who are in "relapse" are not really in relapse, as they never actually reached full recovery in the first please. You cannot judge the state of a person's recovery by their appearance.

I know plenty of people who have been "weight restored" and somewhat better off mentally for years, but not fully recovered. If you are almost all better, but not all the way, there is still work for you to do. Getting lulled into the "this is good enough" mentality will cheat you out of what you can attain. Your recovery process is your own. You deserve the fully recovered version of life, and it is never too late to decide to get all the way there. Nobody on the outside (doctor, therapist, parent, spouse) gets to decide if you are fully recovered or not, or label you as such. Only you really know the true mental state that you are living in.

I want you to know that full recovery means you get out of this. The urges to count calories, or restrict, or compulsively exercise, or move all the time, or eat orthorexically, or plan all your meals meticulously, or say no to that dinner invite because you don't know what people will be serving ... dissipate, until they are memories of a past version of you. Full recovery should look like freedom from all this. Do not settle for anything less.

Of course getting there is hard work. But it is so very worth it. Every bite you take and every doubting thought you ignore will be worth it. And yeah, recovery is bloody hard. But let's face it, sustaining anorexia isn't exactly a barrel of laughs, is it?

I know plenty of people who have made full, utter, total, recovery from anorexia. Many of whom had anorexia for a long time. You are capable of this too. Don't sell yourself short. Don't settle for anything less than complete recovery. Life is so worth that.

Learning how to eat for *your* body

Okay, so imagine that you are two or three years old. You're a toddler. You're exploring the world, you are also learning about your body, and how to operate it. Kids get to learn how to operate their bodies in terms of eating food all through childhood. Most people don't have to think twice about eating to hunger and stopping at fullness by the time they are an early teen. It comes naturally. For those of us who have been through anorexia, we have relearn this whole glorious relationship after we reach nutritional rehabilitation and our hunger and fullness signals begin to regulate.

This is one of the reasons I try and get people to eat to physical/mental hunger rather than a set caloric "minimum" as soon as they can trust themselves to be able to do so without restricting. There will come a point where you need to stop eating to numbers, and start learning to eat for *your* body. Eating for *your* body will involve listening to *your* body — a skill most of us have to relearn. Of course this will get easier and more decipherable as your body comes out of energy deficit. So if you can't trust yourself not to restrict, put safety measures in place.

Feelings of hunger and satiation change throughout the process. For me, satiation went from being an all or nothing affair, to some sweet spot in the middle.

When I was in recovery, anything other than feeling fully stuffed to the brim felt unsatisfying. My body would feel irritated and annoyed unless my stomach was crammed with food. This is understandable, as my body was in malnutrition and constantly wanting what it was lacking in: food. As I became more physically rehabilitated, I noticed that I could eat to satisfaction without having to stuff myself full to the point of discomfort anymore.

The key here is erring on the side of caution by eating if you are not sure. But gradually allowing yourself to be more relaxed about ... everything. Your body is constantly communicating with you, and these, more often than not, are not egregious signals, but more subtle. When we have anorexia we become used to ignoring communications from our bodies and learning to listen again is a process. Once you are no longer underweight for your body, and you can trust yourself to not restrict intentionally, or undereat, you can focus on re-establishing this natural, uncomplicated relationship with food. And the best part is that there is no rush. You take your time. You put safely nets in place if you need them. You listen and learn and explore. Enjoy the process of learning your body again.

Full recovery

- ❏ No desire to restrict.
- ❏ No tendency to be compulsive about exercise.
- ❏ No OCD-ED.
- ❏ No fear around eating.
- ❏ No excessive emotions around food.
- ❏ No hyper-awareness of food all the time.
- ❏ No constant mental hunger.
- ❏ A return of the pre-anorexia you (if you remember what that was).
- ❏ Being at a healthy weight for your body

Rather ... a relaxed attitude to food and eating. You should notice that movement and food are no longer linked in your head. They are independent of one another. You will enjoy the mental state shifts as outlined previously.

Becoming trigger proof

Becoming trigger proof allows you to sustain recovery with greater ease. It takes time and effort, but if you keep countering the messages that society gives you about needing to be thin or exercising you'll get there eventually.

Egregiously, we live in a culture where everywhere you look there are messages telling you to eat less and move more. In your doctor's office. At the dentist. In the mall. On the side of your packet of cookies. And that's not to mention the marketing behind the diet and fashion industry. That bias towards thinness on every billboard. You cannot, possibly, remove all triggers from your life. You cannot change our thin-obsessed diet culture, but you can change your reaction to our thin-obsessed, diet culture. If you can achieve this (and you can) nothing can touch you.

The most effective tool for becoming trigger proof for me was the "Fuck it!" attitude.

The industry can throw all the marketing messages at me that they want telling me to change my body. I don't care. My body is just fine. My friends can bleat on about the diets that they are on until the cows come home. I don't care. I'll eat what I want.

My doctor can ask me if I am eating enough fruit and vegetables and if I exercise enough. I'll tell her I do what is right for my body.

It's all like water off a duck's back to me now. After what I have been through I know how to look after myself. In order to recover I had to learn not only how to do that, but I had to teach myself mental astuteness. That is one of the gifts of recovery. You are forced to learn mental and emotional discernment that many people never have to acquire.

Another aspect of becoming trigger proof is developing different reactions to stress. For the first couple of years in recovery, I had to force feed myself again through times of stress — bereavement, career changes, moving etc. My brain's default reaction to stress was still to reduce appetite and yearn a little for restriction. Force feeding myself was a super-skill that I had learnt, and I kept it handy in my back pocket until my brain had learned that losing my appetite was no longer an appropriate reaction to stress or anything else. Don't be disappointed in yourself if you find stress sparks an increase in the urge to restrict even a while past the acute recovery stages. Your brain needs time to re-wire all these things, but if you keep eating, it will learn not to react to stress with loss of appetite eventually.

So keep going. Fully recovered means trigger proof. It means unwavering. If you are not there yet, then keep working on getting there. Keep rejecting the thoughts and reactions that don't serve you. You'll discover that you really *do* get to decide whether or not you allow that woman in front of you at the checkout having a discussion with the cashier about her juice cleanse to influence you. There really is a choice every time you react to something. You will get there so long as you keep trying.

You could plaster your diet or cleanse all over my Facebook feed and I won't bat an eye. I laugh in the face of diet talk. It actually makes me feel strong to do so. Fuck that shit, I know better!" - M, adult recovered from anorexia.

Being recovery proud

In order to recover from this illness you have to walk ... no, run ... you have to run into fear all day every day. Full recovery is not just about eating more and doing less. For me, restriction and OCD-ED infested every thought and movement. Therefore, in recovery there were no safe spaces where I got to hang out and take a breather. No, I had to change it all, and run into the resistance at every moment. Recovery is a process of finding the very edge of your comfort zone and sitting there for months and months.

In order to win that mental shift out of anorexia, I had to sit in the snake pit for months. It is the difference between touching a tame grizzly bear at the zoo and moving in with one in a cave in the wilderness — and staying there. It is not the one-shot bravery of eating a burger as much as it is the living in a body that invokes your fear reaction.

And you will come out from this experience a total fucking champion.

"It's bloody incredible how my general disposition has altered. I often just laugh for no reason, I fool around, I giggle a lot because I can and it feels natural. I haven't felt that way since I was a kid. Since before." - Anon, adult recovered from anorexia.

Recovery is mental strength training

As my brain acclimatized to my new body, and as the mental recovery progressed, I learnt a hell of a lot about my own mental processes. Want to talk about mental strength? Ask someone who has recovered fully from anorexia. Ask someone who has had to live within their greatest fear before their brain stopped perceiving it as a threat. Ask someone who stood with their hand in the fire and didn't move away from it — for months. Ask me what it is like to keep eating despite being petrified of the weight I was gaining.

It is hard to think of any other life situations that require a person to sustain a place of intense fear for the sort of time period that anorexia recovery requires. A fear of one's own body is different from most as it is not a fear that one can step away from physically. We get to stay there with the fear until we step away from it mentally.

In recovery I learnt that my perception creates my reality, and anorexia warped my perception, therefore my reality was distorted. This taught me to not assume that a thought or feeling is the truth, and to question it. I am very glad to have learned such personal discernment, even if it did mean 12 years of hell to get there.

About my recovered body. About your recovered body

One of the things that I hated about anorexia was that it turned me into this small insignificant person — or at least, that is how I felt.

I went from being a boisterous teenager into a walking apology. I looked liked someone who couldn't look after herself, and people treated me accordingly. I felt like I didn't have respect from people. And why would I? I could not blame anyone for thinking that they could walk all over me when I looked like someone who couldn't even feed herself. That was my harsh reality of being an adult with this illness in a time when it was even less understood than it is now.

I love to meet people who knew me when I was emaciated and looking like death. I love to see them stare at me like I am a different person — a respected, larger, significant person.

Initially, in earlier recovery and when I was in the middle of The New Body Problem I feared other people's reaction to my changed shape. I would wince at the look of surprise on their faces as they noticed the change in me. As the mental shift in perspective progressed, I learned to watch for that reaction with pride. Yes, you saw it right, I put on weight!

Recovery healed my body and my mind, but so much more than that. It changed the way that I walk through the world, and it changed the way that people perceive me. My pride in my own recovery gave me a lot more confidence in other areas of my life.

Recovery will be your greatest achievement ...
... that nobody understands!

You had the strength to gain weight despite the fact that everything in your body and mind was screaming at you not to. You overcame a mental hurdle that many people will never experience. You developed a degree of mental dexterity that many people will never need to.

It can be frustrating that nobody other than someone who has experienced anorexia themselves really understands the significance of the type of courage that one has to rev up all day every day in order to get oneself into a recovered body. I wish it were something that you could put on your CV and be respected for in that way. It is your greatest achievement, after all.

" I don't' sweat the small stuff. I have fried (and eaten!) the biggest fish already." - Anon, adult recovered from anorexia.

You are a champion

I am excited for you because I am anticipating where you are headed so long as you keep going. I am excited for you to experience the unrestricted, unsuppressed version of your already wonderful self.

If I could give you a taste of full recovery I know that there would not be any doubt in your mind about continuing. Because full recovery is so much more than the physical. It is the mental relaxation, and the change in perception that turns the world of energy (be it food, money, or any other energetic exchange) into a blissful place — rather than that hellhole of anxiety.

You should be proud of yourself. This process is insane. It is wild. Nobody other than a handful of people in your life can really understand it. Give yourself the respect and authority that you deserve. As your perspective continues to shift your confidence will grow too.

Something that just about everyone I work with says to me at some point is they fear that once recovered they will be a failure. That they won't succeed in work or relationships or anything else. I say, if you can recover from this, how on earth can you fail at anything?

Be brave and curious.

"I'm sleeping better, and the mental hunger has reduced drastically and I haven't binged in a long while now." - Mike, adult recovered from anorexia.

Full Recovery

There is no white line that signifies full recovery. There isn't a day when you will wake up and look out your window to see a marching band and a parade. There are no tests to pass to see if you got there. It is a case of a very gradual mental state shift.

"Yesterday a workmate asked me to go to lunch with her and it was only 11:30 so early for me, but I didn't even hesitate to say yes and grabbed my coat just like that. But there was no stress. That's the part that I appreciate more than anything. It was like nothing. I sometimes wait for the stress to hit me, and it doesn't. And every time I do something small and normal -- things that most people would not even notice -- like that, and it is easy, it still makes me so happy!" - JJ, adult, recovered from anorexia.

Recovery is a process of noticing that you haven't felt that knot in your stomach when walking into a restaurant for a while. Recovery is about getting to the end of the day and being so busy with other things that you order and eat takeout without thinking twice about it. Recovery is when you realise that you cannot remember what you ate for lunch yesterday, or maybe even today. Recovery is about not counting calories — not because you are not allowing yourself to, but because you have no desire to. Recovery is about moving because you want to, not because you feel that you should. Recovery is about asking someone else to make dinner and serve it to you just because you don't care enough anymore to totally control the kitchen. Recovery is about sitting and talking to a friend for hours and hours and not for a second missing something that they were saying because you were thinking about food. Recovery is having chocolate cake in the fridge and eating some when you want, not because it is on a meal plan. Recovery is about just about every other aspect of your life feeling more important than thinking about food. Recovery is about having the time to have friends. Recovery is about food being unremarkable — just part of life.

Recovery is a process. Your, unique, process.

"Frankly, I am often stunned at how normal I am around food. I'll never take it for granted."- Anon, adult in recovery from anorexia

Cover art was drawn by my sister, Bethany Alderson.

Manufactured by Amazon.ca
Bolton, ON

27337953R00323